China's Economic Powerhouse

China's Economic Powerhouse

Reform in Guangdong Province

Edited by

Tung X. Bui

David C. Yang

Wayne D. Jones

and

Joanna Z. Li

palgrave
macmillan

First published 2003 by
PALGRAVE MACMILLAN
Houndmills, Basingstoke, Hampshire RG21 6XS and
175 Fifth Avenue, New York, N.Y. 10010
Companies and representatives throughout the world

PALGRAVE MACMILLAN is the global academic imprint of the Palgrave Macmillan division of St. Martin's Press, LLC and of Palgrave Macmillan Ltd. Macmillan® is a registered trademark in the United States, United Kingdom and other countries. Palgrave is a registered trademark in the European Union and other countries.

ISBN 1–4039–0385–9

This book is printed on paper suitable for recycling and made from fully managed and sustained forest sources.

A catalogue record for this book is available from the British Library.

Library of Congress Cataloging-in-Publication Data
China's economic powerhouse : reform in Guangdong Province / editors, Tung X. Bui . . . [et al.].
p. cm.
Includes bibliographical references and index.
ISBN 1–4039–0385–9
1. Guangdong Sheng (China)—Economic policy. 2. Guangdong Sheng (China)—Economic conditions. I. Bui, Tung X., 1953–
HC428.K9 G833 2002
338.951′27—dc21 2002070639

10 9 8 7 6 5 4 3 2 1
12 11 10 09 08 07 06 05 04 03

Printed and bound in Great Britain by
Antony Rowe Ltd, Chippenham and Eastbourne

Contents

List of Figures

List of Tables

Preface

Since the economic reform of China in 1979, Guangdong, a southern province of China, has grown at an average annual rate of 14 per cent per year, far exceeding that of the Four Little Asian Dragons, namely Hong Kong, Singapore, South Korea and Taiwan. Twenty years of hypergrowth has transformed Guangdong from an obscure underdeveloped agricultural region into a modern export-oriented industrial economy with dramatic impacts on the Asia Pacific region and the world. While we are entering the new millennium, it is time to assess the problems and prospects of the Guangdong economy.

We choose Guangdong for our study because Guangdong Province is the forerunner of China's economic reform and economic powerhouse. Guangdong has developed incredibly rapidly in the last twenty years since adopting the policy of economic opening to the outside world, and will continue to do so. Some of its outstanding records are as follows:

1 Guangdong is the fastest growing province in China since economic reform began in China in 1979. In 2000, Guangdong had a gross domestic product (GDP) which surpassed US$115 billion, the highest of any province in China, and which represents 10 per cent of China's national GDP.
2 The average income per capita is the highest among all provinces in China. The average urban annual income per capita of Guangdong was US$1,191 in 2000.
3 Guangdong leads the nation in foreign trade. In 2000, the province's total exports and imports were valued at US$91.9 billion and US$78.2 billion. Roughly 40 per cent of China's trade passes through Guangdong. Hong Kong is Guangdong's number one export market (35 per cent of total exports), and the United States ranks second, receiving 25 per cent of Guangdong's exports.
4 Guangdong, with utilized foreign direct investment of US$12.2 billion in 2000, leads China in utilizing foreign investment, receiving about 30 per cent of foreign direct investment in China.
5 Guangdong's economy is quite international. Guangdong leads China in carrying out the open-door policy and is therefore regarded as China's frontier to the outside world.

Guangdong is one of China's leading industrial and commercial areas. Its location just above Hong Kong helped make it among the first areas to introduce economic reforms after the 1979 economic opening of China. It faces the South China Sea and borders on Hong Kong and Macao. Its capital, Guangzhou (Canton), is the largest city in South China. More than 20 million overseas Chinese, scattered over more than 100 countries, were originally from Guangdong. Through its emigrants, Guangdong is well-connected with Hong Kong and other parts of the world. It will continue to play a leading role in attracting foreign investment and finding new forms of economic cooperation with the outside world.

This book covers the evolution of economic reform in Guangdong, an important economic linkage between Hong Kong and other parts of China, and developmental strategies in different localities of the Guangdong. We aim to give an analysis of the multifaceted factors in economic development in Guangdong involving systemic interactions between the domestic and international economies. The discussion covers the important topics of development of land, human resources, the agricultural sector and industrialization, and reforms of state-owned enterprises and township and village enterprises.

The book consists of 11 essays written by government officials and executives from the Guangdong Province of China. These officials were invited as chapter contributors because they can offer a unique view as insiders, and can communicate effectively with Western readers. All were trained in the United States, and understand management practices of both Western and Eastern cultures. All are also policy-makers, and have profound working experience and knowledge about economic development in Guangdong. These contributors were asked to provide recommendations and food for thought for the chosen economic or business topics, and the papers are arranged according to the logical sequence of the topics chosen by the authors. All in all they offer a mix of subjects that provides a comprehensive review of the economy of modern Guangdong – from its infancy to the current need of migrating into the information age. A common thread among all the essays is the acknowledgement that the New China – as best illustrated by the economic success of Guangdong Province – is undergoing an inevitable economic and social transformation with a recognized need for identifying new strategies, policies and means.

It is intended that this book may serve not only as an informative reference to readers, both business executives and professionals, but also as a textbook or teaching supplement for international business or

Chinese studies at universities and colleges. In addition, we hope that it is a testimony of the achievement and commitment of the authors to provide the reader with innovative and thought-provoking essays about China's economy as it enters a new era.

We thank the Government of Guangdong, China, which was provided financial support to the Guangdong Leadership Training Program at the College of Business Administration, University of Hawaii. We also acknowledge the assistance of the Department of Business, Economic Development and Tourism of the State of Hawaii and the faculty and students at the University of Hawaii in providing our chapter contributors an 'out of the box' perspective. We gratefully acknowledge the helpful and able editorial assistance of Ziaojin (Iris) Zhu and Kim Fujiuchi. Finally and most importantly, we look forward to feedback from readers. If anything, the purpose of this book it to provide a basis for a meaningful discussion on the evolution of economies in transition.

Organization of the book

In Chapter 1, Zhang Wenbiao provides a succinct overview of the current economic situation in Guangdong in the context of the new China. He offers a quick historical review of the economic development process and enumerates a number of major issues for an economy in transition. He argues for a strategy of industrialization through development of the information industry, the stimulation of domestic demands and the necessity to reform state-owned enterprises. The solutions suggested here seem logical but constitute a daunting task, in particular for those who seek to lead China toward an effective sustainable development policy.

Chen Junqin addresses a critical aspect of industrialization, which is the interaction between industrialization and urbanization. Environmental protection – a policy deemed by many as a policy of the rich – is indeed a major threat, as Chen argues. In Chapter 2, Chen lists a series of public policies to deal with urban forestry in Guangdong. Given the fact that the management of urban forestry is extremely expensive, if not insurmountable in certain agglomeration areas, a particular challenge for the policy-maker is to be able to prioritize these policies and execute them in the most equitable and cost-effective manner. Along the same development context, Yu Jingquan broadens the discussion to that of land resource sustainable development in Greater China (Chapter 3). To Yu, probably one of the most urgent issues revolving around sustainable development is the protection of fertile farmland. He briefly reviews the basic working conditions of implementing a sustainable development policy and attempts to highlight key challenges of the China Land Administration Law. Chen advocates for a comprehensive and scientific approach to deal with this difficult task.

Zhou Liang focuses his research on a key component of economic development, managing the power industry (Chapter 4). With no exception, China seems to have faced the deregulation of the utility industries to deal with the increasingly high cost of energy and the inevitable explosion of energy consumption. Following the evolution of the power industry in California, Zhou advocates the transition to an oligopolistic market that would help increase the industry's efficiency while effectively managing a sector characterized by capital-intensive investment.

In Chapter 5, Yefei Yang continues the debate on sustainable development with a focus on the agricultural sector. Acknowledging that poor agricultural policy and practices would lead to income stagnation of farm households, Yang submits that there are economic, technological and political factors that are critical to sound agricultural development. To substantiate his recommendation, Yang conducts a comparative analysis between China and the United States. Ultimately, his arguments lead to a series of recommendations at both micro-economic and macro-economic levels.

Biao Chen and Wayne Jones address state-owned enterprise (SOE) reform – a major effort for the Chinese economy (Chapter 6). Despite the impressive contribution to modern China, SOEs have been slow to adapt themselves to the new market conditions. The difficulties range from production inefficiency to lack of marketing know-how. The authors explore a number of possible solutions to include the separation between the State and the SOE, tax reform, and better human resource management.

It is widely acknowledged that human resources remain the most important asset of any economy. The next four chapters share a common set of issues: human resource management, leadership, and strategic planning. These issues are further framed in the context of an economy in transition – from a planned economy with state-owned enterprises to a new enterprise structure required for a market-driven economy.

In Chapter 7, Jingchao Geng addresses the dramatic development of township and village enterprises (TVE) in Guangdong. In essence, his analysis suggests that, in general, TVE have proved to be more effective than the SOE. And, if managed properly, they have a better chance to adapt themselves to compete in the twenty-first century.

Minsheng Chen elevates the discussion to the national level (Chapter 8). He conducts a comparative study at the global level and claims that in China, human capital is undercapitalized. He then outlines the basic components of quality human resources (for example, education reform and investment) and lines up a series of suggested policies to prepare Chinese labour for a knowledge-intensive economy. With his extensive leadership experience, Yongling Zhu supports the arguments discussed in the previous chapter. Using his company as a case study, he provides a thorough analysis of the role that the government can take to improve the quality of the workforce of SOEs (Chapter 9). Among others, he advocates for the creation of a more competitive labour market based on competencies and a human resource management that is comparable to that of the private sector.

Leadership remains a key critical success factor for any economy that seeks to be forward-looking in a fast-changing and increasingly competitive environment. Linhai Fang (Chapter 10) samples the characteristics of a number of successful American business leaders, and suggests a number of basic qualities that future Chinese business leaders should possess. These qualities include, but are not limited to, the willingness and ability to learn, innovate, communicate and act.

Last but not least, Joanna Li and David Yang examine in Chapter 11 the major contributing factors of Guangdong's economic achievement in the past two decades, discuss the present situation, especially the opportunities and challenges facing the province, and how they might influence the future development of Guangdong.

Honolulu, Hawaii

TUNG X. BUI
WAYNE D. JONES
JOANNA Z. LI
DAVID C. YANG

Notes on the Editors and Contributors

Tung X. Bui has, since 1997, held the Distinguished Professorship of Global Business endowed by the Matson Navigation company, at the University of Hawaii at Manoa. He holds a doctorate in managerial economics from the University of Fribourg, Switzerland, and a PhD in information systems from the Stern School of Business, New York University. Prior to joining the University of Hawaii, Professor Bui was on the faculty at the US Naval Postgraduate School, Monterey, California, New York University, the Universities of Fribourg and Lausanne, Switzerland, the University of Quebec, Montreal, Canada, and the Hong Kong University of Science and Technology.

Professor Bui has published seven books and over 140 papers. His current research interests focus on effective management of large organizations, electronic commerce, sustainable development and collaborative technology, including group decision and negotiation support systems. In 1993, a research journal nominated him as 'one of the most influential researchers in the field of decision support systems'. He also won the best paper award at the 1996 Hawaii International Conference in System Sciences and two of his 1999 papers were nominated best papers in the *Journal of Information Systems Education* (October 1999). He also won the *best* paper award at the Decision Science Institute conference (April 2000). Professor Bui is journal department editor of *INFORMS Group Decision and Negotiation*, and the *Database for Advances in Information Systems*. He is also associate editor of the *Journal of Management Information Systems*, the *Journal of Decision Systems*, the *Journal of Electronic Commerce*, and the *European Journal of Information Systems*.

Professor Bui has been a regular consultant and advisor to both governmental and private organizations on a number of public policies, including national and regional planning and business process reengineering. He is the Director of the Pacific Research Institute on Information Systems Management and the co-director of the Asia-Pacific Economic Council (APEC) UH Studies Center. He has chaired five major international conferences worldwide, and is a regular programme committee member of international meetings and workshops. Among other professional activities, he is also an active member of the International Public Management Network which is interested in reinventing government.

In Hawaii, he is promoting the use of information technology to support the state economy. He is the author of an annual report on *E-commerce Trends in Hawaii*. Prof. Bui's recent activites can be found on his website: http://ec.cba.hawaii.edu/tbui.

Wayne D. Jones is currently a doctoral candidate in the University of Hawaii's International Management programme where he is specializing in strategic management and entrepreneurship. He received his MBA in management and human resources (with an additional entrepreneurship concentration), as well as his Master of Science degree from the University of Wisconsin, Madison. He also received his Bachelor of Science degree from the University of Wisconsin, Madison, with majors in geology and geophysics and physical geography. He has worked as an environmental scientist, analytical chemist and international consultant.

Mr Jones has taught courses for the University of Hawaii College of Business Administration and University of Wisconsin School of Business in general business, global management and organizational behaviour, strategic management, entrepreneurship and executive education. His research publications include studies related to trust in student groups and cross-cultural strategic decision-making. His research interests include innovation and technology management, cognitive decision-making, international new ventures, and private and governmental initiatives to assist small- and medium-sized enterprises in developing countries and economies in transition.

Joanna Z. Li is currently the academic coordinator of an executive education programme of Chinese government officials and business executives at the College of Business Administration of the University of Hawaii. She received her BA degree in American and British literature from Zhongshan University of China and her MBA degree from the University of Hawaii at Manoa. Her other academic qualifications include being a Parvin Fellow at the Department of Journalism, University of Hawaii, and an East–West Centre participant of the Communications and Journalism Programme (1993–94).

From 1988–95 Ms Li was a reporter for *China Daily*, the sole national English-language newspaper in China, where she acquired thorough understanding of China's business and economic environment. She published more than 1,000 news reports on international trade and investment, economic reforms in China and their impacts on the social, political, cultural and financial aspects of people's life in China. She has also published many news reports in the *Windows* magazing in Hong Kong.

Ms Li was also a business development executive of Jardine Matheson Group (1995–96), where her responsibilities included identifying opportunities in international trade, retail distribution, merchant banking, estate development and property management. She also participated in the company's joint venture operations and negotiations with government officials, local businesses and international companies.

David C. Yang received his BA degree from the National Taiwan University, his MBA degree from the University of California at Berkeley, and his PhD degree from Columbia University. Specializing in financial accounting and reporting, financial analysis and international accounting, with a particular emphasis on Chinese and Asian-Pacific accounting systems, Professor Yang has been honoured with numerous awards for teaching excellence, including the Outstanding Professor Award by the Delta Theta Chapter of Beta Alpha Psi, the Dennis Ching/First Interstate Memorial Teaching Award and the University of Hawaii College of Business Administration Teaching Excellence Award. Professor Yang is a member of Beta Alpha Psi and Beta Gamma Sigma. His biography appears in *Who's Who in the World*.

Currently he serves as the president of the Association of Chinese Scholars in Hawaii (2000–1), and is an executive member of the Centre for Chinese Studies at the University of Hawaii. Previously he was the President of the Chinese Accounting Professors' Association, North America (1997–98), and Associate Director of Beijing University's Research Centre for International Accounting and Finance (1996–98). Having taught at Beijing University and the National Taiwan University, he has consulted on financial and accounting management concerns for major firms in China and the United States.

Professor Yang served as Director of the School of Accountancy from 1992 to 1994 and from 1997 to 2000. He is currently a Professor of the School of Accountancy at the College of Business Administration, University of Hawaii.

Biao Chen was Director of the Economic Development Bureau, Zhanjiang Economic and Development Zone, Guangdong Province, China.

Junqin Chen is Vice-Director of the Guangdong Provincial Forestry Department, China.

Minsheng Chen is Vice-President of the Guangzhou Medical College, China.

Linhai Fang is Deputy General Manger of the Guangdong Textile Import and Export Corporation, China.

Jingchao Geng is Director of the Foreign Affairs and Economic Cooperation Division, Guangdong Provincial Department of Agriculture, China.

Zhou Liang is Director of the Enterprise Administration Department, Guangdong Electric Holding Corporation, China.

Yefei Yang is Deputy Director, Management Office of World Bank Loans, Guangdong Provincial Department of Agriculture, China.

Jingquan Yu is Deputy Director of the Construction Division, Cost Administration, Guangdong Province, China.

Wenbiao Zhang is Vice-Director and Associate Professor of Law, Economic Management Department, Guangdong Executive Institute, China.

Yongling Zhu is Chief Executive Officer of Xinyue Co. Ltd, Hong Kong, China.

1

The Adjustment of Economic Structure and Guangdong's Economic Growth: Past Successes and Future Challenges

Wenbiao Zhang

Introduction

China's economic reform and the opening of its doors to the outside world have resulted in the phenomenal growth of its output. Gross domestic product (GDP) growth has accelerated, so that between 1984 and 1999 real GDP grew by 9.4 per cent annually according to Chinese statistics. This growth rate is not unprecedented, and in fact mimics rather closely earlier East Asian success stories. Japan's GDP grew by 10.4 per cent annually between 1950 and 1973, while in both South Korea and Taiwan GDP grew by about 9 per cent annually between 1950 and 1990. China's real distinction is its vast size and enormous population, which make it more difficult to sustain a high growth rate.[1]

Guangdong Province has been at the forefront of China's economic boom that has brought tremendous prosperity to the country's coastal areas over the last 20 years.[2] However, the province was hit hard by the Asian financial crisis in 1997 that affected many major companies. For example, Guangdong International Trust and Investment Corp. (GITIC), the province's key investment institution, went bankrupt. With greater competition from Southeast Asia over the last few years, exports of the province are also down, except for those to the United States.

To sustain economic growth in the long run, Guangdong must push through tough structural adjustments. According to economic theory, GDP growth could be achieved in a short period with increased investment:

$$\text{GDP} = \text{Consumption} + \text{Investment} + (\text{Exports} - \text{Imports})$$

GDP growth is not a problem as long as the government speeds up investment. However, overall economic development is a more complicated concept than mere GDP growth. Economic development should factor in such important elements as improvements in living standards, environmental protection, and so on. Since this development is the result of both growth and structural adjustment it is a long and painstaking process.

Since 1992, Guangdong, like the rest of China, has carried out a policy of economic structural adjustment and achieved great progress, but difficulties remain.

This chapter attempts to discuss the issue of economic structural adjustment in Guangdong Province and is divided into three parts: (1) the development phase of Guangdong's economy surveyed by its economic structure, (2) the problems existing in Guangdong's economic structure, and (3) some thoughts on the adjustment of Guangdong's economic structure.

The developing phase of Guangdong's economy surveyed by its economic structure

Guangdong leads China in GDP, the number of foreign-funded enterprises, total foreign investment, exports, per capita income and consumption. The province accounts for 10 per cent of China's total GDP, 30 per cent of its foreign investment, and 40 per cent of its exports. Exports account for 80 per cent of Guangdong's GDP, as compared with only 20 per cent for the country as a whole. Guangdong's GDP totalled 793.7 billion yuan (US$95.8 billion) in 1998, up 10.1 per cent from 1997. Guangdong has the country's highest household income, with Shenzhen and Guangzhou ranked first and second in cities. Consequently, Guangdong leads the country in retail sales and pays the most taxes to the central government.[3]

Guangdong's economic growth has attracted numerous foreign investors. *China Daily*, China's official English-language newspaper, estimates that up to 70,000 foreign invested enterprises (FIEs) have set up operations in the province, and many of them have established their headquarters there.[4] The presence of FIEs has further boosted the local economy. FIEs employ seven million workers, make up half of the province's industrial output, contribute 40 per cent of the province's capital investment, and account for 26 per cent of its tax revenue. Most projects are in labour-intensive industries, particularly those producing consumer goods. Forty-one per cent of foreign operations are in manufacturing, 31 per cent in real estate, and the rest in other sectors.

Factors for Guangdong's rapid growth

Why has Guangdong achieved such brilliant progress? As some experts put it, the salient feature of Guangdong's success is its better utilization of its comparative advantage at each stage of development.[5]

Location. Proximity to Hong Kong, with its complementary comparative advantage and common dialect, is one of the province's major advantages. On the one hand, Hong Kong has served as China's gateway to the world for over a century, providing foreign companies with a powerful incentive to set up their China operations in Guangdong; on the other hand, Hong Kong itself has become Guangdong's biggest investor. It accounted for three-quarters of the province's total investment in 1999.[6] Hong Kong-invested factories provide millions of jobs and offer technological and managerial skills.

Thousands of Hong Kong's companies have relocated their manufacturing facilities to Guangdong to take advantage of the province's relatively cheap and abundant labour and land. According to one study, goods produced in Guangdong have a 70 per cent profit margin compared to the 20 per cent margin for goods made in Hong Kong. Trade and investment flows have thus skyrocketed since the late 1970s. Hong Kong accounted for 80 per cent of the investment in Guangzhou and 65 per cent in Shenzhen from 1993 to 1998.

In addition, Hong Kong has become a bridge of economic cooperation between mainland China and Taiwan. With direct trade between them still prohibited, the most common indirect route for Taiwanese companies to invest in mainland China is through Hong Kong. Taiwanese companies invest in mainland China for similar reasons as those from Hong Kong, and many companies have relocated their manufacturing facilities there, particularly to Guangdong and Fujian provinces where labour and land costs are lower than those in Taiwan. In mainland China, Taiwan invests more in Guangdong than in any other regions including Fujian, which is closer to Taiwan not just geographically but also in heritage and language. By the end of 2000, Taiwanese investment in 11,000 firms in Guangdong had exceeded US$7 billion.[7] In line with Guangdong's development goals, Taiwan companies are shifting from labour-intensive investment to high-tech projects.

Infrastructure. The province has well-developed energy, transportation and telecommunication systems. It has 91,862 kilometers of highways, the highest density in the country. Guangdong boasts 163 trading ports and has been China's telecommunication pioneer, hosting the country's first wireless paging station, digital telecommunication network, 900 megahertz analog and digital cellular network, advanced 2.5 gigahertz synchronized digital hierarchy transmission, and digital cellular network based on Code Division Multiple Access (CDMA) technology. Moreover, Shenzhen-based Guowei Electronic Corp. was the first company to make digital mobile phones in China. Mobile telecommunication revenue in Guangdong accounts for 15 to 20 per cent of China's total.

Government. As Guangdong was the first province to benefit from China's economic reform, local officials are well-trained in the art of doing business. The consensus among foreign companies in Guangdong is that the local government is more straightforward and sophisticated than elsewhere in China.

Consumers. Much like their Hong Kong neighbours, Guangdong residents are avid consumers. Guangdong ranks first in the country in household consumption, spending nearly 3.2 billion yuan (US$386 million) in 1998. Jiangsu province ranks second, at 2.4 billion yuan (US$289 million). Guangdong's urban consumption jumped 7.8 per cent in the first half of 1999 over the same period in 1998. The rural consumption growth rate was even higher, at 11.6 per cent.

Strong consumption growth appears to be here to stay. The provincial government has been encouraging domestic consumption to avoid the effects of falling demand for exports to Southeast Asia. The government aims to sustain consumption growth over the long term in part by increasing investment in education. Province-run colleges and universities expect new student enrolment to jump 64 per cent this year.

Consumers in Guangdong tend to look for quality. For example, three of the top shampoos in Guangdong are American brands. One company representative explained simply that a 'buy local' campaign may have worked 5–10 years ago, but today business and society are more open, and Guangdong consumers cannot be coerced into purchasing local products that are inferior.

Three stages of Guangdong's economic structural adjustment

Guangdong's economic structural adjustment can be divided into the following three stages:

- *First stage (1979–84).* Guangdong paid attention to light industries such as textiles, electronic appliances, toys and footwear. In this period, Guangdong moved from an agricultural economy to a more industrialized economy.

- *Second stage (1984–92)*. Guangdong paid attention to infrastructure investment in highways, subways, power plants, railways, and so on. In this period, Guangdong's industrialization continued.
- *Third Stage (1992–present)*. Guangdong has paid attention to macro development strategy and prepared for a highly industrialized economy. Compared to the first and second stages, this period has some special features. First, the relationship between demand and supply changed, with supply surpassing demand for some merchandise such as textiles and electronic appliances; an economy featuring supply shortage came to an end. Second, the Asian financial crisis in 1997 affected the province's economic growth, especially in exports. Third, state-owned enterprise reform faced more and more obstacles, including the lack of a social security system and the huge task of dealing with unemployed workers. Fourth, entry to the World Trade Organization (WTO), whose effect is yet unknown, will bring about both advantages and disadvantages to the process of structural adjustment.

In 1999, the structure of three sectors was 12.7 per cent, 50.4 per cent and 36.9 per cent, as compared to 24, 46 and 30 per cent in 1978. Primary industry showed a decline, while secondary and tertiary industries increased steadily. The investment structure accords with the national industrial policies. Investment in basic industry and infrastructure increased, whereas the number of redundant construction projects in general processing industries decreased. The continued downward trend in investment in innovative industries was reversed. Development of sectors such as electronic telecommunications and electric equipment sped up while growth in sectors such as textiles, sugar refining and coal mining slowed down.

Problems existing in Guangdong's economic structure

Guangdong is reorganizing its economic structure in order to prepare for across-the-board increases in market competition expected to come with China's entry into the WTO. The setting of serious production ceilings in many sectors and the closing of many small and inefficient plants, which are sometimes the source of heavy pollution, mark the reorganization. As Sheng Huaren, Minister of the State Economic and Trade Commission, states, 'because of the market conditions, controlling the overall production of some important products has become a very urgent matter if we are to adjust our economic structure and improve economic efficiency.'[8]

Serious oversupply of many industries

Oversupply has reduced market activity and has exerted downward pressure on prices. The specific production capacity of some enterprises is too small to reach a rational economic scale. This problem exists not only in Guangdong but also in other provinces, affecting earning performance. Meanwhile, outdated technology and equipment are hindering the progress of these industries, and such a fragile industry structure is incapable of competing with international firms.[9]

Policy discrimination in the non-state sector

The non-state sector has not become a major economic power. Guangdong's government, however, has not redirected investment to non-state firms, hence, this sector still suffers from policy discrimination and tight credit.

The structural changes in Guangdong's economy over the past two decades have significantly increased the economic power of the non-state sector, which includes private firms, township and village enterprises, and Sino-foreign joint ventures. The non-state sector has been the major source of employment and output growth, accounting for over 50 per cent of the province's urban employees and 70 per cent of its industrial output. However, 86 per cent of all state bank lending goes to the SOEs, leaving only 14 per cent for the non-state sector, of which the private sector receives only 0.3 per cent. Banks are reluctant to lend to non-state companies because of both government policy and their own risk aversion.

At the same time, Guangdong is investing a lot of money into its state-owned sector, which has yet to be completely restructured. China has used state banks as vehicles for policy lending to keep SOEs afloat. While these loans are not based on sound business principles, SOEs have government guarantees so their credit risk is perceived to be much smaller than that of private companies. In addition, the government often waives taxes and bank-loan interest to SOEs experiencing financial trouble, but does not give the same treatment to firms in the private sector.

Despite all of the efforts to turn state companies around, over half of SOEs are still losing money. Such a record is hardly encouraging for Beijing's purported goals of revitalizing large SOEs. However, the obstacles to private sector growth have not stopped the number of private firms from growing rapidly. Many of these new firms are start-ups set up by laid-off workers, but large numbers go bankrupt quickly, an indication that the growing industrial output of the private sector does not necessarily mean that the sector is enjoying an environment conducive to further development.

Investment suffering from the Asia slump

The number of new investment agreements signed fell 40 per cent in the first half of 1999 compared to the same period in 1998, and foreign direct investment dropped 4.2 per cent. To some extend, the province's overall investment environment is no longer as enticing as before. It no longer enjoys nearly exclusive preferential status in trade and investment. This status, once unique to Guangdong, has now spread to other parts of the country. The cost of land and labour in the province though still low compared to Hong Kong and other East Asian economic 'tigers', has risen over the years, prompting some companies to relocate to other parts of China.

Deterioration in bank asset quality

The deterioration in bank asset quality remains unchecked and resolving the debt problems in the state banks will be a long process. The entire banking system reflects serious conflicts of interest between lending practices and political interference. The difficulty facing China's international trust and investment companies (ITICs) is a clear indication of this problem. The main function of ITICs, investment instruments for national and local governments, is to raise foreign capital, ranging from direct investment to loans and financial derivatives, for local governments and businesses. They are not run as profit-maximizing institutions. As a result, politically-driven lending has been a serious problem.

ITICs also have the balance-sheet problems common to many Asian banks. They have borrowed short-term foreign money to finance long-term local projects, and such mismatches have exposed ITICs to the risks of rising interest rates and withdrawal of foreign funds. This problem was evident during the Asian crisis. Meanwhile, poor regulatory oversight and supervision of the ITICs has resulted in capital forbearance and asset quality deterioration. Until recently, funding from local governments or increased overseas borrowing enabled the institutions to muddle through. However, high real domestic interest rates, and a sluggish economy have finally exposed the ITICs' problems aggravated by the currency withdrawal of foreign funds.

The closure of GITIC in October 1998 showed Beijing's determination to tackle structural problems in the financial system.[10] In GITIC's case, the People's Bank of China (PBOC) made it clear that it would bail out neither debt-ridden financial institutions nor non-foreign creditors if the loans were not properly registered with the State Administration of Foreign Exchange. The refusal to bail out all creditors indicated that Beijing is confronting the difficult problem of moral hazard in its financial system. If Beijing pursues a consistent policy with other ITICs, the closure of GITIC can be seen as a direct attack on the system's root problems. Thus, it is a positive sign for reform.

The fact that Beijing is pushing through painful reforms amid rising economic stress and weak public confidence shows that it understands the urgent need for reform. By offering much higher yields on deposits, ITICs and other non-bank financial institutions, such as credit cooperatives, have threatened to erode the deposit base of state banks, which hold almost 70 per cent of total deposits and are seen as the foundation of economic stability.[11] In addition, ITICs' speculative nature and imprudent management suggest that their competition with the banks is unhealthy at this stage. Stabilizing the financial system by shutting down the inefficient, non-bank financial institutions will help pave the way for state bank reform.

It is apparent that the government will thus proceed with its financial restructuring strategy to reform the ITICs and provincial banks before restructuring the large state banks. Continuing with this reform strategy, PBOC, China's central bank, has announced that starting in 2000 it will allow only 40 out of 240 ITICs to survive, depending on their asset quality and size. The central bank is likely to allow one ITIC to remain for every 10 billion RMB yuan (US$2.4 billion) of assets, or two ITICs for the same amount after restructuring, provided that their asset quality meets certain criteria.[12]

The deflation trend

The deflation trend has not been curbed and insufficient demand remains a prominent factor restricting economic growth. There is an emergence of structural and low-level supply surplus and commodity retail prices and the capital goods price index were down in 1999. A large volume of production capacity is lying idle, except for that of the processing industry. Even commodities that had long been in short supply, such as energy and means of transportation, began to witness a surplus in 1999. In addition, investment growth slowed down, with an increasing trend of investment by the state-owned sectors being slower than the non-state sectors. The dependency of investment growth on state debt is rising considerably. The market lacks new attractions for consumers, and some system and policy factors that restrict consumption are yet to be eliminated, thus holding back consumption in other markets such as housing, transportation and education, from beginning. The low purchasing power of farmers due to the slow increase in their income makes it difficult to develop a rural market.

Reform of the macro-policy environment has lagged behind

The fundamental reason for the failure of economic development in Guangdong, as in the rest of China during the pre-reform era, was the adoption of the leap-forward policy and the heavy-industry-oriented development strategy, as contrasted to the more recently employed comparative advantage strategy.[13]

A mistake of the traditional socialist system was to promote capital-intensive heavy industry in order to construct a self-contained industrial economy for national security within an agrarian economy with scarce capital resources. In order to develop then unprofitable capital-intensive industries, a number of input prices had to be lowered artificially. Thus, interest rates and wages were suppressed, the exchange rate was overvalued, and raw materials and energy were underpriced. In order to sustain the living condition of low-wage urban workers, the prices of agricultural products had to be reduced, which necessitated the formation of collective farms to produce cheap food. This highly distorted price structure required the replacement of market mechanisms with planned allocation mechanisms. Additionally, in order to secure scarce capital for the development of heavy industries, profit incentives had to be suppressed, which led to the nationalization of industrial enterprises.

In this way, the trinity of the traditional socialist system was formed as a logical consequence of the adoption of a heavy-industry-oriented development strategy. The system features a distorted macroeconomic or price environment, a planned resource allocation mechanism, and non-private micromanagement institutions consisting of state enterprises and collective farms. Thus, despite a commendable average annual growth rate of GDP, 6 per cent annually between 1953 and 1978, the standard of living was persistently low due to underdevelopment of the consumer goods industries.[14] Planned allocation resulted in inefficient resource allocation, which was exacerbated by the inefficient operation of state enterprises and collective farms driven by lack of work and management incentives. Thus, the economy grew due to capital accumulation with minuscule improvement in efficiency.

It is important to note that the Chinese government has not yet abolished a heavy-industry-oriented, leap-forward strategy, as is evident in its support of inefficient large- and medium-sized state enterprises engaged mainly in heavy industries.[15] Being inefficient, many state enterprises require subsidization under the distorted macroeconomic policies particularly in the form of low-interest loans supplied by state banks. This explains why the reform of macro-policy environment has lagged behind. It is important to realize that such a distorted macro-policy environment has serious consequences for reform of enterprises. Because of the distortion, profit levels do not necessarily indicate the efficiency of enterprise management.

The approach to the adjustment of Guangdong's economic structure: goals and strategies

Development goal

Guangdong is implementing and should adhere to three major development goals, namely having an export-driven economy, emphasizing sustainable development, and promoting rejuvenation through science, technology and education.[16] Based on these three major goals, new and better performance will be achieved in economic structure, industries, science and opening up to the outside world in a bid to enhance Guangdong's competitiveness and maintain rapid and sound economic growth, Guangdong's provincial government will initiate economic restructuring as follows:

- *Readjust and optimize industrial structure*. In the wake of home and world market changes in the 1990s, predominantly labour-intensive industries in Guangdong have failed to meet the changing market demand,[17] and a shift is needed to a technology-intensive industrial structure. Guangdong will encourage increasing adjustment in industrial structure and the product mix of businesses, and priority will be given to three major pillar industries:

    1. Electronic information
    2. Electrical machinery
    3. Petrochemicals

The proportion of these three major pillar industries to the total industrial output is expected to be 32.1 per cent by the year 2000 and 37.5 per cent by 2010.[18] Meanwhile, new and high technologies shall be introduced to upgrade the three conventional industries in Guangdong – textiles and garments, food and beverages processing, and building materials. The government will also support automobile, pharmaceutical and paper industries, and foster and promote high-tech industries with biotechnology at the core. Prioritized industrial projects in the next five years include:

1 A polyethylene plant (800,000 tons/year) in Huizhou City
2 A PTA manufacturing operation (250,000 tons/year) in Zhuhai City
3 A paper pulp mill (500,000 tons/year) in Guangzhou City
4 A Honda sedan plant in Guangzhou City
5 Fenghua Company's facility to manufacture new types of electronic components in Zhaoqing City

- *Product-mix restructuring*. The short-term objective in product-mix restructuring is to create 5 to 10 world-known brand names by 2010 in Guangdong. The long–term objective is to create another 100 brand names in the province.[19]
- *Enterprise restructuring*. The provincial government will focus its support on 70 conglomerates, which will become powerhouses of industrial development in Guangdong. The government expects that the dominant industries may secure over 30 per cent shares of China's market by the year 2005 and a number of strong multinational corporations should emerge from Guangdong Province by 2010.[20]
- *Rational regional distribution of economic sectors*. According to the strategy in which Guangdong's central region plays a leading role, the development of the western areas and the northern hilly and mountainous areas will be accelerated.[21] The Pearl River Delta will serve as the focus of the whole province. Priority will be in developing natural resource effective, environment-friendly, high value-added and technology-orientated industries. Development of high-performance agriculture, high technologies, and the service industry will also be encouraged.

Development strategy

Guangdong should continue its strategy to maximize its comparative advantages. The salient feature of the East Asian success is the utilization of comparative advantages at each stage of the region's development. Guangdong should implement a shift in development strategy from a heavy-industry-oriented to a comparative-advantage-led strategy in order to sustain growth momentum. The adoption of the latter strategy implies that government support for inefficient state enterprises will become unnecessary. This suspension of support for inefficient state enterprises will accelerate the reform of the macro-policy environment.

In the process of adjusting Guangdong's economic structure, how should Guangdong carry out the strategy of using its comparative advantage? First, Guangdong should maintain its advantage of an export-oriented economy and continue to enhance export competitiveness. It should replace low-tech and labour-intensive 'sunset' industries such as textiles and footwear, with high value-added 'sunrise' industries, such as machinery and electrical equipment.[22] This process has been occurring since 1997; the share of low-tech, labour-intensive products in China's total export dropped over 6 per cent, while that of high value-added products rose more 8 per cent in 1999.[23]

Second, the government should grant private businesses equal access to capital and markets as the rising importance of a market economy ensures that small- and medium-sized businesses, many of which are private companies, will become the backbone of the economy. Small- and medium-sized enterprises are a characteristic of Guangdong's economy. There are already signs that Guangdong's government has started to realize the importance of the private sector. For example, it has cut the valued-added tax for small businesses by 2 per cent to 4 per cent, effective since July 1998. Guangzhou has also given state commercial banks the autonomy to lend to small- and medium-sized companies, easing their credit crunch.

Guangdong needs to facilitate capital allocation through the capital markets. However, the feasibility of this depends largely on the central government's willingness to focus its securities regulation on the quality of listings rather than their sizes and political ties. The Securities Law passed recently addresses trading irregularities, but ignores the limitations on new listings. Current domestic and overseas listing rules are based on a quota-allocation system and limit public listings to large SOEs. The rules essentially exclude market-oriented and efficient private enterprises from the securities capital market, allowing SOEs to continue to consume the country's savings.

Third, Guangdong, like the rest of the country, should go through a financial sector cleanup. The key to resolving the SOEs' woes is the establishment of an institutional framework for the financial system.

Indonesia and Malaysia are two other countries whose institutional weaknesses were put under a magnifying glass once the Asian crisis began; but these weaknesses also occurred in Guangdong and the rest of China. Allocation of funds based on political connections and government favours rather than the standard credit analysis should also be eliminated. The Asisan crisis has warned us that anti-competitive practices are harmful to healthy economic development and should be abolished. Banks were routinely protected from competition forcing them to lend to government-favoured customers instead of choosing their customers based on net worth calculations.

Guangdong should continue to take the expansion of domestic demand as the top task of macro-economic control. The expansion of domestic demand, which will remain the primary task of macro-economic control in the year 2000, should be further enhanced. With the proactive fiscal policy continuing to be implemented, efforts should be made to accelerate enterprise reform and to heighten the reform of the investment and financing system. The goal is to facilitate the increase of investment in fixed assets and the formation of a system and mechanism for a normal demand growth, and to gradually reduce the dependency of investment growth on government loans. Measures should be adopted to encourage the enthusiasm of enterprises and various social sectors for investment and to create a social environment favourable for the expansion of investment.

Active efforts should be made to encourage and guide non-government investment. Except for the areas that are related to national security and must be controlled by the state, all other areas should allow non-governmental capital to enter, and all restrictive and discriminatory regulations should be suspended in regard to taxation, land use, opening of businesses, import and export, and development of private economies. Moreover, with regard to stock listing, private enterprises should enjoy equal opportunities with their state-owned counterparts, and procedures for the examination and approval of non-government invested projects should be simplified.

It is important to treat deflation, but it is more important to treat the economic environment for business development.[24] One key is to ease controls and encourage competition. At present, banking, telecommunication, insurance, railway transportation and so on still operate under an administrative monopoly. Maintaining a monopoly, especially an administrative monopoly of the rapidly expanding industries, has suppressed non-governmental investment and expansion of investment demand. High costs created by the monopoly have suppressed consumer demand for the products of these industries and related products.

Consumption by urban and rural residents should be promoted to bring into play the role of consumption in stimulating economic growth. However, while encouraging residents to consume, it should be kept in mind that under the market economy it is very important for consumers to adopt a prudent attitude towards consumption when the social security function cannot be put in place quickly. Too much stress on consumption by the government is tantamount to consumption for consumption's sake and consumption for the sake of production.[25] The government should not be impetuous in encouraging consumption, and must not let the people feel that they are forced to consume, or that the aim of reform is to rob people's pockets.[26]

Consumption is an inherent characteristic of a human being, and there must be some reason when consumption declines. To encourage consumption, the government should remove the cause that restrains consumption. Policies that restrict consumption in electricity, automobiles, and telecommunications should be rectified, and consumer credit expanded. Efforts should be made to strengthen the development of tourism resources to stimulate domestic travelling. Focus should also be placed on stimulating consumption in transportation, education and housing, encouraging an active real-estate market in commercial housing and public houses that have been sold to state employees. Most importantly, reform of the income distribution system should be promoted to enhance purchasing power and to increase disposable income.

Another important means to stimulate consumption is to improve the competitiveness and diversification of the province's products. At present, there are few unique products with high scientific and technological content. Primary products in the fields of manufacturing, iron and steel, textile and chemicals are oversupplied,[27] while most of the core technology in producing household electric appliances is imported. In addition, the service industry currently concentrates on traditional food and commerce while modern service industries that tend to focus on information, consultancy, intermediary assistance and finance lag behind.

Guangdong should enhance the management level of township and village enterprises. Township and village enterprises (TVEs) in Guangdong, as those in the rest of China, are widely regarded as one of the major successes of the country's reform of the socialist economy. The discussion of enhancing the management level of TVEs in Guangdong frequently focuses on ownership changes as a means of fostering more efficient managerial behaviour. One viewpoint is that TVEs should sell shares of the enterprises.[28] Which might help to establish a modern enterprise system, giving real control rights to shareholders. However, without the development of financial institutions to monitor enterprise management, selling shares is likely to be an empty gesture from the standpoint of disciplining managers. Selling shares to shareholders should be done through a fair market mechanism. Otherwise, the likely buyers are those who already know the enterprises well, namely current managers and local officials or their relatives and friends.

Another problem with this approach is that the valuation of the enterprises will be difficult to determine, thus buyers might obtain a large windfall at the expense of local communities. Monitoring by people representing the interests of those communities, and not only of its leaders, will be imperative to forestall such an inequitable and socially divisive outcome. Even if sale prices pass the fairness or legitimacy test, there might be ownership by people closely associated with local leaders, many of whom are already resented by community members for alleged corruption.

Reform of state-owned enterprises is critical to the adjustment of Guangdong economic structure. Guangdong's economic structural adjustment also faces the biggest challenge – the reform of state-owned enterprises – which will largely decide the success or failure of the economic restructuring. Guangdong's reform of SOEs is similar to that of the whole nation, and a good understanding of Guangdong's situation can be achieved by examining the situation at the national level. One of the most prominent features of China's recent economic reforms has been the decision to promote large enterprises and enterprise groups with strategic significance. In September 1997, the central government approved a reform programme, the central platform of which is to promote large- and medium-sized enterprises (LMEs). Later, the central government announced three major polices to develop LMEs. First, it hopes to establish three to five large firms in the world's biggest 500 enterprises by the year 2000 and has been channeling extra funds into a selected number of large enterprises to accomplish this.[29]

Second, the central government wants to develop modern enterprises among large-scale SOEs by the year 2010. It has selected 1,000 SOEs to form the core of the 'modern enterprise system'. In 1996, the central government announced that a main bank relationship would be developed in these 1,000 enterprises starting with a pilot programme in 300 firms.

As of 5 September 1996, 279 enterprises had signed 'banking and enterprises cooperation agreements' with major banks. Under these agreements, the firms consult with their main banks before making investment decisions and their main banks support the long-term development and funding of the enterprises. The main bank relationship being developed at the national level is similar to the Japanese main bank system, but the major difference is that, unlike Japan, in China the banks do not sit on the SOE's board of directors.

Third, the central government is developing a number of enterprise groups in strategic sectors and has chosen 512 enterprises to form the basis of this programme. At the national level, the State Council is backing 57 enterprise groups, and a number of large enterprise groups are also being promoted at the sub-national level. Guangdong, for example, is restructuring 70 large SOEs into enterprise groups. The number of large SOEs and enterprise groups has mushroomed in recent years.[30]

However, there are potential barriers pertaining to the decision of Guangdong and the rest of the country to establish large enterprise groups:

1 *There is too much focus on blind expansion.* The main point which critics make is that the government is being too ambitious. For example, well-known Chinese economist Wu Jing Lian has criticized the establishment of enterprise groups on the basis that the authorities should not attempt to 'forcibly weld sampans together to form a aircraft carrier.' He argues that enterprises are subjected to 'forced marriages' or 'high-speed fattening' where entire industries are merged into a few large firms or one or two big enterprise groups.[31] Enterprise groups which have pursued blind expansion often consist of a number of enterprises that have been thrown together in an *ad hoc* manner and hence lack specific business strengths. In these cases the government has not paid enough attention to the transformation of the management mechanism inside the enterprises or to the rational composition of the enterprise groups.
2 *SOEs' debt-asset ratio and level of non-performing loans are too high.* Figures from the State Statistical Bureau indicate that the debt to asset ratio for the state-owned sector as a whole is 75 to 80 per cent. This is similar to South Korea before the financial crisis when the debt–asset ratio was about 85 per cent.[32] The problem is that over 80 per cent of the operating capital for SOEs is borrowed from the banks; most of the debt cannot be repaid because of their continued poor performance, meaning that the number of non-performing

loans has increased. High savings ratios combined with high debt–asset ratios were important catalysts for growth in East Asia over a sustained period. For example, in Japan concerns about the level of bad debts has underpinned recent calls to overhaul Japan's banks. Without a high level of savings and borrowings, it would not have grown as fast as it did in the 1950s and 1960s. In the period of rapid growth between 1956 to 1970, the cumulative deficiency of total enterprise accounts was made up entirely by the surplus funds of residents' accounts through deposits to bank loans.

3 *Financial support for LMEs is diverting funds from more deserving recipients.* Lending to SOEs, and LMEs in particular, is diverting funds from more deserving recipients. For example, the World Bank states that SOEs continue to absorb more than three-fourths of domestic credit and their borrowing makes up about 60 per cent of the total non-financial public debt. This has taken away investment in the non-state firms that have been the engines of China's growth. A similar argument is made in a recent report in *The Economist*. The report states that as long as the largest state enterprises lay claim to the bulk of China's financial resources, there is little incentive for the government to write-off the banks' bad debts, recapitalize the system, and allow credit to reach the most deserving recipients.

The main problem with the statement from the World Bank is the observation that 'non-State firms have been the engines of China's growth'. While it is true that the non-state sector has been growing fast, it is often forgotten that there has also been significant growth in upstream industries where large-scale SOEs are dominant. For example, between 1978–92 the gross output value in heavy industry grew at almost 11 per cent per annum. Over this period, China's ranking in total world output moved from fifth to fourth largest in steel, from third to first in coal, from eighth to fifth in crude oil, from seventh to fourth in electricity and from fourth to first in cement. Rapid growth in upstream industries provided the input needed to fuel growth in downstream industry. Hence, rather than attribute China's growth to the non-state sector in isolation, the better view is that there has been balanced growth. From this perspective, LMEs have not diverted financial resources from the non-state firms, but instead have contributed to the strong growth record of the non-state sector.

4 *The relationship between enterprise groups and government is too close.* Not enough attention is given to separating the functions of enterprises and government. Since the crisis, critics of China's approach

have argued that the experiences of Japan and South Korea show the danger to China if the relationship between enterprises and government is too close.[33] It is argued that in South Korea the role of government became muddied, which generated two related problems. First, too much emphasis was placed on government support through bank loans and not enough attention was given to developing robust business groups that can compete in the marketplace. Second, failure to separate business and government provided opportunities for the later to interfere in the decisions of management. It also tilted government policies in favour of large enterprises that made economic growth too dependent on the performance of these enterprises.

Conclusion

The restructuring of Guangdong's economy is a complicated issue. Guangdong government's implementation of the three major development goals, namely having an export-driven economy, rejuvenating Guangdong through science, technology and education, and assuring the sustainable development of the province, has formed the basis for the adjustments in Guangdong's economic structure. With the rapid changes in the world's economic situation, Guangdong must achieve a great breakthrough in developing strategic choices, exploiting external and internal markets, stimulating domestic demand, enhancing the level of management practices in state-owned businesses as well as township and village enterprises, and continuing reform in state-owned enterprises. It is believed that Guangdong's economic restructuring will be successful in the near future and the province will catch up with the economic development of the world's most developed areas.

Notes

1 Lin, Justin Yifu, Cai, Fang and Li, Zhou (1996) *The China Miracle: Development Strategy and Economic Reform. Hong Kong,* Chinese University Press, Hong Kong.
2 Krugman, Paul, 'The Myth of Asia's Miracle', *Foreign Affairs,* 7 November/ December, 1994.
3 *Ibid.*
4 'Guangdong Trade Group Looks to HK for Investment', *China Daily,* 16 May 2000.
5 Lin, Justin Yifu, Cai, Fang and Li, Zhou (1996) *The China Miracle: Development Strategy and Economic Reform. Hong Kong,* Chinese University Press, Hong Kong.
6 'Guangdong Trade Group Looks to HK for Investment', *China Daily,* 16 May 2000.

7 Wang, Rong, 'Taiwan Firms Keen on Guangdong', *China Daily*, 4 June 2001.
8 Sheng, Huaren, 'Some Thinking to the Adjustment of China's Economic Structure', *Management Science*, vol. 2, 1998.
9 *Ibid.*
10 Qian, Wen, 'Economic Fluctuation and Policy Regulating Responses', *Social Science in China*, vol. 1, 2000.
11 *Economic Daily*, 23 July 1998.
12 *Ibid.*
13 Bia, Heijin, 'The Strategic Choice for China's Economic Development in the 21st Century', *Reform*, vol. 6, 1999.
14 *Ibid.*
15 Qin, XiaoHua, 'View on China's Economic Trends for 2000', *Economic Research Journal*, vol. 4, 1999.
16 *Nan Fan Daily*, 6 October 1998.
17 World Bank, 'The State in a Changing World', *World Development Report 1997*, Chinese version, Finance and Economic Publishing House, 1997, China.
18 Qin, XiaoHua, 'View on China's Economic Trends for 2000', *Economic Research Journal*, vol. 4, 1999.
19 *Ibid.*
20 *Ibid.*
21 *Guangdong HK Information Daily*, 24 June 1999.
22 'The Strategic Blueprint to Realize the Modernization of Guangdong', *Guangzhou Daily*, 28 June 1999.
23 *Guangdong HK Information Daily*, 27 December 1999.
24 Zhou, Yonge, 'Multi-Level Financial Support System Needed for the Development of Small Enterprises', *Macroeconomics*, vol. 3, 1998.
25 Wu, ShaoPen, 'Is China's Current Consumption Rate Too Low?', *Macroeconomics*, vol. 1, 2000.
26 Lian, Jing, 'Some Thinking on China's Consumption Issue', *Economic Research Journal*, vol. 2, 1998.
27 Jiao, Pin, 'Economic Transformation and the Treatment of Un-appropriate Effective Demands', *Economic Research*, vol. 1, 1999.
28 Xia, Ying, 'China's TVE: Problems and Strategy Choices in Long Term Development', *Problems of Agriculture Economy*, vol. 6, 1999.
29 *People's Daily*, 23 March 1999.
30 *Ibid.*
31 Zhou, Jin Ming, 'Function Orientation of Chinese Enterprises Group', *Social Science in China*, vol. 2, 1999.
32 Zhou, Shulian, 'A Review of Reform in Chinese State-owned Enterprises Over the Last Twenty Years', *Social Science in China*, vol. 1, 2000.
33 Mao, Pin, 'How to Deal with the Relationship between the State-owned Enterprises and the Government', *Social Science*, vol. 4, 1996.

2

The Sustainable Development of Urban Forestry in Guangdong's Urbanization

Junqin Chen

Introduction

Urbanization is the inevitable trend of Guangdong's social and economic development. Since the beginning of reform and opening up in 1978, with the development of industrialization and commercialization, the rural population has been shifting to cities. More cities are emerging and existing cities are becoming larger. According to 1998 statistics, there were 71,434,300 permanent residents in Guangdong. Urban areas accounted for 31.2 per cent of the total population, up from 20.6 per cent in 1982.[1] The number of cities had increased from 13 in 1982 to 54. As the urban population grows, new living areas and facilities of all kinds are also being constructed.

Such increased development also brings with it certain negative effects as well, such as traffic jams in medium-sized and large cities, and air, water and noise pollution. Acid rain and other toxic materials seriously damage the living environment. As in other cities around the world, urban greenhouse and 'hot island' effects are becoming more prominent. The urban environment in Guangdong is quickly degrading, causing concern for the populations affected and posing challenges for regulators and policy-makers.

The growth in urban forestry can help to alleviate some of these problems. People are becoming aware that green space in cities is important. Forests have many benefits; as the major component of the terrestrial ecosystem, they represent nature's richest reservoir of resources, biological genes, water, carbon and energy. It is thus of vital importance to improve the environment and sustain the ecological balance. To a certain extent, without urban forestry, the sustainable development of cities as a whole is problematic. Therefore, developing urban forestry, increasing public green areas, and improving the urban environment have become the major goals of sensible sustainable urban development.

The government of Guangdong is starting to place greater emphasis on ecological and environmental issues. For more than a decade, the government has carried out a large-scale afforestation campaign. It has helped to bring Guangdong's forest coverage from 27.7 per cent in 1985 to 54.7 per cent in 1999.[2] In recent years, the province has been actively engaged in urban forestry. Many cities have outlines of their own urban forestry plans, and are building greenbelts around city perimeters as well as shelter forests and urban forest parks. Some cities are attempting to transform themselves into what has been termed 'forest cities' and 'garden-like cities'. Currently, the forest coverage in the urban areas is 30.7 per cent and the per capita public forest area is 8.5 square meters.

The concept of urban forestry was introduced into China as recently as the early 1990s; its implementation is just in the beginning stages. An urban forestry system that fits China's unique characteristics has yet to be formed. In particular, there is little research regarding its impact on the development of urbanization. This chapter attempts to discuss issues related to developing urban forestry in Guangdong and its efforts to achieve sustainable development.

Features and problems of Guangdong's urbanization

A city is the political, cultural and economic centre of a certain area or region. As the economy of the province as a whole is growing, the cities also are quickly increasing in size. This is particularly true in recent years as the reform and opening policy has generated a great influx of rural dwellers into cities. There are certain characteristics associated with the urbanization process.

Counties are transformed into cities and cities at the county level increase in size quickly

Cities are the products of economic development. They are also the propagator of still further economic development, and a result of the industrialization process and marketing efforts. As populations converge on a delimited geographic area, cities emerge. Since the introduction of the reform and open-door policy, small enterprises, village enterprises (which have come to be known as 'township and village enterprises') and foreign ventures are proliferating in rural areas, especially in the Pearl River (Zhujiang River) delta region. These businesses employ a large number of rural residents and bring them into the cities. What used to be farmland is turning into industrial sites. Villages are transforming into towns and continue to grow in size. Peasants are becoming workers in the manufacturing or service sector as economic development brings with it new opportunities.

Many counties in Guangdong have followed this pattern of development. In 1982, there were 13 cities and 112 towns in Guangdong. In 1998, there were 54 cities (among them, 2 at the sub-provincial level, 19 at the prefecture level, and 33 at the county level) and 1551 towns in total. At the end of 1998, there were 71.4 million permanent residents in the province. Among them, 22.2 million were non-agricultural workers, which accounted for 31.2 per cent of the total population. This indicates that the percentage of urban population rose 10.6 per cent from that in 1982. The Pearl River Delta Area has thus become a major city cluster in the country. The urbanization rate in the province is 34.6 per cent, higher than the national average of 13.6 per cent.[3]

Cities are enlarging; city clusters around large-size cities are emerging

As new cities are emerging, older cities are continuing to get larger. At present, the population in Guangzhou is over 5 million.[4] The population in Shenzhen, Shantou, Fuoshan and other cities exceeds 1 million in each. As more counties are turning into cities, the surrounding countryside is being incorporated into metropolitan areas. For example, in the Pearl River Delta Area there are now 432 towns and 24 small cities with populations ranging from 20,000 to 100,000.[5] There are over 100 towns and cities in every 10,000 square kilometers, creating a system of metropolitan areas with large cities as cores and small cities and towns as supplements.[6] The borders between cities and other cities are becoming blurred and the surrounding countryside being integrated into cities.

City functions are changing and industries are beginning to differentiate themselves

Until recently, cities in Guangdong were mostly comprehensive in their functionality, usually serving as regional centres of political, cultural and economic activities. In light of the economic development, industrialization and urbanization have had a synergistic effect on each other. Most cities have become industrialized, and focused on different sectors. For example, Shenzhen has gradually specialized in hi-tech industries, Huizhou in the manufacturing of electronic goods, and Maoming in petrochemical products. In addition, industrial development has reached its limits in some regions. In certain cases, the investment environment deteriorated, and some sectors became less profitable. Consequently, some businesses decided to relocate to other places or disappeared altogether. The space they vacated became occupied by the service sector. Now, some cities are focusing on developing service industries (e.g., tourism and banking). For instance, Zhaoqing is committed to developing tourism and has established a reputation as being among the best tourist destinations in the country.

Urbanization has played a role in altering the social and cultural environment as well. In many places, people have ignored the sustainability of the development of their cities. Many problems have occurred due to this oversight, including a number of environmental problems, managerial conflicts, and an imbalance of urban ecology. The following are some of the most prevalent problems:

First, the population explosion in recent years has created pressure on the administration and environment of cities. Since the beginning of the reforming process, Guangdong's urban population has sharply increased, especially in large- and medium-sized cities where rural labourers flocked to find new jobs. Guangdong has been the centre of the nation's population movement since the 1980s. 'Peacocks fly toward the southeast and millions of people move to Guangdong' was the commonly stated description of the population flow at the time. In the Pearl River Delta Area, newly formed businesses have attracted a large number of workers from other provinces and cities. More than one million professionals have come to the delta since the 1980s, while the number of labourers has increased to five million.[7] The transient population has increased the population density that was under considerable pressure even before the migration caused by new economic activity. The current population density in the Delta is 494 people per square kilometer.[8] The pressure has become even more serious as city planning and administration functions have lagged behind economic development.

Second, basic urban facilities are insufficient and environmental pollution is severe. As mentioned, with industrialization and urbanization, the population is exploding in many places. People's lifestyles have also changed. Manufacturing operations are substantially escalating and increasing with them are solid waste, air and water pollution. In addition, because of the lack of funding, such wastes have not been treated properly. According to governmental studies, in the delta areas where business activities are concentrated, the sources of drinking water are in greater danger than ever.[9] Many cities are technically experiencing drought conditions, although water is plentiful in their regions. In Guangzhou, the sources of eight water plants have been polluted to such an extent that they can not be used from time to time. Guangzhou has been forced to import water from outer regions. The same thing also has happened in Shenzhen. In Guangdong, acid rain frequency occurs more than 50 per cent of the time. In Guangzhou, it is present over 70 per cent. Air pollution also is increasing; visibility in Guangzhou is very low because of the foul air. Sunshine time per year has decreased by 400 to 500 hours, the biggest drop among all provincial capital cities.[10]

Third, older districts in cities are becoming degraded, and small- and medium-sized cities are expanding too quickly. Some of the districts in some of the older cities are experiencing dramatic changes: old municipal facilities are outdated and overused, economic development is lagging compared to suburban areas, long-time residents are moving out, and the surrounding areas are playing more active roles in the urbanization process. Hence, peripheral areas are developing faster than the older districts and the boundary between urban and rural regions is disappearing. Ecological problems are of even greater concern. In some small- and medium-sized cities, because of rapid urbanization, there is a growing number of disputes between cities and their adjacent regions as well as between different departments within the same region. Problems such as these create increasing difficulties for maintaining sustainable development in terms of planning, administration, public health and general security.

The role of urban forestry in Guangdong's urbanization

Urban forestry is a municipal service industry, a specialized branch of forestry that has as its objective the cultivation and management of trees for their present and potential contribution to the physiological, sociological, and economic well-being of urban society. Its goal is to build up forests in cities, and to embrace cities with trees, shrubs and grass. It could improve the ecological environment, maintain the ecological balance, and beautify the cities to enhance the quality of life. Urban forestry is part of the urban ecological system that involves the usage of energy and materials, and their interaction with the natural system. In addition, it plays a critical role in maintaining the fluctuating balance within the ecosystem.[11] The various benefits of urban forests are as the follows:

Amelioration of climate

The major elements of climate that affect city dwellers include solar radiation, air temperature, air movement and humidity. With the proper placement of trees and shrubs, a microclimate can be created that could potentially improve the climate sufficiently for residents. During the summer cities in the region are usually hot and dry. Trees and shrubs can serve to lower the temperature and increase the humidity. It is reported that for every percentage of increase in forest coverage, the highest temperatures in summer could be reduced as much as 0.1 degrees centigrade.[12] If the forest coverage in a city can reach 50 per cent, the urban 'hot island' effect can be contained for the most part.[13] The humidity under a tree is usually higher than an open field and that generated by a single tree could be ten times the amount generated by water in the same area. Well-distributed and maintained urban forests using the right tree species can increase the relative humidity by 54 per cent.[14] In winter, urban forests can reduce the forces of chilly and strong winds while they can mitigate the effect of hot and dry winds. The shelter forests can also reduce the speed of winds. The windward side of a shelterbelt, can reduce the wind speed for a range that is two to five times of the height the trees; on the leeward side, the range affected tends to be about 30 to 40 times the tree height. Within a range of 10 to 20 times of the trees' height, wind speed could be reduced by as much as 50 per cent.[15]

Abating air and noise pollution

Some have suggested that plants perform an important role in reducing air pollution through the processes of oxygenation (the introduction of excess oxygen into the atmosphere) and dilution (the mixing of polluted air with fresh air).[16] Thus, it is reasoned that when polluted air flows in and around plants and through the freshly oxygenated air, dilution occurs and pollution is lessened. Particulate air pollutants also can be reduced by the presence of trees and other plants in several ways. They aid in the removal of airborne particulates such as sand, dust, fly ash and smoke. Leaves, branches and stems tend to trap particles that are later washed off by precipitation. Trees also aid in the removal of airborne particulate matter by air washing. Transpiration increases humidity, thus aiding the settling out of airborne particulates. Studies show that for every percentage point increase in a city's forest coverage, the dusts falling on an area of 1 sq km can be reduced by 23 kilograms, and airbound flowing dusts by 22 kilograms, 45 kilograms in total.[17]

City forests can also reduce bacteria. Certain types of trees can discharge materials that can kill bacteria, thereby reducing the air-bound bacteria in the proximity. In addition, when dusts are reduced, the carriers of bacteria decrease too.

In addition, city forests can absorb noise. The gentle surfaces of leaves and branches serve to absorb sound waves. Therefore, a dense and high forest can decrease the noise level by 10 dB.[18] In many cases, if there is a 30-meter forest belt between the source of noise and an inhabited area, the surrounding region can actually be very quiet. A 12-meter-wide greenbelt that is composed of trees and shrubs over a road can reduce noises by 3–5 dB.[19]

Controlling soil erosion and protecting watersheds

Because of environmental impacts associated with most construction activities, soil erosion control is perhaps the most important engineering use of plants. Plants reduce water-caused soil erosion by intercepting rainfall, by holding soil with their roots, and by increasing water absorption through the incorporation of organic matter. In addition, urban forest can preserve the sources of water and provide cities with clean water. Rapid population growth accompanied by expanding cities has greatly increased the demands on water resources. This growth is also creating ever-increasing wastewater problems. Urban forest can assist in alleviating these problems by providing cleansing of partially treated municipal wastewater and by recharging urban water supply aquifers.[20,21]

Increasing municipal income

Urban forests not only generate great ecological benefits, but economic benefits as well. A city with a developed forestry can produce a substantial amount of timber, fruits, flowers and other forest products. For example, in recent years the production of flowers and garden stock in the Pearl River Delta Areas has been blossoming. In this region, there are about 6,500 hectares of flower and garden stock production bases. The annual sale of flowers and garden plants reached 1.3 billion RMB yuan (US$156.6 million).[22] Of this, US$60 million worth of products are exported to other countries.[23] This business has become a pillar for many cities, and generates a major part of municipal income.

Forest tourism is another big source of income and has become a hot spot in recent years. Forest parks are now the ideal destination for many people. The Liuxihe Forest Park near Guangzhou receives over three million visitors each year, with revenue of over US$3.6 million.[24]

Urban forests may also increase the value of real property in the vicinity and induce the development of new construction. A home located within a city forest could be priced double that of others. A house with trees can be valued five to 15 per cent more, whilst apartments near parks or public playgrounds are worth 15 to 20 per cent more.[25]

Keeping control of the size of cities and beautifying urban regions

Urban forests can control the rapid expansion of cities, and rejuvenate the appearance of old districts within. In recent years, the peripheral areas of large cities have quickly become industrialized, and the sizes of cities are getting much larger. Therefore, the development of urban forests, especially in the city surrounding areas with the aim of building up urban shelter forests and separation greenbelts can effectively contain the expansion of cities. Such forests, flower plants or plant nurseries can serve to delineate city communities and promote the upgrading of older city regions. Afforestation projects can lead to increased beautification efforts in areas otherwise plagued by urban blight. The seasonal changes of plants, spring flowers, summer greenery, fall fruits and winter branches can change the appearance of cities at different times of the year. The colourful plants can supplement the rigid appearance of cement buildings in many cities and make buildings look more attractive.

Adding jobs in cities

The development of city forests can provide more job opportunities. Plant care, the management of forests, forest byproducts processing and tourism, are all labour-intensive. Because most of the labourers currently living in the cities originally come from the countryside, they should know more about planting and maintaining trees than people born and raised in urban areas. It is also likely that with their background in agriculture, many workers probably know more about this field than other services and industries. Therefore, it is possible that urban forestry can help ease the pressure on city employment levels.

Some may argue that using land for planting trees or timber production in urban regions is a poor investment when analyzed from a strictly financial perspective. Indeed, demand for land in urban regions is high, so there are numerous alternative uses for forestland in these regions, provided that the land can be physically developed. These lands can be sold for other uses, for example for factories, stores and highways which would generate income to the community in the form of jobs, tax dollars and increased economic development. However, for the sustainable development of cities and the benefits of the urban forest, in the case of public forestland many urban residents would rather bear the opportunity cost associated with parks or open spaces in cities, rather than dedicate the land to other more potentially damaging uses.

Futian Natural Mangroves, a 180-hectare tract of forestland in the city of Shenzhen, is used primarily as recreational land and is the location of a nature preserve. A proposition was made in 1994 to use a portion of this nature preserve for a highway corridor to Hong Kong. Many residents of Shenzhen, concerned with the developing economic base of the city, saw immediate economic benefits to the community, including construction jobs and better access to Hong Kong and other cities which they hoped would make it more attractive to new industries. Other residents did not want to lose a portion of the land to highway development, and this sparked a five-year-long debate over the fate of Futian Natural Mangroves. In 1998, the government of Shenzhen finally ruled out Futian Natural Mangroves as the location for the highway and maintained this open space as a natural mangrove preserve.

The current situation of urban forestry in Guangdong

The development of urban forestry is part of the solution for the many problems facing cities in the urbanization process. Especially for environmental problems, it is the inevitable choice. Guangdong has been ahead of the country in social and economic development and urbanization, but also in the deterioration of the environment. To solve the problem, in 1985 the government of Guangdong called on people to launch a campaign to 'eliminate bare mountains [i.e., to plant trees] in five years and afforest Guangdong in 10 years'.[26] Soon there was a great upsurge called the 'green revolution'. By 1990, a total area of 3,386,000 hectares of barren hills and mountains in the province had been afforested and the State Council designated Guangdong 'the number one province in waste mountain afforestation' in 1991.[27]

After much time and effort, Guangdong realized its goal of having the whole province afforested within a decade two years early. As a result, the area of afforested land increased from 4,637,000 hectares to 8,884,200 hectares in 1985, and the forest coverage rate rose from 27.7 per cent to 54.7 per cent in 1985.[28] To maintain this momentum, Guangdong has moved on to put urban forestry as its top priority project. Although the concept of urban forestry still awaits greater recognition from the populace, its development has actually been relatively fast, especially in the delta cities such as Guangzhou, Shenzhen, Zhuhai, Zhongshan, and so on. Many cities have incorporated urban forestry projects into their urban planning and economic development blueprint. They also stress adding on their own new features so that they can differentiate themselves from other cities. Such features include: (1) fully exploiting the spaces in cities for planting, (2) centring on the cities, building up circle-city greenbelts and radiating green corridors, and forming ecological circles around cities, (3) building several tourist spots with stylish buildings and plantations around the cities, and (4) setting up some fruit trees, flower and garden stock production bases in the suburban areas.

Although Guangdong's urban forestry has been successful in its practice, several problems have created obstacles for its sustainable development.

First, for historical reasons, there is little comprehensive and rational planning in the big picture of urban planning. Space saved for forestry is not enough, and little attention has been paid to this point. In some cities, existing forests and green fields have been occupied and eliminated. This situation brings difficulties related to comprehensive planning and development. At present, there is a tendency of decline in the forest coverage of some cities.

Second, because of the lack of technologies and equipment, and the lack of proficient management professionals, urban forests have been badly managed. Such a situation has hurt the development of urban forestry. In many cities, plants and trees are not properly nourished and watered and they are slowly dying or have stopped growing. In addition, some cities did not choose the right plant species when starting the planting projects, or used the wrong composition of plants that cannot fight pollution by themselves. In some cases, pests and diseases killed them. In other cities, there is only a single variety of tree for many streets.

Third, since urban forestry is still in its beginning stages in China, management of urban forest resources requires a set of relevant laws and regulations. In particular, China's urban forests involve different administrations such as the forestry department, park administration, environmental protection agency, land control and transportation departments. As a result, there are difficulties coordinating these relationships and administrative efforts, and this creates obstacles for the sustainable development of urban forestry.

Solutions for problems in Guangdong's sustainable development of urban forestry

The rapid urbanization process in Guangdong has brought opportunities and challenges to the development of urban forestry. In light of the unique features involved in Guangdong's urbanization and urban forestry, several policies should be adopted to achieve sustainable development.

Public education efforts should be strengthened in order to enhance awareness regarding city forestry

In China, urban forestry is a new branch of science and a concept introduced from abroad. Society as a whole is not yet familiar with it, and few people know how important it is. Therefore, education is needed, and people should know that urban forests are relevant to their living and working environment, and their health. They should realize that urban forestry is a necessary condition for the sustainable development of their cities and an inevitable rule of social development. At the same time, they should also be educated on the technology and practice of urban forestry to be both the beneficiaries and practitioners of city forestry. They can be involved in the planting and caring of trees so that they can improve their environment in part through their own efforts. Additionally, education should be incorporated into forest tours and citizens should be allowed to enjoy the beautiful forest so that they understand its value. Different methods can be used to enhance their incentive to participate, for example declaring a city flower and tree, or creating an Arbor Day holiday or forest week.

Urban forestry should be well planned

In urban development planning, the relevant authorities should consider sustainability in the development of urban forestry. Sustainable development is a frequently cited development strategy around the world. Urban development is a major threat to natural green space in cities, so in urban planning, urbanization and urban forestry should be planned and implemented simultaneously.

In planning for urban forestry, several principles should be followed. First, the authorities should refer to the general urban planning schemes for the region of interest, create an overall distribution plan of forests, and understand how many forests are needed. Second, the features of the cities and their industrial structure should be considered to define the goals and the tasks of urban forestry. For famous historical, cultural or tourist cities, the emphasis should be on scenic forests and forest parks; for industrial cities, because of the pollutants they generate, fighting pollution is their main task. Third, forest types and tree species should be scientifically chosen. There should be many types of forests – for example tourist forests, entertainment forests, shelter forests in suburbs, and separating forests between the cities and suburbs to limit the growth of city areas. In choosing trees, some species that can fight pollution and some that have beautiful appearances should be considered.

Urban forestry should be administrated and managed scientifically

The fundamental goal of city forestry is to improve the urban environment and to make cities more attractive, safer and more effective. For beautification purposes, forest planners should choose the right species of trees with the right shapes and colours so that they can match and enhance the environment. Safety is about citizens' health and security. For example, dying or weak trees could fall down in winds, and could damage power lines. Surface roots on streets can trip people. Even falling fruits and flowers could rot and pollute the environment. These are all threats to human safety and health.

Urban foresters should adequately manage their activities. They should choose the right species of trees, orderly plant them, check on their growth regularly, care and nourish them frequently, and clean out and cut down dying branches thus reducing risks to a minimal level. To achieve high effectiveness, highly efficient systematic management of the forests should be adopted for more ecological, social and economic benefits. The reason for effectiveness is that cities are congested, and traffic is heavy. Effectiveness is important so that urban forestry should not become a burden or adversely affect citizens' working and living activities.

In order to realize these beautification goals, safety and effectiveness, manpower, capital and equipment must be invested, and modern scientific management methods and technologies such as geographic information systems and information technology must be adopted. In addition, high-standard and intensive management practices should be introduced.

More professionals should be trained and research on urban forestry should be strengthened

Urban forestry in China is still in its infancy, and there are a lack of professional managers and researchers. Therefore, emphasis on these fields is necessary. More urban forestry courses should be offered in colleges and universities and the subject should be introduced to students majoring in garden, forestry and urban planning. More professionals in city forestry should be trained, and research institutes in urban forestry should be set up to organize studies combining ecology, park studies, forestry, economics, systematic science and urban planning. Cross-departmental studies are also necessary linking researchers in forestry, park studies, environmental protection, city construction, public administration, land control and traffic management. They should together develop a strategy for Guangdong's urban forestry, develop new technologies, and solve technical problems emerging from urban forestry practices.

Investment in urban forestry should be increased

Lack of capital is the major obstacle in forestry planning and effective urban forestry engineering. In order to sustain the development of urban forestry, the government should increase investment in this field by not only increasing its financial input but also seeking diversified sources of funding. Additionally, more support from citizens should be sought and a foundation for urban forestry should be set up.

An administration of urban forestry should be established and laws and regulations should be formulated

Due to historical reasons, two different departments manage urban forests in China; one is the Forestry Department and the other is the Park Administration. This situation is not conducive to the development of urban forestry, and the government should set up a new administration to coordinate their relationship so that funding can be utilized to its fullest extent and urban forestry can be better managed.

Moreover, laws on urban forestry must be formulated to define its legal status. As of September 1994, China formulated and promulgated four statutes or legal documents for forestry as a whole throughout the country, 10 sets of administrative rules and regulations, and over 60 departmental regulations. In addition there are a total of over 200 local bylaws and regulations, forming a basic legal framework for forestry regulation.[29] However, China still does not have any laws or regulations specifically addressing urban forestry, and special comprehensive laws and regulations dealing with this area should be formulated and implemented to promote and bind together all the activities associated with urban forestry.

Notes

1 Chen, Lie (1998) 'A Study on the Rual Urbaniation in the Pearl River Delta', *Tropical Geography*, vol. 18, no. 4, December.
2 Guangdong Editorial Department (1999) *The Research Office of the People's Government of Guangdong Province*, Guangzhou.
3 Forestry Department of Guangdong Province (2000) 'Forest Resource Data', Guangzhou, China.
4 Li, Ling (1997) 'Administration System Changes and Population Urbanization in Guangdong', *Tropical Geography*, vol. 17, no. 4, December. See also note 1 above.
5 Op. cit.
6 Li, Juan (2000) 'The Trend of Urban Forestry in The Pearl River Delta Area', *Forestry Development Workshop*, Guangzhou, China.

7 *Ibid.*
8 *Ibid.*
9 *Ibid.*
10 *Ibid.*
11 *Ibid.*
12 Cong, Richun (1997) 'Discussions on the Position of Urban Forestry in City Development', *Journal of Beijing Forestry University*, vol. 19, no. 2, April.
13 *Ibid.*
14 *Ibid.*
15 *Ibid.*
16 *Ibid.*
17 *Ibid.*
18 *Ibid.*
19 *Ibid.*
20 *Ibid.*
21 *Ibid.*
22 Miller, Robert W. (1996) *Urban Forestry*, Prentice Hall, Upper Saddle River, New Jersey.
23 Op. cit.
24 *Ibid.*
25 *Ibid.*
26 Op. cit.
27 Op. cit.
28 *Ibid.*
29 *Ibid.*
30 Ministry of Forestry, People's Republic of China (1995) *Forestry Action Plan for China's Agenda 21*, Beijing.

3
Sustainable Land Resource Development in Guangdong: What are the Current Issues?

Jingquan Yu

Introduction

Sustainable development includes many facets. Among them, land issues have always been of key concern to the Chinese people due to China's basic scarcity of per capita land. In the 1930s and 1940s, the Communist Party launched the so-called 'land-reform' campaign, confiscating lands from owners and redistributing them to peasants. This helped the Party win grassroots support, and eventually acquire the power of the state. Deng Xiaoping's economic reform in the late 1970s and early 1980s also started with assigning land and farm work to households in the rural areas. This system is called 'the Household Contract Responsibility System (HCRS)'.

China has made great strides in land resource development and has established a system with farmland protection at its core. However, the challenge facing China is still very serious and can be summarized as follows:

Shortage of arable land

China is a populous country characterized by a shortage of arable land. The total area is 960 million hectares, among which cultivated land, forest land, pastures, land for construction sites, bodies of water and unexploited land account for 13.8 per cent, 20.7 per cent, 27.55 per cent, 2.95 per cent, 3.8 per cent and 31.3 per cent, respectively, as revealed by the statistical survey finished in 1996.[1] China is also a hilly country with mountainous regions making up two-thirds of its territory. The per capita land and cultivated land comparison is shown in Table 3.1.

The table shows that the per capita cultivated land area in Guangdong province is less than the minimum warning limit of 0.05 hectare set by

Table 3.1 Per capita land and cultivated land by country (hectares)[2]

	World	Australia	Canada	Russia	USA	Japan	China	GD*
Per capita land (ha)	2.4	43.7	33.6	11.4	3.7	0.3	0.7	0.3
Per capita cultivated	0.25	2.90	1.67	0.87	0.73	0.03	0.11	0.04

* Guangdong Province.
Source: Data adapted from 'Special Research Report on Land Resource and its Sustainable Development', Guangdong Provincial Land Department, 1997.

the Food and Agriculture Organization of the United Nations.[2] There is a total of 666 counties where the per capita cultivable land is lower than the minimum warning limit.[3] Among the sparse cultivatable land, a large portion is dry, deteriorated and marked by soil erosion. The average per unit area output is only about 3,000 to 3,750 kilograms per hectare, which is about 1,500 kilograms less than that of developed countries.[4]

According to the results of the land resource survey finished in 1996,[5] China has about 13.33 million hectares of reserved land, of which 8 million hectares can be cultivated. Considering the delicate ecological balance, the land that can be reclaimed is quite limited.

Urbanization and urban sprawl

China is in the process of urbanization. In 1950 the total urban population in China was 58 million; by 1990, the figure had quadrupled to 214 million.[6] The number of cities increased rapidly and most of the cities doubled in size. In 1980 there were 223 cities throughout China; by 1990 the number had more than doubled to 467. In the last decade, the number of large cities has increased from 70 to 119, small cities from 108 to 289 and towns from 2,887 to 12,084.[7] The vigorous development of village and township enterprises in rural areas has also greatly accelerated the process of urbanization and industrialization.

At the end of 1999, the total urban population was 376 million which was about 30.9 per cent of the total population, according to official data from *China Daily*.[8] At present, more than 800 million people live in rural areas. During the transition to a market economy, surplus rural labour tends to move into urban areas, and consequently the migrant population has already reached 80 million and will increase substantially in the future. Demographic estimates indicate China's urbanization rate will reach 50 per cent by 2030, when China's total population is expected to jump to 1.6 billion.[9] Based on this calculation, approximately 15 to 16 million transient farm workers will head to the cities annually during the next 30 years. Provision of appropriate living conditions for these people inevitably has to occupy some of the land which is currently cultivated.

Inefficient land use

From 1986 to 1996, the total urban area increased by 106.8 per cent and there had not been rational planning and land utilization. Per capita land in cities stood at 133 square metres, which was 50 per cent more than the world's average of 83 square metres.[10] Roughly 5 per cent was vacant land and approximately 40 per cent was used in low efficiency ways.[11]

In rural areas, dispersed housing occupies a considerable amount of arable land; the per capita housing area is up to 182 square metres,[12] much more than the upper limit set by the State government. This poses a potential threat to sustainable development.

Guangdong Province is a good example of this situation. From 1987 to 1996, the expanded industrial and urban area was about 89,000 hectares, contributing 56.1 per cent of the construction land in that period. About 50 per cent of the expanded area was cultivated land.[13]

It was estimated that each 100 million RMB yuan (US$12 million) investment has occupied about 15 hectares of land and every 1 per cent of GDP growth can be regarded as the result of the cost associated with sacrificing about 1823 hectares of cultivated lands.[14] If Guangdong is unable to change its traditional extensive mode of land use, the reserved arable land will run out very soon. According to the survey of land resource finished in 1996, there are about 110,000 hectares of reserved arable land available,[15] which could run out within seven to ten years if Guangdong maintains its 10 to 13 per cent GDP growth rate without improving its land use. Of course, other factors such as, land degradation, soil erosion and desertification have reached all-time highs and should be of great concern.

The following sections provide definitions and a review of concepts related to sustainable development, and major land-use reforms made over the last 20 years in China are summarized. Emphasis if given to measures and processes related to farmland protection, particularly the new Land Administration Law and its implementation. Other actions and achievements are also briefly described. Finally, the challenges confronting China's sustainable development of its land resources are discussed and some strategies are suggested.

Concepts of sustainable development

Definitions and concepts associated with sustainable development are provided in order to have a better understanding and overview of sustainability.

Definitions of sustainability

Sustainable development will be the main concern of the world in the twenty-first century. No single term or definition can precisely capture the concept of sustainable development, and there are in fact many operational definitions.

Towards the end of the nineteenth and the beginning of the twentieth century, the prosperity of Western economies created an optimistic view of the future. Natural resources were no longer seen as posing severe restrictions on economic growth as new technology made far more efficient use of both old and new resources. The fragility of this economic growth was revealed, however, by the world oil crisis and economic recession of 1970s. Neo-Malthusians began to have doubts about unlimited growth, stressing once again the importance of conserving natural resources by setting limits to economic growth.[16]

In April 1968, the Club of Rome gathered to discuss the present and future predicament of the Earth and its finite resources. The results of its deliberation were published in *The Limits to Growth*.[17] The book predicted that the limits of growth on Earth would be reached sometime within the next 100 years if the economy continued its exponential growth in global population, resource depletion and industrial pollution. In 1992, 20 years after this controversial book was published, the same authors published its successor, *Beyond the Limits*, which reexamined the situation of the Earth.[18]

Another sustainability concept can be found in the 1960s' notion of carrying capacity in resource management. This concept can be described in wildlife management as 'the maximum number of animals of a given species and quality that can, in a given ecosystem, survive the least favorable conditions within a stated time period.'[19]

The most recent concept of sustainable development is a modified derivative of the concepts of growth limits and carrying capacity. It not only stresses the importance of resources in setting limits to economic growth, but also draws attention to the need to develop methods that emphasize the potential 'complement' between economic development and environmental improvement.

The 1987 report *Our Common Future from the United Nations World Commission on Environment and Development* (WCED) set forth the most widely used definition of the concept: 'Sustainable development is development that meets the needs of the present generations without compromising the ability of future generations to meet their own needs.'[20] The central goal of sustainable development is intergenerational equity, which implies fairness to coming generations.

Sustainable development does not mean *no* development. It means improving methods for resource management in an environment where there is an increasing demand for resources. Sustainable development represents a new synthesis of economic development and environmental protection. Economic activities are inevitably associated with the consumption of natural resources, and as populations increase and the pace of economic development quickens, there is a widespread concern about the scarcity of natural resources.

Sustainable land use

'Land' means something quite different to us now compared to what it meant to our grandfathers' generation. In the nineteenth century, for example, wetlands were once characterized as 'useless,' but are now thought of as having 'value.' As we increasingly understand the science of ecology and the web of connections between the use of any particular piece of land and the impact on the environment as a whole, we are increasingly aware of the need to protect wetlands and other areas that were formerly ignored. This concern over the interrelation of land uses had led to a recognition of the need to deal with the entire ecological system rather than small segments of it.

Sustainable land use has been defined in a number of ways, although the FAO (Food and Agriculture Organization) definition has gained common acceptance (See Box below). The essential feature is that sustainable land use achieves production combined with conservation of the natural resources on which production depends. The simplified definition can be compressed still further into a pseudo-equation:[21]

Sustainability = Production + Conservation

Land use and land-use policies are absolutely crucial items in the sustainability debate, and this can be demonstrated in two broad ways.

First, land is an essential ingredient of all human activity and a fundamental requirement for any form of production or development. There is almost universal evidence from recent history that population growth and the patterns of development and wealth creation that Western nations have pursued have created massively increased demands for land. Urbanization and industrialization in developing countries have greatly accelerated the conflicts between people and land. Second, the system and institutions of planning that promote and regulate both economic development and environmental protection have always been firmly based upon land use. Planning is centrally concerned with allocating land between competing uses and it is clear that when growing demands upon a fixed amount of land exist alongside increased environmental awareness and heightened concerns about sustainability, it is a field where potential conflict becomes more acute.

According to the FAO of the United Nations,[22] sustainable agriculture and rural development is the management and conservation of the natural resource base, and the orientation of technological and institutional change, in such a manner as to ensure the attainment and continued satisfaction of human needs for present and future generations. 'Such sustainable development conserves land, water, and plant and animal genetic resources, is environmentally non-degrading, technically appropriate, economically viable, and socially acceptable.'

Kivell simplifies this definition.[23] To him, sustainable land use is that meets the needs for production of present land users, whilst conserving for future generations the basic resource on which that production depends. In other words:

Sustainability = Production + Conservation

Chinese land reform over the last 20 years

The household contract responsibility system

China's economic reform started in rural areas. In the early 1980s, China abolished the administrative commune system and adopted 'The Household Contract Responsibility System (HCRS)' – rural lands were distributed among farmers according to their family size, and each family undertook sole responsibility for cultivating the land. The new system has at least three advantages:[24]

1 The separation of land-ownership (collective ownership) and the right to use it makes the farmers independent, thus arousing enthusiasm, promoting farm production and increasing incomes;
2 The principle of 'more pay for more work' can be realized; and
3 It may help to promote the transformation from a self-sufficient natural economy to a commodity economy.

Furthermore, the labour surplus freed from agriculture has stimulated the development of small enterprise and tertiary industries in towns or rural areas. This system had created agricultural miracles in the initial period of reform, but the later stagnation of agriculture shows that there is still more room for improvement. One of the problems, for example, is that with scattered, fragmentary agricultural plots it is hard to achieve scale operations and increase agriculture infrastructure. To some extent, this restricts the increase of farm production, and grain production in particular. A survey of 28,000 farm households in 300 counties in 1986 showed that 37 per cent of the households had less than five mus (0.8 acre) of contracted land.[25] Zhang[26] listed four disadvantages of HCRS, namely:

1 Peasants lost the sense of stability and permanence with relation to their land ownership. This resulted in eagerness for quick success and instant benefits, and predatory overexploitation of the land.
2 The land use is small in scale and scattered so it is difficult for agriculture to operate at the optimum scale or to specialize or modernize.
3 The arbitrary occupation and abuse of croplands by rural collectives cannot be controlled.
4 The uncontrolled felling of forests cannot be forbidden and forest cultivation is difficult to promote on a large scale.

With respect to achieving a scale operation, some scholars believe that rural land should be nationalized – a good idea to pursue for greater operation scale, farm mechanization and improvement of land-use efficiency. Some promote the privatization of rural land, so that farmers are self-supporting and self-managed. Others are in favour of leasing the rural collective land to farmers in the belief that leasing is more suitable to China's specific conditions because it will not only consolidate the collective economy, but also help to consolidate the scattered land and facilitate scale operations.

Although the nationalization of land is theoretically tenable, it would be difficult to implement due to the strong attachment of Chinese farmers to the land and the lack of alternatives for subsequent surplus labour. This would result in creating panic and resentment among the peasant farmers.

Privatization of the land does not fit China's specific conditions, and it would be a riskier proposition. Some peasants might annex land and others would lose land. Peasants who lose land and could not be immediately employed by other industries would face additional hardships. This would result in two opposing extremes and social turbulence.

Leasing might seem a reasonable alternative, but it still has the problem of transformation of the subsequent surplus labour and also requires a relatively high management cost.

Another method that has been adopted in Shunde, the most developed area in Guangdong, is that of bonding the land. In this system, individual households hold the land-share bond instead of the land itself. The collective then leases the land to farmers by tender (*zhaobiao*).

It is the opinion of the author that there is no single solution that can fit all of China. Because China is so large with an unbalanced economic development, any reform should be done in accordance with specific situations and should not be carried out with undue haste. For the developed areas, such as Shunde, leasing or bonding of the land is probably appropriate due to the capacity to transfer the surplus labour to secondary or tertiary industries. For most undeveloped areas, especially those found in mountainous regions, there are more disadvantages than advantages in changing the present system (that is, HCRS).

The basic dilemma is that HCRS has become intimately tied to protecting the farmer's households and is now absolutely dominant in China, although household production is probably destined for slow growth. With greater industrialization, HCRS would give way to industrial or corporate farming based primarily on hired labour. Because there are 800 million people in rural areas, reform of HCRS will eventually focus on the transformation of the subsequent surplus labour. Therefore, the central government should encourage those local governments that have the capacity to transfer the surplus labour to the non-agricultural sector to adopt leasing or bonding reform strategies.

Urban land-use reform

Up to the 1980s, a system of land distribution called 'administrative allocation' was adopted in China. Under this system, the state, as the monopolistic owner, allocated land to users and transferred the use rights to users without compensation. Land use was determined by a designated unit, and the rights to use the land were not allowed to be exchanged. As a non-valued commodity, demand and consumption of urban land was huge and wasteful. Much of the urban land allocated to units in inner cities remained undeveloped or underdeveloped.

The emergence of a market economy in China led to a growing demand for urban land-use reform, and the concern for foreign investment provided a chance for a reexamination of the administrative allocation system. The 1979 Sino-foreign Joint Venture Enterprises Law marked the start of the change in the traditional land-use system. The policy was further specified in the State Council's document, *A Tentative Regulation About Land-use Concerning Sino-foreign Joint Enterprises* (1980).[27] It required all Sino-foreign joint or foreign solely invested enterprises to pay a lump-sum fee for land-use rights. In November 1981, the Shenzhen Special Economic Zone started to levy a land-use fee, and the following year *A Tentative Regulation on Land Management in Shenzhen Special Economic Zone* (*shenzhen jingji tequ tudi guanli zanxing guiding*) was issued.[28] However, land was still forbidden to be sold and land-use rights were not allowed to be transferred. Furthermore, the land-use fee was normally too low to reflect the land value.

In September 1987, Shenzhen took the lead in experimenting with land-use rights transfer. On 9 September 1987, the land-use rights of a 5321.8 square metre parcel were sold to a Shenzhen company at a price of 200 yuan (US$24) per square metre through negotiation (*xieyi*).[29] This practice was regulated by law in 1988. In the revised constitution approved by the First Session of the Seventh National People's Congress, Article 10 section 4, the statement 'No organization or individual may seize, buy, sell or lease land or make any other unlawful transfer of land' was rewritten as 'No organization or individual may seize, buy, sell or lease land or make any other unlawful transfer of land. The right to use of land may be transferred according to law.' The Chinese government has adopted the separation of land ownership and use rights and allows the purchase and sale of land-use rights. The government can sell land-use rights to users and the land-use rights can be exchanged through the market.

Since then, the traditional administrative allocation system and the non-gratuitous land-use system coexist for different purposes. The former remains to be applied to state administrative units, social non-profit organizations, the armed forces and schools. These administrative allocated land-use rights are not permitted to be transferred, leased or mortgaged. If the administrative-allocated land occupiers want to dispose of their land-use rights, they have to get the approval of the local land management authorities and they also have to make payments to the state upon the completion of their transactions. If the land-use rights are offered through the non-gratuitous land-use system, it has a limited period of occupation. For example, the longest period is 70 years for residential use, 50 years for industrial use, and 40 years for commercial use. This kind of land-use right can be transferred, exchanged, mortgaged or denoted within its valid term. A land-use right can also be renewed on the expiration of its terms. This system is equivalent to the leasehold land system in Hong Kong.

Distribution of non-gratuitous land-use rights takes one of three forms: negotiation, tender or auction. Currently in some of the larger cities such as Guangzhou, the negotiated price is no longer allowed to be applied to commercial-use lands. Open auction is the unique way that commercial land is distributed. In December 1999, the Ministry of Land Resource requested that all the land used for real-estate purposes be transferred through auction.

Protection of farmland

Farmland is the most precious land resource in China due to its scarcity. In the last 40 years, total grain output has increased from 110 million tons to 490 million tons.[30] Since the policy of reform and opening up was adopted in the early 1980s, the structure of agriculture production has undergone some improvements. Township and village enterprises have been developing rapidly, and are changing, to some extent, the backwardness of rural areas. But on the other hand they have caused an increasingly serious pollution problem in agricultural environments. Accompanying the rapid economic development, the limited agricultural resources have been increasingly exploited (e.g., the non-agricultural use of farmland, over-grazing and deforestation). The Chinese government has been aware of the problem since the middle 1980s, and a series of reform measures for the establishment of a macro land administration system have been undertaken since 1985. First of all, a special agency – the Land Administration Bureau (LAB) – was established at various government levels, the duties of which include:[31]

1 Completing administration of the entire process from land ownership to land use in both urban and rural areas, and handling of applications for non-agricultural land use;

2 Surveying land resources and designing general land-use plans in urban and rural areas;
3 Supervising land-use patterns and land quality change, and protecting land resources from degradation; and
4 Strengthening research and education programme for land use and administration.

The first land law – the Land Administrative Law (LAL) – and the first 'Land Management Ordinance' were issued by the National People's Congress in 1986. Since then, a series of policies and measures for protection of farmland have been adopted, namely:[32]

- Carrying out national awareness education and improving people's understanding about the importance of protecting farmland;
- Strengthening administrative management and establishing the responsibility of local government leaders in those selected areas for farmland protection during their tenure (according to the *Regulations on the Protection of Basic Farmland* as established by the State Council);
- Strengthening the construction plan of urban and rural land use in order to control the scale of land use for residences;
- Delimiting basic farmland protection areas and strengthening the legal protection of farmland;
- Using economic devices to keep the dynamic balance of the total amount of farmland;
- Increasing investment in farmland, building key irrigation works, strengthening farmland's capability to resist natural disaster, and improving the quality of farmland and per unit area output;
- Strengthening technical management of farmland and carrying out the dynamic monitoring of farmland;
- Developing comprehensive management of rural farmland, water, roads, forests and villages (the estimated farmland to be increased by this measure is 6.67–13.34 million hectares); and
- Developing reserved farmland resources.

By the end of 1996, 2,100 counties had finished the delimitation work and 65 per cent of farmland was under effective protection according to the revised *Regulations on the Implementation of Law on Land Management*, and over 80 per cent of the farmland must be delimited into the reserves.[33]

Furthermore, extreme concern about the loss of farmland has arisen since the mid-1990s. In 1997 the Chinese central government made the decision to adopt the sternest policy to protect farmland and urged revision of the Land Administration Law. Meanwhile, all cultivated lands were 'frozen' in agricultural use until the new law was issued and took effect in January 1999. Moreover, illegal land use was included in the revised *Criminal Law of the People's Republic of China* (issued in 1997).[34] Qu and collegues[35] suggest that two factors triggered the change. One was the grain-market crisis that erupted at the end of 1993 and 1994; a shortage of rice in some southern areas led to price increases. The second factor was a prediction made by Lester Brown in 1995. Based primarily on his observation of the rapid decline in cultivated land, Brown predicted that by 2030 China would not be able to feed itself. The surplus of the rest of the world would also not be enough to fill China's grain shortfall.[36] Although Brown's projection received intense criticism both within China and abroad, it drew the concern of the loss of cultivated land and China's food security to an all-time high. Another factor which should be mentioned here was that China applied modern remote sensing methods to monitoring changes in cultivated land in five large cities in 1996. Comparing land satellite images from two periods, 1986 and 1992, astonishing decreases in the amount of cultivated land were found.

In order to halt the decline of cultivated land, a strategy called 'maintaining a dynamic balance of cultivated land' was initiated in 1996.[37] This strategy was later formally written into the new Land Administration Law. Provincial governments are required to take the responsibility to maintain a dynamic balance of cultivated land within their jurisdictions, and losses of cultivated land have to be compensated by somehow reclaiming an equivalent amount of new land. To some extent, China has curbed the rapid decline in cultivated land by implementation the new Land Administration Law.

The new Land Administration Law and its implementation

The core of the new law

The first land administration law was issued in 1986, but due to the fact that China lacked market economic experience at that time, the first land law proved to have some vital defects not suitable to a market economic system. According to the old land law, county or upper-county-level governments had the right to requisition farmland from the collectives. This was one of the main reasons that the rapid decline of cultivated land could not be curbed. The new Land Administration Law was promulgated in 1998 and took effect in January 1999. The core of the new law is to protect farmland and put land use under surveillance. The central government wants to change the former land-use mode of mainly providing construction land, to for the most part preserving cultivated land and controlling the increase of construction land, as well as encouraging circulation of vacant land in the cities. Before the new law was promulgated, mainly city or county-level governments determined land use. Now, the new law makes it clear that only the central government and provincial governments have the decision-making authority to occupy farmland for construction purposes; the county-level governments only have the execution right.

According to the new law, the central government deploys quotas to provincial governments and the provincial governments disperse the limited increment quotas to municipal governments or county governments. Land users must compensate for the valuable farmland lost for non-agricultural purposes. New farmland of equivalent quality and quantity should be reclaimed for the compensation of occupied farmland. In cases without reclamation conditions, a cultivation fee must be turned over to the provincial government for reclaiming the new farmland with equivalent quality and quantity in order to keep a dynamic balance of the total amount of farmland.

Implementation of the new land law

The new law took effect in January 1999, and the seizure of cultivated land has been alleviated.[38] The following year, while 205,369.3 hectares of cultivated land were occupied by various construction projects, 199,899.9 hectares more were preserved. Twenty-four provincial regions have achieved a balance in their seizure and replenishment of cultivated land. Also, far fewer illegal seizures of cultivated land occurred that year.[39]

The seven other provincial regions were warned by the Ministry of Land Resource that they had not kept their total farmland in dynamic balance and were instructed to guarantee to do so in 1999 for 2000 and formulate a plan for filling the gap created in.[40]

The implementation of the new land law showed that it still needed to be improved as it lacked specific penalties for violations and the present administration system still needed reform. Some local governments still tend to sacrifice cultivated land for short-term economic benefits and their subordinate grassroots land administrations could not effectively stop such activities.

In 2000, there were 168,309 land-related violations involving 28,732 hectares of land, of which 10,983 hectares were cultivated. Local governments themselves accounted for only 15.3 per cent of the violations.[41] However, their inadequate enforcement of the land law allowed local businesses to engage in illegal land use in pursuing rapid economic development. Some local governments have attempted to influence the work of grassroots land administrations in enforcing the law and some have even ignored land laws as they pushed economic development projects.

Supervision of the implementation

China's top legislators dispatched three inspection teams to check on implementation of the Land Administration Law in May and June of 2000.[42] The Ministry of Land Resource established a monitoring group composed of 140 experts. With the application of the highly differentiating remote sensing data and the aid of aerial photography, it monitored land-use transformation in 66 large cities (e.g., Beijing and Shanghai) which have more than 500,000 people, involving 714,000 square kilometers, among which there were 376 million mu (25 million hectares) of cultivated lands. The Ministry also investigated eight cities that reported falsified data. The illegal use of cultivated lands was up to 2,800 mu (187 hectares).[43]

The Ministry of Land Resource has taken strict measures to enforce the law while working out a complete set of administrative regulations on land management. A total of 689 government officials who illegally approved land use were punished in 1999.[44]

Rules to punish land law breakers

Because the law lacks specific penalties for violations, it allows an estimated 95 per cent of such lawbreakers to escape punishment.[45] When violations occur, the usual practice in many places is to fine the lawbreakers and have them go through the land-use application process. This actually aids offenders and encourages others to ignore land laws because the regulations are rarely enforced.

In order to enforce the new land administrative law effectively, the Chinese central government has issued new regulations to punish officials for violating state rules on land distribution.[46] A new regulation issued jointly by the Ministry of Land Resource and the Ministry of Supervision stipulates punishments for those found to have violated the state law on land management. The Ministry of Land Resource has received 4,049 reports of illegally distributed land, more than 57 per cent of which involved local officials.[47]

The regulation is expected to put some teeth into the Land Administration Law. It outlines specific criteria and procedures for the punishment of officials who illegally distribute land, and there is no doubt that the regulation will make implementation of the Land Administration Law easier and more practical.

Other actions and achievements

Surveying of land resources

From 1985 until October 1996, China spent more than 1 billion RMB yuan (US$120 million), with over 500,000 officials and land management experts participating in the first overall and unified land resources investigation. This super-scale survey of land resources was based on 1/10,000 topographic mapping, combined with new aerial photography and field surveys, which is thought of as the country's most systematic, complete and accurate survey to date.

Based on the investigation results, China promoted its famous policy 'strictly protecting cultivated land' and came up with fundamental programmes for the development of western regions. Based on the investigation results, China completed a three-level land-use overall planning (i.e., provincial, city or county and town level). The results were also used to settle over 1,000 land disputes.[48] On 5 July 2000, the Ministry of Land Resource vowed to update data on regional land resources every year to make it accurate, dynamic and comprehensive.[49] Whether or not this goal was attained will be demonstrated when data acquired in 2001 are analysed.

Land rehabilitation and augmentation of usable land

Since 1988 when the Chinese government promulgated the *Regulations on Reclamation of Land*, great progress has been made in the rehabilitation of abandoned land. According to statistics, 163,300 hectares of abandoned land have been rehabilitated or reused, 75 per cent of which have been used for farmland or other agricultural purposes. In 1995, the State Coal Industry Ministry arranged 10 key demonstration projects such as the project in the area at the conjunction of Shanxi, Shaanxi and Inner Mongolia which rehabilitates 4,500 hectares of land annually (this being 22.5 per cent of the total subsided area caused by coal mining in that year). Moreover, 1,770 hectares of slag hills were rehabilitated in open-cut coal-mine areas (amounting to 33 per cent of the total slag-hill area created that year). Since the early 1990s, Huaibei City of Anhui

Province has made great efforts in the rehabilitation of subsided land caused by coal mining. The accumulated rehabilitated area was 4,700 hectares, a rehabilitation rate of over 50 per cent.

Soil and water conservation

In recent years, the Chinese government promulgated and enforced the Law of the People's Republic of China on Water and Soil Conservation and the Regulations on the Enforcement of Law of the People's Republic of China on Water and Soil Conservation. Additionally, the National Programme for Water and Soil Conservation was formulated. All of these have stepped up the control of soil and water loss. Twenty-five major soil-erosion control areas have been established at the national level, and soil and water conservation projects have been carried out in the seven large river basins. The accumulated eroded soil area under control is 67 million hectares. The integrated soil-erosion control area in the Loess Plateau is 15 million hectares, putting 30 per cent of the eroded soil area under control to some extent and decreasing the annual discharge of silt to the Yellow River by more than 300 million tons.

Enhancement of grassland construction[50]

Guided by the Grassland Law of the People's Republic of China, governments at all levels have strengthened their protection and management of grassland resources, and strictly prohibited overgrazing and overcultivation. Grassland construction has been enhanced, and from 1991 to 1995 the average net increase of grassland was 598,000 hectares annually. A scientific experiment network and several bases for introduction and breeding of herbage have been established. The reserved herbage seed land has reached 350,000 hectares and the yearly production of herbage is 47,000 tons. There are 49 comprehensive animal husbandry demonstrations that have been organized by the government with outstanding results. By the end of 1994, the area of man-made grassland was 5.64 million hectares. This has created a new means for the development of highly effective animal husbandry in the areas sensitive to drought, desertification and soil erosion.

Combating desertification[51]

Since 1990, the Chinese government has taken a series of steps to control desertification. It has formulated the National Planning Programme for the Control of Desertification in 1991–2000 and National Action Plan for the Control of Desertification of China. It has also set up the Chinese Research and Development Centre for the Control of Desertification, as well as several training and monitoring centres. It has also promulgated the Principal Technology Programme for Monitoring Desertification. The Chinese government has also laid down and promulgated the Comments on Several Policies and Measures for the Control of Desertification, which gives preferential loans with low deducted interest towards desertification control. To counter different types of desertification, the government focused on 20 major counties and established nine experiment areas and 22 experiment and demonstration bases. From 1991 to 1995, 4.29 million hectares were brought under control, of which 1.22 million hectares were subject to sandy-land enclosure, afforestation and grass planting. Another 470,000 hectares were subject to sandy-land control, cultivation and low-yield farmland transformation.[52]

China promoted a new plan to reduce deserts and dust in North China in 2000.[53] In this plan, the Ministry of Science and Technology has divided the target areas of North China into four different ecosystems: the capital circle, the agriculture and animal husbandry belt, the grassland belt and the desert and oasis belt. It has also come up with four corresponding strategies to address the four categories. The Ministry has budgeted 20 million yuan (US$2.4 million) for its anti–desertification campaign in the capital circle, which has already begun. The goal of the plan is to basically control desertification in the capital circle by 2010.

Challenges and strategies

Challenges

The main challenges confronting the sustainable development of China's land resources can be summarized as follows:

Population pressure and food supply

Although China's overall population has continued to increase, the country has made some improvement with respect to its rate of population growth. The country's population increased from 962.59 million in 1978 to an estimated 1.25 billion people in 1999.[54] The crude birth rate decreased from 20.9 per thousand people in 1982 to 17.7 in 1990 while the average household decreased from 4.5 to 4.1 individuals during the same period.[55] Another important trend has been the migration of people to cities. The urban population as a percentage of total population increased from 20.6 in 1982 to 26.2 in 1990.[56]

China is currently self-sufficient in food. In 1996, the national grain output reached 490 million tons.[57] When the Chinese population reaches its peak of 1.6 billion, 640 million tons of grains will be required each year; even assuming China can achieve the goal of 'maintaining a dynamic balance of cultivated land' the field production must increase by 31 per cent ((604–490)/490=0.306) in order to meet the basic demand.

Some argue that China can produce enough milk and meat products to solve the food shortage problem because its pastures are double the area of cultivated land, but they may be ignoring the fact that the major sources of meat, eggs and milk are from forage produced on croplands rather than pasture. Also, most of the pastures have already been overgrazed.[58].

Still others argue that China can solve its food shortage problem by importing grain, but may forget that there are more than a hundred countries needing to import grain.[59] The world population may reach 10 billion by 2050, and therefore the crisis will become more serious. On the other hand, due to the disadvantage in industry and technology in China, it is almost impossible for China to earn enough foreign exchange by exporting industrial products and services. Thus, even if the international market could supply enough grain, China could not afford it. Transportation is also a big obstacle to importing grain. So, overall, China must rely on its own land. Achieving the goal of self-reliance in food supply is not only an important component of China's overall sustainable development strategy, but also a major task for China to ensure its social stability.

Soil erosion and desertification

Soil erosion is one of the main causes of the destruction of the limited cultivated lands of China. Erosion has plagued a total of 3.7 million square kilometres or over one–third of China's total territories. Annually, some 5 billion tons of soil are washed away, causing the loss of more than 66,000 hectares of arable land. Erosion is currently expanding at a rate of 10,000 square kilometres each year.[60]

Desertification is another severe disaster in China, where an average of 2,460 square kilometres of land is swallowed annually by quickly advancing deserts.[61] Soil erosion is particularly serious in the country's western region. Some local governments in the west, where most of the desertified areas are located and where subsistence is still the priority, yield to impulse to boost the local economies without thinking of the results. The major cause of erosion and desertification is overuse by humans through overlogging, overgrazing and overreclamation.

Land degradation

Since the policy of reform and opening up was adopted in the early 1980s, the structure of agriculture production has undergone a number of improvements. Village and township enterprises have been developing rapidly and their production now accounts for over 30 per cent of gross domestic industrial output[62]. They are changing, to some extent, the backwardness of rural areas, but on the other hand they have caused increasingly serious pollution in agricultural environments. Due to rapid economic development, the limited agricultural resources have been increasingly exploited; for example the non-agricultural use of farmland, overgrazing, deforestation and excessive fishing. There is an annual trend of decreasing quantity and quality in agricultural lands. Furthermore, pollution and environmental degradation has accelerated the process of destruction of resources. Over 20 million hectares of cultivated lands, or about one-fifth of the total farmland, have been contaminated to some extent.[63]

Land degradation is a serious problem and severe natural disasters are common. At present, as a result of industrial development and the excessive use of chemicals, the agro-ecological environment is suffering from serious pollution. Each year, 7 to 13 million hectares of farmland are directly affected by fertilizer or pesticide contamination.[64] Industrial emissions and wastes eventually affect the agro-ecological environment. In recent years there have been thousands of claims resulting from environmental damage, and environmental conditions are still deteriorating. Moreover, due to the irrational use of lands and lack of adequate measures to protect the agricultural environment, the depletion of resources and soil degradation continue to be serious concerns.

Strategies

In view of these severe challenges, and taking into consideration existing policies, the following strategies are suggested as a way forward:

1. *Upholding the strategy of 'maintaining a dynamic balance of cultivated land' and reinforcing environmental protection policies*. Due to the scarcity of cultivated land, adhering to the strategy of maintaining a dynamic balance of cultivated land is absolutely necessary. Only if China insists on this policy can the rapid decline of cultivated land be cured. On the other hand, it should be pointed out that merely maintaining cultivated land in quantity is not enough to guarantee the long-term food supply. As a matter of fact, quality is more

important than quantity. Hence, any policy aiming at upholding the cultivated land quantity has to be incorporated with the protection of the environment and land productivity. Solely emphasizing a dynamic balance of cultivated land could intensify environmental damage, and hence potentially do more harm than good to the long–term food supply. People should never forget that disasters are the main causes of the destruction of cultivated land, and human abuse of land resources has been a major cause of those disasters. Two kinds of monitoring system should be established as soon as possible. Monitoring systems are needed for land-resource planning and policy design – undertaking long-term development plans with enhanced sustainability outcomes, and also for land-use early warning and intervention – meeting the needs of emergency planning and for presenting short-term critical impacts of natural resource degradation.

2 *Strengthening land administration and supervision.* Land administration and legislation have been strengthened in recent years, but nevertheless the present land administration system should be improved further to be more effective, and supervision of law enforcement should be undertaken. Under the present administration system, when local governments sacrifice cultivated land for short-term economic benefits, their subordinate grassroots land administration authorities cannot effectively stop such activities. Some local governments even attempt to influence the work of grassroots land administration in enforcing the law.

Implementing the law through intensified supervision over law enforcement is one of the best ways to conserve land resources and protect the environment. Supervision should include administrative supervision and legislative supervision. The form should focus on the implementation of the overall land-use planning. Legislative supervision dwells on the implementation of land law and other relevant laws and regulations. Both administrative supervision and legislative supervision should be combined with technical supervision. With the help of new advanced technology, supervision will be more effective and powerful. The use of remote sensing for the purpose of monitoring the changes in cultivated land in five cities in 1996 heightened awareness of the decline of cultivated land and became one of the factors triggering the rise of a series of strict measures to protect cultivated land. China has actually enlarged its monitoring areas, which has played a very important role in supervision for the implementation of the new land law. This method will be extended to more areas through the programme 'remote sensing monitoring on coastal urbanization and the environment' within China's Agenda 21.[65]

3 *Establishment of land banking to tap the land potential in cities.* Because of the low-efficiency land-use in cities, the potential of tapping the land-use in cities is huge. At present there are about 300,000 state-owned enterprises dispersed in 668 cities, which occupy about 700,000 hectares distributed by 'administrative allocation'.[66] Many of these enterprises are near the edge of bankruptcy.

   How to bring back into circulation the inefficient-used land while facilitating the reform of state-owned enterprises has been one of the main concerns in recent years. Some policies and measures are under formulation, and land banking has been proposed by the Ministry of Land Resource. Some cities, like Hangzhou, are undertaking experimentation of this kind, and as a matter of fact land banking played a very important role in Western Europe's urbanization. It is widely accepted as a desirable means of implementing land-use plans.

4 *Increasing investments in land.* In the protection of cultivated land, the reclamation of wasteland, intensification of used land, and the protection of the environment demand inputs of capital and labour. China has a rich manpower resource and a tradition of intensive labour cultivation. So far, the capital investment level aspect in China has been very low. Annual capital investment for fundamental construction in each hectare of cropland averages only 45 RMB (US$5.4) in China, but 2040 (US$245) in Japan, and 390 (US$47) in France. State investment in agriculture has been only 5 to 10 per cent of total expenditure,[67] and should be doubled at least.

5 *Reforming from fees to taxes and establishing a social security system.* Reforming from fees to taxes is an experiment being undertaken in Anhui Province as well as in some other rural provinces.[68] According to Vice-Premier Wen Jiabao's remarks at a provincial conference in Wuhu, Anhui Province, on 14, April 2000,[69] the fee-to-tax policy is bound to regulating the rural distribution system, stimulating farmers' enthusiasm in production, and contributing to the long-term stability and prosperity of rural areas. It will also be implemented in a package with rural institutional and education reforms to achieve maximum results. Once the new policy is implemented, the random collection of unwarranted fees and illegal charges will be halted, while fees approved by the central government will be collected in the form of an agricultural tax. This policy will be the third significant rural reform in China after the land reform and adoption of the

household contract responsibility system, and it will revitalize the stagnant rural economy.

Establishing a social security system in rural areas is significant to the long-term strategy and it should be spread gradually. It will change traditional concepts, such as people raising more sons because they could rely on them in old age. It will facilitate the implementation of the population control policy and reform of the present HCRS system.

6 *Increasing inputs on R&D and education.* Producing substitute synthetic fibres for cotton, wool and silk, and replacing wood by plastics have helped mitigate the conflict between people and land. In order to produce more substitutes for land products, greater research and development (R&D) investment is needed. R&D in agriculture could help to increase the production capacity of fields, and improving land productivity should be very effective in sustaining a desirable food supply. Compared with the average per unit area output of developed countries, yields could be increased by a relatively large amount. Realization of the goal of self-reliance in food supply in the twenty-first century will mainly rely on R&D in agriculture.

Education can help peasants to improve their skills, lead to the cultivation of land by means of modern science and technology, and enhance the efficiency of labour and land productivity.

Conclusion

China has made remarkable achievements in its sustainable development of land resources and we can see that the challenge is huge.

It is almost a universal idea that land resources play a critical role in human welfare, and improvements in land-resource management can only come about if they are preceded by awareness of the problems and recognition of the need for action. In China, there is no lack of awareness of the problems of sustainable land development at the national level. Population control, environmental conservation, resource conservation and rational use are the stated fundamental policies of China. Ten years ago the Chinese central government declared 25 June to be National Land Day in order to promote national awareness of the importance of land sustainability. Especially in recent years, the land management system has been strengthened as a result of legislation, control mechanisms and supervision.

The present land administration system should be improved further to be a more effective system of preventing violations of the land law.

The defect of the new land law is that it lacks specific penalties for violation and this may be corrected by new regulation. But the prevailing situation of 'strict rule while loose execution' lets most lawbreakers escape punishment which encourages people to take risks in ignoring the laws. This common failing must be overcome.

Remote sensing is a powerful method for monitoring changes in land use. The government has determined the 'remote sensing monitoring on coastal urbanization and the environment' programme to be one of its top priorities for China's Agenda 21.[70] It will play an important role in China's sustainable development of its land resources.

So far, among all the efforts made by China, it appears that designating basic farmland protection areas and strengthening the legal protection of farmland have been the most effective efforts, which basically provides a fundamental guarantee to the relatively good quality of farmlands and guards against their loss and degradation. Guangdong serves as a good example. Since 1993, basic farmland protection areas of 2 million hectares were delimited, a three-year slide in grain output was reversed, and there have been four years of successive increases. Moreover, this measure has not brought about any negative outcomes.

Considering the limitation on potential reclaimable cultivated land resources and the fact that China is in the process of industrialization and urbanization, the decrease in cultivated land is almost inevitable. Policies aiming to protect the environment and stimulate improved land productivity are urgently needed.

On the other hand, tapping the potential of land in cities is essential and possible in China. China's Land Resource Minister, Tian Fengshan, said recently that most Chinese cities, towns and villages will not need any more cultivated land in 10 years, if they can utilize the potential of the land they already have.[71] Some policies and measures for tapping the potential use of land in cities are being tried, and only if China taps such use can sustainable development of land resources be effectively achieved.

In the end, it should be pointed out that protecting cultivated land from further decline is necessary; however, just focusing on the quantity of land to be protected is not enough. China has excessively emphasized protecting the quantity of cultivated land and has more or less ignored the protection of its quality. China now has the rules in place to punish those who destroy cultivated land but lacks the rules to punish those who destroy the environment. Many large projects are approved without enough evaluation. There are many lessons to be learned from the past. Some local governments have taken some policies or projects for granted without enough scientific proof and have suffered losses. Without a clear understanding of their potential impact, some projects could prove to be very detrimental. Most in China can clearly recall the exceptionally large Yangzhi River flood disaster in 1998, one of the main causes of which was the artificial filling of a lake for cultivation in Hunan Province. In order to avoid this kind of disaster the decision-making process should be developed with the support of scientific studies.

Notes

1 http://www.acca21.edu.cn/indexe7.html (1997) *China's Agenda 21 Chinese National Report On Sustainable Development* (June).

2 Special Research Report on Land Resource Sustainable Development (1997), by Guangdong Provincial Land Department, unpublished.

3 Yongkan Zhou (2000) 'Tapping the Potential of Land and Using Land Intensively', *Chinese Land 2000*, Beijing, Chinese Earth Publishing House.

4 Special Research Report on Land Resource Sustainable Development (1997), op. cit.

5 http://www/.acca21.edu.cn/indexe7.htm (1997) *China's Agenda 21 Chinese National Report On Sustainable Development* (June), op. cit.

6 Special Research Report on Land Resource Sustainable Development (1997), op. cit.

7 http://www.acca21.edu.cn/indexe7.html (1997) *China's Agenda 21 Chinese National Report On Sustainable Development* (June), op. cit.

8 http://wwwl.chinadaily.com.cn/news/cn/index.html/(2000)Tang Min, 'Protection of Limited Cultivated and Land Priority',<China Daily>, 26 June.

9 *Ibid.*

10 Yongkan Zhou (2000), op. cit.

11 *Ibid.*

12 *Ibid.*

13 Special Research Report and Land Resources Sustainable Development (1997), op.cit.

14 *Ibid.*

15 *Ibid.*

16 Cheng Zhou (1999) 'Exploration to State-owned Urban Land Estate Right of Annual Rent System', *China Land Science*, vol. 13, no. 4, July, Beijing, Chinese Earth Publishing House.

17 D. H. Meadows, D. L. Meadows, J. Randers, and W.W. Behrens III (1972) *The Limits to Growth*, New York: Universe Books.

18 D. H. Meadows, D. L. Meadows and J. Randers (1992) *Beyond the Limits*, London: Earthscan.

19 R. Y. Edwards and C. D. Fowle (1955) *Transactions of the 20th North American Wildlife Conference*, Washington, DC: Wildlife Management Institute.

20 Gro Harlem Brundtland (1987) *Our Common Future*, World Commission on Environment and Development, Oxford: Oxford University Press.

21 Anthony Young (1998) *Land Resources: Now and For the Future*, Cambridge: Cambridge University Press.

22 Food and Agriculture Organization of the United Nations (FAO) (1992).
23 P. T. Kivell (1999) 'Land Use Policy and Sustainibility', in M. Redclift (ed.) *Sustainability: Life Chances and Livelihoods,* London: Routledge.
24 Xiaoying Wang (1999) 'Changes of Land System and Land Contraction System', *China Land Science,* vol. 13, no. 4, July, Beijing, Chinese Earth Publishing House.
25 *Ibid.*
26 Xing Quan Zhang (1997) 'Urban Land Reform in China', *Land Use Policy,* vol. 14, no. 3, p. 187–99.
27 *Ibid.*
28 *Ibid.*
29 *Ibid.*
30 http://www.acca21.edu.cn/indexe7.html (1997) *China's Agenda 21 Chinese National Report On Sustainable Development* (June), op. cit.
31 Lawrence Wai Chung Lai (1995) 'Land Use Rights Reform in China', *Land Use Policy,* vol. 12, no. 4, p. 281–9.
32 http://www.acca21.edu.cn/indexe7.html (1997) *China's Agenda 21 Chinese National Report On Sustainable Development* (June), op. cit.
33 *Ibid.*
34 Hong Yang, Xuibin Li (2000) 'Cultivated Land and Food Supply in China', *Land Use Policy,* vol. 17, pp. 73–8.
35 Futuan Qu, Nico Heerink and Wanmao Wang (1995) 'Land Administration Reform in China – Its Impact on Land Allocation and Economic Development', *Land Use Policy,* vol. 12, no. 3, pp. 193–203.
36 Hong Yang, Xuibin Li (2000), op. cit.
37 Futuan Qu, Nico Heerink and Wanmao Wang (1995), op. cit.
38 http://www1.chinadaily.com.cn/news/cn/index.html/(2000) Tang Min, 'Country's Land to be Protected', <China Daily>, 23 June.
39 *Ibid.*
40 *Ibid.*
41 http://www1.chinadaily.com.cn/news/cn/index.html(2000) Hai Min, 'Land Law Poorly Enforced', <China Daily>, 18 May.
42 http://www1.chinadaily.com.cn/news/cn/index.html/(2000) Meng Yan, 'Legislators to Check for Cultivated Land Protection', <China Daily>, 20 April.
43 http://wwwl.chinadaily.com.cn/news/cn/index.html/(2000) Liang Chao, 'Soil Protection Vital to Nation', <China Daily>, 30 June.
44 http://www1.chinadaily.com.cn/news/cn/index.html(2000) Meng Yan, 'Legislators to Check for Cultivated Land Protection', <China Daily>, 20 April, op cit.
45 http://www1.chinadaily.com.cn/news/cn/index.html/(2000) Tang Min, 'Protection of Limited Cultivated Land Priority', <China Daily>, 26 June.
46 D. H. Meadows, D. L. Meadows, J. Randers, and W. W. Behrens III (1972), op. cit.
47 http://www1.chinadaily.com.cn/news/cn/index.html (2000) Meng Yan, 'Rule to Punish Land Law Breakers', <China Daily>, 7 March.
48 http://www1.chinadaily.com.cn/news/cn/index.html/(2000) Tang Min, 'Ministry to Update Land Data Yearly', <China Daily>, 7 May.
49 *Ibid.*
50 http://www.acca21.edu.cn/indexe7.html (1997) *China's Agenda 21 Chinese National Report On Sustainable Development* (June), op. cit.

51 *Ibid.*
52 *Ibid.*
53 http://www1.chinadaily.com.cn/news/cn/index.html/(2000) Guo Nei, 'New Tax Policy to Ease Farm Burden', <China Daily>, 15 April.
54 National Bureau of Statistics of China. (2002) http://www.stats.gov.cn/ndsj/zgnj/2000/D01c.htm.
55 *Country Profile 2000: China, Mongolia* (2000) London: The Economist Intelligence Unit: p. 24.
56 *Ibid.*
57 http://www.acca21.edu.cn/indexe7.html (1997) *China's Agenda 21 Chinese National Report On Sustainable Development* (June), op. cit.
58 Xing Quan Zhang (1997) 'Urban Land Reform in China', op. cit.
59 *Ibid.*
60 http://www1.chinadaily.com.cn/news/cn/index.html/(2000) Liang Chao, 'Soil Protection Vital to Nation', <China Daily>, 30 June.
61 http://www1.chinadaily.com.cn/news/cn/index.html(2000) Meng Yan, 'Combating Desertification', <China Daily>, 25 May.
62 http://www.acca21.edu.cn/indexe7.html (1997) *China's Agenda 21 Chinese National Report On Sustainable Development* (June), op. cit.
63 *Ibid.*
64 *Ibid.*
65 *Ibid.*
66 Yongkan Zhou (2000) 'Tapping the Potential of Land and Using Land Intensively', *Chinese Land 2000*, Beijing: Chinese Earth Publishing House, op. cit.
67 Xing Quan Zhang (1997), op. cit.
68 http://www1.chinadaily.com.cn/news/cn/index.html/(2000) Guo Nei, 'New Tax Policy to Ease Farm Burden', <China Daily>, 15 April.
69 *Ibid.*
70 http://www.acca21.edu.cn/indexe7.html (1997) *China's Agenda 21 Chinese National Report On Sustainable Development* (June), op. cit.
71 http://www1.chinadaily.com.cn/news/cn/index.html/(2000) Tang Min, 'Country's Land to be Protected', <China Daily>, 23 June.

4

Restructuring Guangdong's Power Industry: Is It Possible?*

Zhou Liang

Guangdong's power industry at a glance

Guangdong's power industry has developed rapidly over the last few decades. However, as Guangdong's economy has been growing at an even faster pace, the shortage of electricity was not eased until 1997. Driven by strong demand, electricity supply capacity has increased significantly over the last two decades.

Electricity generation

Installed generating capacity increased over 10 times from 2,760 megawatts (MW) in 1979 to 30,333 MW in 1999. The capacity of both single power plants and single units increased noticeably. In 1979, the biggest power plant in Guangdong province was that of Huangpu with a total installed generating capacity of 375 MW and single unit capacity of 125 MW. However, Shajiao power plant has become the biggest today with a total installed generating capacity of 3,180 MW and a single unit capacity of 660 MW. Fossil fuel-powered plants contributed over two-thirds, or 21,937 MW to the total installed generating capacity. The capacity of nuclear power plants is 1,800 MW, hydropower plants 4,497 MW, and water-storage plants 2,100 MW. Total electricity generation in the province increased 9.77 per cent to reach 114 GWh in 1999 (see Figure 4.1).

Participants in the electricity generation market consist of five power generation groups and hundreds of small-size generator owners. The

* The data related to Guangdong's electricity industry in this chapter are from GEPH internal reports.[1]

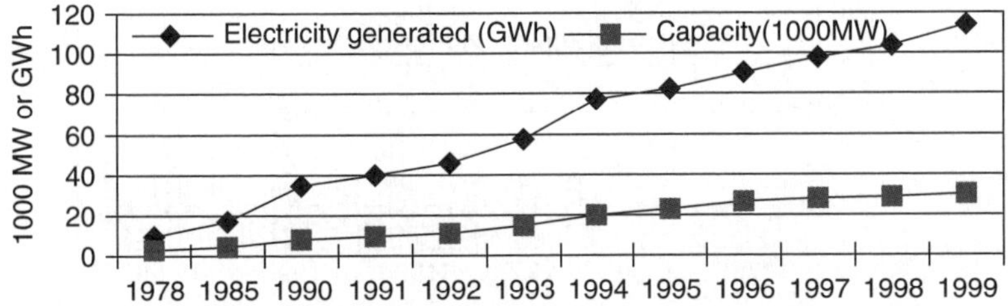

Figure 4.1 Installed generating capacity and electricity generated
Source: Adapted from Guangdong Electric Power Holding (GEPH), Internal Reports, 1979–2000.

five groups are Guangdong Electric Power Holding Corporation (GEPH), responsible for 30.96 per cent of the province's total installed generating capacity, ShenZhen Energy Group (SZEG) (8.06%), Guangdong Nuclear Power Group (GNPG), (5.93%), Guangzhou Power Group (GZPG) (3.96%) and Huaneng International Power Development Corporation (HIPDC) (1.98%).

Transmission and distribution system

Guangdong's electricity grid has quickly developed not only in total circuit length of transmission lines, but also in voltaic grade of transmission lines. The voltage of transmission lines has been upgraded from 220 kV and 110 kV in 1985 to 500 kV and 220 kV. An electricity transmission circle has been formed at 500 kV around the Pearl River delta, the central part of Guangdong and the main load areas of Guangdong province. Transmission lines of 500 kV have also reached the north, the east and the west of the province. Guangdong electricity grid connected with Guangxi and Guizhou provincial grids at 500 kV and with Hong Kong's network at 400 kV (see Figures 4.2 and 4.3).

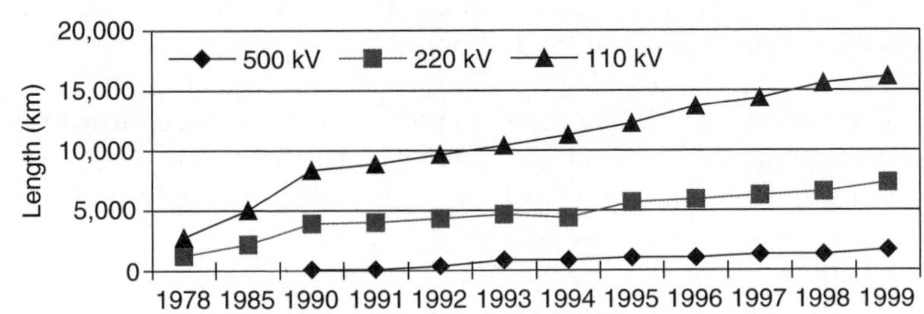

Figure 4.2 Transmission lines of Guangdong grid
Source: Guangdong Electric Power Holding Corporation, internal reports 1979–2000.

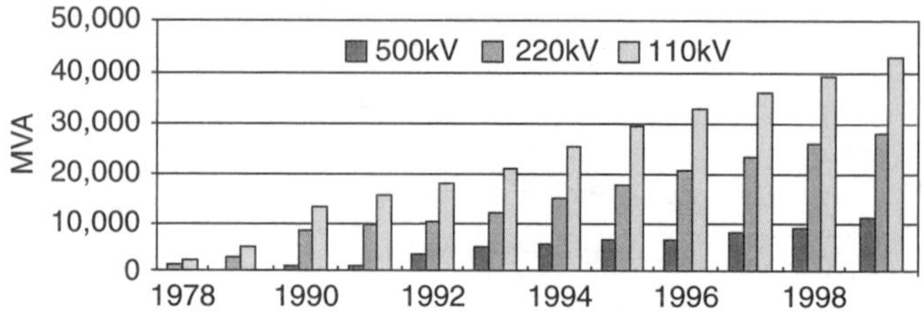

Figure 4.3 Capacity of transformers in Guangdong's grid (MVA)
Source: Guangdong Electric Power Holding Corporation, internal reports 1979–2000.

Demand and supply

The demand of electricity in Guangdong maintained a high growth rate over the last two decades. Total consumption of electricity increased 9.96 per cent to 108.62 GWh in 1999. Industrial demand was 69.57 GWh, or 64 per cent of total demand, while residential and commercial electricity consumption was 25.43 GWh and agricultural electricity consumption was 3.41 GWh. Despite the high increase in the rate of the electricity generating capacity, the supply of electricity could not meet the needs of peak demand until 1998.

Demand in electricity is expected to average 7.7 per cent growth from 2000 to 2005, 6.6 per cent from 2006 to 2010, and 5.6 from 2011 to 2015.

Background, current situation and problems

Monopoly and vertical integration

GEPH, a state-owned enterprise, is a major participant in Guangdong's electricity market. Its business covers electricity generation, transmission, distribution and customer service. Under the current system, GEPH is given a legal monopoly called 'franchise', which extends to all of the following aspects of the utility business:

- Generation – producing power in power plants or purchasing it from other generators or neighbouring power networks;
- Transmission – carrying power from power plants over high-voltage transmission line to load centres;
- Distribution – delivering power to the customers at reduced voltage, through substation and distribution lines;
- Customer services – rendering services such as metering and billing which are traditionally considered as part of the distribution function.

GEPH was also given certain governmental power, working as a functional department of the government, to deal with matters related to the power industry such as power industry policy, new utility facilities planning, and approval of new facilities connected to the electricity grid. These functions no longer existed after August 2000.

In exchange for being granted a monopoly franchise, GEPH had the obligation to meet electricity needs in the social and economic development of Guangdong province, to guarantee the quality and safety of the electricity supply, and to serve all customers under the terms and at the rates set by related departments of the government.

Independent power plants

The shortage of electricity in the 1980s and early 1990s was the key factor for the establishment of many independent power plants. The shortage was seriously affecting economic growth and the daily life of residents at the time; factories could only work three or four days per week due to the shortage. As a result, policies were made to encourage local entities as well as foreign companies to invest in electricity generation. The policies included the so-called 'high cost, high price' policy – the price of electricity generated by certain generators was set according to the cost of production.

Independent power groups emerged quickly at that time. By the end of 1999, SZEG had built a coal-fired power plant with four units of 300 MW each and some combined cycle power plants. The total installed generating capacity is 2,445 MW. GNPG owned a nuclear power plant with two units of 900 MW each with a total installed generating capacity of 1,800 MW. Another nuclear power plant with two units of 900 MW each was under construction at that time. GZPG owned a coal-fired power plant with four, 300 MW units. HIPDC had a coal-fired power plant with two 300 MW units. Except for combined cycle power plants, all of these power generation facilities are managed by Guangdong Dispatch Centre – a subsidiary of GEPH. The amount of electricity to be produced by each power plant was negotiated at the beginning of each year. All the above power groups are now listed on the stockmarket except the nuclear power group.

At the same time, small (under 50 MW) independent generators were built more quickly due to the fact that the large-size power plants needed heavy investment, long construction periods, and long approval processes by the central government. The provincial or local governments could approve generators under 50 MW. The installed generating capacity of these small power plants totalled 12,151 MW, of which diesel

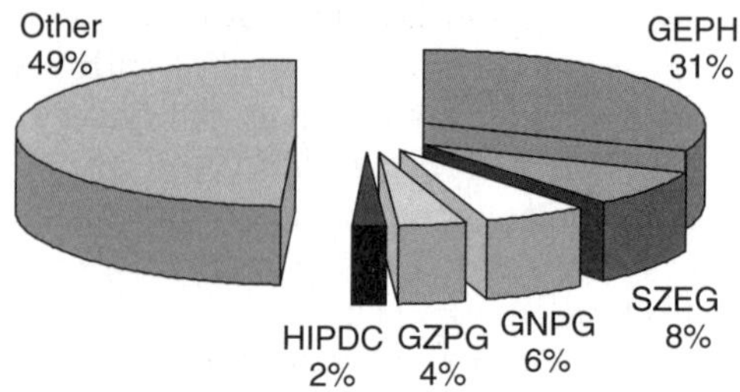

Figure 4.4 Installed generating capacity share in Guangdong, 1999
Source: Guangdong Electric Power Holding Corporation, internal reports 1979–2000.

generators contributed 5,530 MW. These generators have something in common: they are owned by small power producers and used as distribution generators or out of dispatch centres (see Figure 4.4).

The ability to meet peak demand

The total installed generating capacity of Guangdong electric network was 30,333 MW in 1999. Only 16,140 MW was dispatched by Guangdong Dispatch Centre and about 2,000 MW was used by Hong Kong according to contractual arrangements. The rest of the total installed generating capacity, which was not dispatched by GDDC, was contributed by small-size generators included 5,530 MW diesel generators and 3,540 MW small hydro-generators. The output of most diesel generators was below their capacity, and the output of the small hydro-generator was affected by weather conditions. Although the total installed generating capacity was 30,333 MW, the actual output that could be used by Guangdong province was around 22,000 MW. The peak demand in 1999 was 19,540 MW.

Price of electricity

The price of electricity paid to generators varies. As mentioned above, in order to solve the problem of electricity shortage, the policy of 'high cost, high price' was adopted. The prices paid to generators were approved on a case-by-case basis, according to their construction costs, loan interest, return on equity, and variable costs of operation.

Investors were less concerned about the total investment of the power plants. Instead, they made great efforts to convince the authorities that approved prices to accept their operating budgets. It was impossible for the authorities to control or evaluate the costs of construction and operation of power plants because the authorities cannot be too deeply involved in the business of running such a facility. On the other hand, the rate of return on investments varied from 13 per cent to 18 per cent.

As the result, the price paid to generators was rising quickly, and varied from 0.3 RMB yuan (US$0.0357) per kWh to 0.6 RMB yuan (US$0.0714) per kWh. In addition, most of these generators were also guaranteed a quota, which was the amount of electricity to be generated each year at a fixed price.

Consequently, the price the end users paid also varied widely from 0.6 RMB yuan (US$0.0714) per kWh to 2 RMB yuan (US$0.238); the price had dropped to 1 RMB yuan per kWh by the end of 1999. The factors affecting the prices are as follows:

- Electricity generating cost – if a city has large capacity from local power plants with high cost, the price of electricity in that city should be higher.
- Electricity loss in distribution – bad conditions in distribution access to rural areas is the main factor causing high electricity prices. In general, the prices in rural areas are higher than in urban areas.
- Efficiency of the distribution facilities.

Investment in electricity generation

Investment in electricity generation came from two main sources. One was from the government, the other from investors attracted by the favourable policies. On 20 March 1987, Guangdong provincial government approved the establishment of an electricity development fund as a government investment in the electricity generation industry. A fee of 0.025 RMB yuan per kWh (increased to 0.045 RMB yuan per kWh on 1 January 1997) was collected from the final consumers as part of the fund. The tax paid by GEPH was also transferred to the fund. GEPH invested the fund in new electricity production projects (see Figure 4.5).

The policy of 'high cost, high price' attracted a great deal of investment to the power industry. As shown in Figure 4.5, heavy investments were put into new projects in the early 1990s. However, this trend did not continue into the late 1990s, three reasons caused the decline. First, as supply has slightly surpassed peak demand since 1998, some officials of the central government believed that development in Guangdong's electricity generation had proceeded too quickly, and it became difficult to get approval for new power supply projects. Second, the 'high cost, high price' policy with a guaranteed amount of electricity to be generated

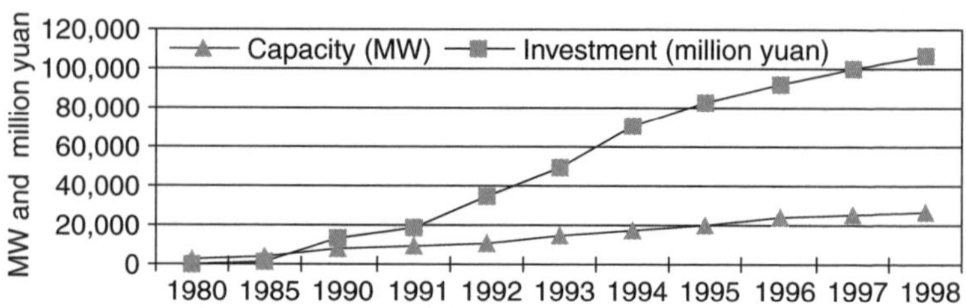

Figure 4.5 Installed generating capacity and investment
Source: Guangdong Electric Power Holding Corporation internal reports 1979–2000.

and sold at a fixed price no longer applied, but a new pricing mechanism had not been set up. Third, electricity development funds collected from the end consumers had dropped from 0.045 RMB yuan per kWh to 0.02 RMB yuan per kWh since 1 January 1999.

Problems

Favourable policies to develop the power industry and strong demand for electricity accelerated the growth of the industry. However, the fast growth has caused negative effects to the industry as well:

- *Low efficiency of the power industry as a whole.* Between 1985 and 1996, the growth rate of labour productivity of China's power industry was only 60 per cent of the country's average. The annual profitability of investment in China's power industry dropped by 0.8 per cent while the average profitability of the country's industries increased by 3 per cent annually.[2]
- *Irrational structure of electricity sources.* As shown in Figure 4.5, small generators accounted for nearly half of the total installed generating capacity. Two-thirds of them are small fossil-fired generators, which are not only low in efficiency but also high in pollution to the environment. These generators also have low reliability and are more difficult to dispatch affecting the ability of the grid to meet peak demand.
- *Unreasonable electricity price.* The price paid to generators differs from one to another. Some are too high, while some are too low. The pricing structure fails to encourage investors to achieve high efficiency.

The shortage of electricity in Guangdong will again appear between 2001 and 2005, as the favourable policies will no longer work and a new market mechanism has not been put in place. The demand of electricity will maintain high rates of increase over the next two decades and it is estimated that the shortage of electricity generating capacity will be 8,000 MW in 2005. It is projected that 15,000 MW of additional installed generating capacity should go into operation between 2001 and 2005, but 7,000 MW is the most that can possibly be put into operation.

Restructuring of the electricity industry

Restructuring of the power industry in developed countries

Vertical integration was considered best for the power industry because electricity is a special commodity with unique characteristics. It cannot be stored economically, so it is generated, transmitted and consumed at the same time. Electricity flows between two points via all possible paths between them, and the operation of utilities within the interconnections requires coordination to ensure the safety of facilities and reliability of the supply. Therefore, a power supply network has the characteristic of requiring economy of scale. No matter how efficient competition is, the benefit does not exceed that of a vertically integrated monopoly system.

During the past two decades, however, advances in generation and metering technology have eroded the justification for a monopoly in generation and customer service activities, and for the 'bundling' of generation, transmission, distribution and customer services into one entity. Since the early 1990s, some Western countries have restructured their electricity industries. At the core of the restructuring is the unbundling of the natural and non-natural monopoly activities, introducing competition to the non-natural monopoly business in the electricity industry.

California is the front-runner in the United States in power industry restructuring.[3] In order to introduce competition into the electricity generation and customer service aspects of the business, vertical integration of utility companies has been separated; utility companies no longer control generation, transmission, distribution and customer services. Although the investor-owned utilities (IOUs) are still permitted to engage in all types of business, their control is functionally unbundled as if there were four separate companies. A new market structure has been created:

- *An oversight board* oversees the Independent System Operator (ISO) and Power Exchange (PX). It appoints the members of the ISO and PX, and serves as an appeal body for decisions of the ISO.

- *An independent system operator* is a non-profit entity and provides day-to-day efficient and reliable use of the state's transmission system. It participates in filings at the Federal Energy Regulatory Commission and adopts transmission standards.
- *A power exchange* provides an open nondiscriminatory auction to all suppliers.

The generation aspect of the utility business has generally become competitive and operates under free-market principles. Anyone can own and operate a power plant and sell power to any customers. Sellers and buyers can participate in a centrally coordinated market in which prices are set by daily bids (the Power Exchange, or PX), or they can enter into longer-term 'direct access' contracts between individual buyers and sellers. Whether in the PX or through a direct-access market, customers may make individual arrangements with suppliers or they may aggregate in order to increase their negotiating power. Customers do not need to participate directly in the PX or in direct access; they may choose to stay with their existing utility company. All generators and consumers connected to the ISO-controlled grid will have to comply with the ISO's rules.

Generators and customers participating in the PX will submit bids for the price at which they are willing, respectively, to sell and buy power. Customers may also, in the case of 'demand bids', indicate the price at which they are not willing to buy. A demand bid may be expressed as a price above which the customer will purchase no more power, or as a price at which the customer will reduce his or her power consumption. When there is enough supply to meet demand, the bid of the most expensive generator necessary to meet demand will set the market-clearing price (MCP), which will then be paid by all buyers to all generators. When supply is inadequate to meet demand, the MCP will be a customer's energy use and thus restore the balance between supply and demand.

No longer restricted to buying power only from the local monopoly utility company, customers will be able to compare one deal with another and choose the one that meets their preferences. It is possible that packages of power and other services (metering and billing, conservation devices, even cable TV and telephone) will be offered. Customers will also have the opportunity to get customized products and services. For example, some customers may not need high levels of reliability, while others may need exceptional reliability. Some customers may be able to shift the timing of their electricity use to take advantage of lower prices during off-peak periods.

Prices for generation will generally be set in the free market, and power plant owners (both public utilities and others) will have their profits go up and down accordingly. Certain plants, such as nuclear facilities and those critical for reliability, will have specialized pricing arrangements.

The IOUs currently own most power plants in California. Because of this, even when generation is opened to competition the utilities may be able to dominate the market and set generation prices at an artificially high level. In order to prevent the utilities from exercising undue market power, the California Public Utility Commission (CPUC) has required Pacific Gas & Electric Co. (PG&E) and Edison to divest half of their power plants that operate with fossil fuels, and, during the transition period, to sell and buy all their power through the PX. In addition, the Federal Energy Regulatory Commission (FERC) will not give final approval to California's restructured system unless the agency is satisfied that market power is at acceptable levels.

In the transmission aspect, the IOUs give control, but not ownership, of their transmission lines to a central operator called the Independent System Operator (ISO). The ISO will be responsible for ensuring that all power sellers have equal access.

Each utility still owns and operates the local distribution system as a monopoly, and distribution rates will be regulated by the CPUC. However, rate-setting will be more market-oriented; 'performance-based ratemaking' (PBR) will set a target revenue and profit level but the utilities will have more flexibility to manage costs and services.

The metering and billing functions will be unbundled from the distribution function and opened up to competition. Utilities can still provide services in this area, but they will do so in competition with others and with the free-market determining pricing and profits.[4]

Restructuring Guangdong's power industry

The restructuring of Guangdong's electricity industry began in August 2000. GEPH no longer has a governmental function, and a new market structure is under consideration. Restructuring Guangdong's power industry should include two steps. The first step is to form a competitive generation market, while maintaining monopolistic vertical integration in transmission and distribution. The second step is to divide the transmission and distribution businesses, unbundling distribution and customer service, from a province-wide monopoly in transmission towards regional distribution, and open market competition in customer service.

There are several reasons for the two steps. First maintaining vertical integration in transmission and distribution will help build an efficient transmission and distribution system. Guangdong is in an industrialization period, and the demand for electricity in will increase by 6 to 8 per cent annually in the next 15 years. As regards the transmission and distribution system, not only does the current system need improvement, but also large-scale construction is needed to expand the system to meet the projected demand. Transmission and distribution are widely recognized as natural monopoly activities, and maintaining a monopoly and vertical integration in them will be more helpful in building an efficient transmission and distribution system.

Second, this approach helps to develop the power industry in rural areas. Guangdong's power industry development was driven by demand; unbalanced development in the economy led the unbalanced development in the electricity transmission and distribution system. The transmission and distribution system in the Pearl River delta is much better than in the rest of the province, and in rural areas it is still very poor. Maintaining a province-wide monopoly and vertically integrated utilities in transmission and distribution is helpful to development in rural areas.

In generation, however, the foundation for competition has been formed. First, the capacity of electricity generation has exceeded demand at present, which is the fundamental factor in creating a competitive market environment. Second, independent power generators contribute 60 per cent of the total installed generating capacity. Five electricity generation groups exist in the market, of which four are listed companies. Meanwhile, investment in electricity generation is still the major part of investment in the power industry over the next two decades. A competitive market for power generation could attract public investment to support development of the industry.

In addition, the current structure has affected the development of the power industry. As previously discussed, quotas were promised to new independent generators in order to attract investment in electricity generation in the 1990s. The quota was usually based on the amount of electricity produced by the generator, but the quota system will not work today since electricity supply has exceeded peak demand. Newly installed generators no longer have quotas, and even for those generators with quotas, the quotas are not always honoured. As a result, investors or potential investors hesitate to invest in electricity generation because the market rules are not clear. If this problem persists, serious electricity supply shortages will emerge again, and Guangdong's electricity industry will repeat its history from the early 1990s.

In short, based on the current situation, the establishment of a competitive market in power generation must be the first step in restructuring Guangdong's power industry. In order to be fair to other competitors, GEPH, as the transmission and distribution monopolist, should no longer be involved in the generation business except for the operation of generators used for voltage and reliability support, such as water-storage plants. An electricity generation company should be set up to take over the power plants operated by GEPH.

Fostering competition in the electricity generation market

There is no competition in the current electricity generation market in Guangdong although 60 per cent of installed generating capacity is contributed by independent power plants. Each plant sells its electricity at a fixed price approved by the pricing department. The contributions are consolidated into the main grid by the Central Dispatch Centre or local dispatch centre according to their capacity. Generally speaking, the generators with single unit capacity of 200 MW or above are dispatched by the Central Dispatch Centre, otherwise units are dispatched by local dispatch centres.

The Central Dispatch Centre or local dispatch centres make their dispatch schedule mainly based on load demand, grid congestion and safety of operation. The quota for each generator is taken into consideration as well. During times of serious shortage of electricity, this system has made a large contribution. However, it does not work well when supply surpasses demand. In addition, it has caused high electricity prices and low efficiency.

A new market mechanism must be set up to sustain the development of the power industry; competition is the strongest force to drive market participants to perform well. Next we are going to discuss how to foster a competitive market in electricity generation, but before doing so it is important to understand the characteristics of the electricity generating industry.

Characteristics of electricity generation

The characteristics of the industry affect the structure of the market, and we may consider several perspectives.

Table 4.1 Capacity of power plant units, 1999

Power plant capacity		Heat rate (KJ/ kWh)	Person rate (person/MW)
Units	Capacity per unit (MW)		
6	600	9,525	0.22
4	600	9,525	0.28
2	600	9,525	0.40
6	300	9,965	0.40
4	300	9,965	0.50
2	300	9,965	0.72
6	200	10,639	0.55
4	200	10,639	0.70
2	200	10,639	1.00
6	100	11,577	0.94
4	100	11,577	1.19
2	100	11,577	1.70

Source: Guangdong Electric Power Holding Corporation, internal reports 1979–2000.

Power plants may be hydro (water), fossil-fueled (coal-fired, oil-fired, gas-turbine, combine cycle or diesel), nuclear solar powered. In Guangdong, electricity is mainly contributed by fossil-fuel plants, especially by coal-fired plants. A coal-fired plant is the cheapest to operate. The installed generating capacity of coal-fired generators contributes 70 per cent of the total installed generating capacity in China and 80 per cent of total electricity actually generated. It will be impossible to change this situation for a very long time.[5]

Economies of scale. A coal-fired power plant with four units of 300 MW generation capacity is considered the least efficient scale at present. Table 4.1 displays the standards used by GEPH to evaluate the performance of their power plants.

Capital requirements. To build a coal-fired power plant in Guangdong costs approximately 7 to 8 million RMB yuan per MW (about US$1 million). A power plant with a capacity of 1,200 MW is the least competitive and will cost 8.4 to 9.6 billion RMB yuan (US$1 to 1.14 billion) to build.

Access to distribution channels. After restructuring the power supply market, the transmission and distribution systems will be open to all industry participants with all players having equal access rights.

High exit barriers. Power plants can only be used to generate electricity. They are specialized assets with few uses except for generating electricity. According to economic theory, because the electricity generation industry requires heavy investment and has the characteristics associated with scale economies, its barriers to entrants are high. Because power plants can only be used to generate electricity, the exit barriers are even higher. Competition in the electricity generation industry is also very strong because of high fixed costs. In addition, although electricity cannot yet be economically stored, the total capacity should exceed the peak demand; in off-peak times, the supply will be much larger than demand. This fact makes competition stronger.

Creating a competitive market in electricity generation

The critical action needed to create a competitive market in electricity generation in Guangdong is to abolish the current system of fixed prices and quotas for each generator. The essential elements to create competition include both the infrastructure and aspects of the market. In Guangdong, most of the needed delivery infrastructure already exists, but market rules that enable suppliers and consumers to transact do not exist. Market rules are needed to ensure that every potential supplier has open and non-discriminatory access to the market and will be treated fairly. The rules should include new dispatch rules and for price-setting, transmission congestion management and market information release.

Attracting investment in a competitive market

Favourable policies have helped attract enough investment in the power industry during the last decade. As a result, the price of electricity was fixed and the return on investment for investors was predictable and guaranteed. Can a competitive market attract enough investment in electricity generation in the coming decade, while the price of electricity stays reasonable?

In a competitive market, the electricity price is set by daily bids. When there is enough supply to meet demand, the bid of the most expensive generator necessary to meet demand will set the market-clearing price (MCP), which will then be paid by all buyers to all generators. Generators' bids are likely to closely track the operating costs of the power plants.

Electricity is a special commodity and, as noted, cannot economically be stored yet. So the electricity generating capacity of an electric power grid should meet the peak demand. However, the demand of electricity varies widely over time. In Guangdong, most of the time there is enough supply to meet the demand, and generators' bids are mainly based on variable costs. However, the total cost of electricity consists of both fixed and variable costs; the fixed costs contribute to half of the total. As a result, most power plant investors can hardly obtain enough revenue to cover their total costs.

California's power supply market switched to a competitive market structure in January 1998. Although their market was more mature and market information was more available than in Guangdong, the electricity price in the generating sector was unexpectedly low in the beginning. The California Energy Commission *Wholesalers' Electricity Price Review* of 1998 dealt with these issues.[6]

Recognizing these limitations, the authors of this report offer the observation that PX prices for April 1998 were probably too low to allow many fossil fuelled generators to recover their fixed costs. With prices for delivered gas close to $3.00/Mbtu, few of them are likely to have cleared so much as $2.50/kw over operating costs for the month. The most efficient plants would be new combined cycle units, and they probably require net operating income of at least $100 per kW per year. Earning $2.50 in a month is not an auspicious beginning towards earning $100 in a year. Even so, the authors noted that low electricity prices should be expected in April 1998 and PX prices should rise as the weather heats up.

In a word, free market competition may lead to cut-throat competition in the electricity generation market. No investor can get enough income streams to cover their costs, with the result of no new investment in generation projects. When the electricity supply cannot meet demand, not only in peak times but also in off peak times, electricity prices rise quickly and a lot of diesel generators will appear again. Such market failure will cause serious problems in the future market.

To solve this problem, available capacity payment could work for the short term. This is to pay the generator available capacity as one part and electricity as another part. The available capacity payment would be based on fixed costs but should not cover them. The electricity supply is then set by competition market. But the solution for the long-term is to foster several big electricity generation groups, to form an oligopolistic market in electricity generating combined with a pricing cap.

Oligopoly market

An oligopoly is a market having a few firms on the supply side and a very large number of buyers on the demand side, each of whom makes a negligible contribution to the market demand function.

An oligopoly market should benefit Guangdong's power industry at least in the next two decades. At present, nearly half of the electricity generating capacity is owned by hundreds of individual owners, most of whom do not have a long-term plan to run their businesses. The capital they have invested is considered stranded costs. When the market switches to a competitive basis they will make bids according to the variable costs. As a result, the price of electricity will probably be unreasonably low and the distorted price signals will bring down investments in electricity generation.

Consequently, as demand increases, the shortage of electricity supply appears not only in peak demand periods but also in off-peak periods, and the price of electricity would rise rapidly. In this case, a lot of small generators would again be built to meet the urgent need. Myopic investment behaviour leads to an unhealthy cycle.

The new electricity generating capacity will be mainly contributed by coal-fired power plants in the next decades since, as stated above, such plants have characteristic associated with economies of scale. To build a power plant with competitive advantages requires huge investments, and the construction period is also very long. It takes at least five years to build a large coal-fired power plant. In an oligopoly electricity generating market, oligopolies have the ability to build competitive power plants; myopic investment behaviour may be avoided and the market can enjoy the benefits both from competition and economies of scale. More specifically, benefits associated with fostering only a few generating groups and forming an oligopolistic market situation in Guangdong are as follows:

- *Long-term stable development of the power industry*. Electricity generating groups usually have a long-term development strategy and plan; they look at long-term benefits instead of just the current market price. They know the current market as well as future market conditions better than a small electricity producer because they can afford to do research. So an oligopolistic structure in the power generation market would be helpful to the overall health and stable development of the power industry.
- *A rational structure of electricity sources*. Oligopolies should have long-term competitive advantages to compete against rivals. In the electricity generation market, the long-term competitive advantage must be low costs, and in order to generate low-cost electricity it is necessary to build high-efficiency, large-scale power plants. The location of power plants must also be considered in order to have

available access to sell their electricity. These strategies can only be implemented well by a large power group.

- *Relatively lower electricity prices*. In the oligpolistic market, oligopolies have the ability to build power plants with economies of scale; they can distribute their power efficiently to minimize operating costs, and they can finance their operations more easily with lower financing costs. As a result, the price of electricity will decrease.

Sufficient marketing information

Sufficient marketing information is a key to ensuring that the competitive market works efficiently. Unfortunately, competitive markets do not, in practice, operate with the 'perfect information' assumed by economic theory. Furthermore, in the electricity market the essential information flows were structured for the needs of a non-competitive market, and restructuring the power industry will substantially change the types of information needed.

In restructuring Guangdong's electricity market into a competitive market, a marketing information system must be built, and essential information is needed for:

- *System coordination*. Smooth information flows are needed in coordination of the operation, generation, transmission and distribution system.
- *Operation and market activities*. An information system is needed to provide the status of the transmission grid, demand, prices, congestion of the grid, and development of the power supply system. Access to information should be widely available to the public on a non-discriminatory basis.
- *Market monitoring*. Smooth information flows are also needed for the government to oversee and monitor the market in order to avoid significant market failures and potential abuses of market power. Adequate information flows can also help to ensure the reliability of the provincial electricity system, to remove competition barriers, and to promote implementation of public policy.[7]

Conclusion

Attracting investment in electricity generation through favourable policies for investors has solved the electricity shortage problem for now. Both the installed generating capacity and the electricity actually generated annually have increased tenfold in the last two decades, and supply has exceeded demand. However, negative effects on the power industry have accompanied the rapid growth. These effects include high electricity prices, a low efficiency in the industry as a whole, and an irrational structure of electricity sources. Therefore, in the current situation the favourable policies no longer work, but a new market mechanism has not yet appeared. This situation has affected investment in new power supply projects and will lead to a shortage of electricity supply in the coming years. Restructuring the power industry is very urgent and imperative.

Recommendations

Restructuring Guangdong's power industry should be divided into two steps. The first step is to form a competitive market in power generation, while maintaining monopolistic vertical integration in transmission and distribution. The second step is to separate transmission and distribution, to unbundle distribution and customer service to form a province-wide monopoly in transmission, a regional monopoly in distribution, and open competition in the customer service market.

The electricity market has its own unique characteristics, so restructuring the power industry cannot simply abandon the monopoly for complete free market competition. Instead, it is important to design a market structure that enables stable and healthy development. An oligopoly is one possible solution to the problems in Guangdong's electricity generating market.

Sufficient marketing information is a key to ensuring that the competitive market will work efficiently. Restructuring of the power industry will substantially change the types of information needed and the people who need it, and an information system must be built for the needs of system coordination, operation activities and market monitoring.

Notes

1 Guangdong Electric Power Holding Corporation (GEPH), *Internal Reports*, 1979–2000.
2 Shujie Liu (1999) *Study of the Price Reform of the Monopoly Industry*, China Jihua Press, Beijing.
3 Edison Electric Institute (EEI) (2000) Learning From California, October, Washington, DC.
4 California Energy Commission (1997) *Electricity Report*, November.

5 Fengqi Zhou and Dadi Zhou (1999) *Study of Long Term Energy Development Strategies of China*, Energy Research Institute, Beijing.
6 California Energy Commission (1998) *Wholesalers' Electricity Price Review*, April.
7 California Energy Commission (1997) *op. cit.*

5

Restructuring Agriculture in Guangdong Province: A View Based on the American Agricultural Experience

Yefei Yang

Introduction

In China, since 1979, the economic reform – decentralization of decision-making combined with development of commodity production – has encouraged investment and generated rapid increases in agricultural output and farmers' household income. In Guangdong Province, the income of rural households grew rapidly between 1978 and 1993. However, since 1994 the growth rate has slowed down (see Table 5.1).

There is a strong argument that the slower growth in the income of farmers is linked with an unfavourable socio-economic environment in which the relation between agriculture and industry is unbalanced.[1] In this chapter I argue that the main cause of the stagnant farm income is the weakness of Guangdong's agricultural structure. This structural weakness will also be the major cause of challenges facing Guangdong's agriculture when China enters the World Trade Organization (WTO).

The term 'agricultural structure' has been used in the past 10 years rather often in China. Here we use it to refer to a supporting framework of agriculture that consists of factors and conditions related to land tenure, farm organization and the market system.[2]

Overview of Guangdong's agricultural structure

Land tenure system. Since the beginning of the 1980s, a land tenure and farming system has been used. The system is the so-called 'family responsibility system' in which, farmland and some mountain areas are divided into small areas and allocated to individual families. The land is collectively owned and the farmers only own the right to use the land.

Table 5.1 Annual per capita household income and growth of Guangdong's rural area (US dollars)

Year	Net income per capita	Growth rate		Per capita consumption	Growth rate	
		Nominal	Actual		Nominal	Actual
1978	193.25			184.89		
1979	222.72	15.2	13.6	205.18	11.0	10.1
1980	274.37	23.2	19.4	222.22	8.3	3.9
1981	325.37	18.6	11.4	266.05	19.7	12.1
1982	381.79	17.3	12.7	312.44	17.4	16.2
1983	395.92	3.7	7	328.76	5.2	6.3
1984	425.34	7.4	7.2	346.19	5.3	5
1985	495.31	16.5	9.8	388	12.1	5.7
1986	546.43	10.3	7.6	454.06	17.0	11.1
1987	662.24	21.2	11.1	545.25	20.1	9.5
1988	808.70	22.1	2.7	684.67	25.6	3.2
1989	955.02	18.1	2	870.59	27.2	7.3
1990	1,043.03	9.2	1.6	932.63	7.1	−0.3
1991	1,143.06	9.6	9.4	942.40	1.0	1.2
1992	1,307.65	14.4	10.4	1,060.29	12.5	8.8
1993	1,674.78	28.1	6.1	1,391.01	31.2	6.8
1994	2,181.52	30.3	3.8	1,882	35.3	3.6
1995	2,699.24	23.7	6.5	2,255.01	19.8	5.3
1996	3,183.46	17.9	7.6	2,584.16	14.6	6.9
1997	3,467.69	8.9	4.2	2,617.65	1.3	0.3
1998	3,527.14	1.7	3.4	2,683.18	2.5	3.8

Note: Government data in China are public domain. Thus, no permission is needed. Nominal growth rate denotes the increase percentage over the previous year; actual growth rate the increase percentage over the previous year after deduction of price fluctuation.
Source: Data adapted from Agricultural Statistical Yearbook of Guangdong, 1999.

To obtain the land-use right, farmers have to sign a contract with the collective, mainly the village. Because farmland does not belong to the individual farmers, this most important asset of Chinese agriculture can only be used for farming; it does not play any role in the financial and credit markets.

Farm size. There were about eight million farms in Guangdong in 1998. In 2000 the total farmland in Guangdong Province was 5,624,905 acres, the average farm size 0.7 acres and there were 12.7 million farmers. The average farmland per farmer was about 0.44 acres.[3] The pressure of underemployment in rural areas has been tremendous. The older, more traditional farming methods are still used on most farms, with the majority of farming activities still depending on human labour and animal power.

Production structure. Guangdong's agriculture is usually divided into four farming regions, namely the Pearl River Delta Region, the Western Region, the Eastern Region and the Mountain Region. Each region has developed its own unique agricultural products since 1979. For example, the Pearl River Delta Region has developed into a horticulture, livestock and poultry production base. The Western Region has become known for its subtropical fruits such as lychee, longan and bananas. It also produces off-season vegetables. However, this development does not mean that Guangdong's agriculture has already realized production specialization. Until now, except for some farms in the Pearl River Region, most family farms in Guangdong Province still produce many agricultural products instead of specializing in certain products.

Emerging industrialized production. In the past decade, Guangdong's agriculture has partially realized industrialized production. In China, industrialized production means that marketing, distribution, processing and production of agricultural products form an integrated value chain, referred to in China as a 'dragon'. The agribusiness takes charge of processing, marketing and distribution; it is the 'dragon's head'. The body of the 'dragon' is represented by numerous individual farms. Usually the connection between the head and the body of the chain is a contract; at other times they are connected as an integrated enterprise, from production to processing and distribution.

Industrialized production has existed in many types of agricultural production in Guangdong, including poultry, livestock, rice and tea production; however, its development has been uneven. The poultry and livestock industries are the most industrialized sub-sectors, and the Pearl River Delta Region is the most industrialized production area in Guangdong. For example, in Shenzhen, one of the cities in the Pearl River delta, over 80 per cent of agricultural products are produced by agribusinesses.[4]

Economic organization in agriculture. Numerous rural cooperatives have been established in China since the 1950s, with one rural cooperative in each town. However, all of the cooperatives were developed into state-owned enterprises. In recent years, some farmer-owned cooperatives have been developed, though their number and function are limited. There is no legal regulation of farmer cooperatives, and therefore the distribution of most agricultural products depends heavily on the agricultural product middlemen.

Linkage between agricultural extension stations and research units. In Guangdong Province, agricultural extension stations have been established in every town, and there is an agricultural extension centre in every county, administered by the Agriculture Bureau. The government plans to establish extension stations in every village, supervised by the centre. There are often no direct links or very weak links, if any, between the extension stations and agricultural research units, such as agricultural academies or colleges.

The causes of income stagnation of farming households. Since the beginning of the economic reform in China, agricultural output has increased greatly, and some traditional products have started to have relative surpluses (the so-called 'structural surplus') in the country. Such surpluses tend to depress prices.

Secondly, farms are too small and their marketing abilities are often very poor. In a market economy such small family farms suffer from lack of information and high transaction costs. In addition, they suffer other disadvantages such as a lack of economies of scale, limited financing abilities and poor competitiveness.

Thirdly, another important factor is that the agriculture product structure is not rational; the proportion of low value-added crops and grain is still too high. This is a very complicated issue but the major causes include the influence of a self-sufficiency policy and poor marketing ability. Because of this poor marketing ability, the safest choice is the production of grain so that in the mountainous areas grain production is still the dominant agricultural production even though in those areas it is not as competitive as fruit or vegetable production.

A fourth factor is relatively low productivity. Economic reform has stimulated individual farms to increase physical investment, such as in fertilizers, and improve management. Thus, agricultural productivity grew rapidly from 1980 to 1994; this is the so-called 'catch-up' effect. While the catch-up effect was fading in farming, the structure remained the same, not responding to the changing economic environment quickly enough so that the growth of agricultural productivity slowed down.

Finally, there is a lack of a comprehensive financial support system. After the catch-up effect faded, agriculture had no other way to continue developing quickly in the absence of effective financial and insurance support.

From the above analysis, we can conclude that in order to increase rural household income, optimizing the agricultural structure is crucial.

The bottom line is to improve the agricultural sector's marketing ability and competitiveness, and increase its productivity through structural adjustment.

An analysis of the US agriculture structure

How can Guangdong adjust its agricultural structure and are there any implications that Guangdong can derive from US agricultural development and structural adjustment? The following is an analysis of agricultural development in the USA with the purpose of answering these questions.

Production specialization

The United States is usually divided into 10 major agricultural production regions – the Pacific region, the Mountain region, Northern Plains, Lake States, Northeast region, Corn Belt, Appalachia region, Southern Plains, Delta States, and Southeast region. Each region specializes in certain types of agricultural production. For example, the Northeast States and the Lake States are the nation's principal milk-producing areas. Climate and soil in these regions are suited to raising grains and forage for cattle and for providing pastureland for grazing, while vegetables, fruit and cotton are important in California. About 55 per cent of farms produce only one commodity, 75 per cent produce only one or two commodities, and only 11 per cent produce four or more commodities.[5]

Agricultural mechanization and large-scale production

In 1997, the United States had 2.06 million farms, and 968 million acres of farmland. The average farm size was 471 acres, with sizes ranging from 65 acres to 2,773 acres. Since the 1950s, American farms have realized mechanization; with the help of large-scale machinery a farmer and his son, and perhaps a hired hand or two, can operate a large farm up to 1,000 acres.[6]

Industrialization and dualistic structure

In American agriculture, industrialization has led to a dualistic structure. Large farms produce and sell most of the farm products. In 1990, for example 5 per cent of large farms produced and sold over 56 per cent of all farm products. In the most industrialized sectors, such as that of eggs and vegetables, the largest 5 per cent of farms controlled over 80 per cent of the products. On the other hand, 61 per cent of farms are small, with gross sales of less than $20,000. In 1997, these small farms accounted for only 16.9 per cent of the acreage operated and less than 10 per cent of the total US agricultural production.[7]

Legal structure and land tenure system

American farms may be broadly classified as individual operations (proprietorships), partnerships or corporations. Individual operations account for the largest share of farmland (71 per cent) and gross farm sales (74 per cent), while corporate farms have the highest average farm sales. Average acreage was higher for corporate farms (1,165 acres) and for partnerships (856 acres) than for individual operations (373 acres) in 1999.[8] Land-tenure categories include full owners who own all the land they operate, part owners who own some and rent the remainder of their land, and tenants who rent all of their land or work on shares for others. The majority (53 per cent) of farms in 1996 were reported as under full ownership, while 38 per cent owned part and rented part of the farmland they operated. Only 9 per cent of operations rented all of their land.[9]

Diversified and high farm household income

Labour use on US farms has decreased dramatically over the past several decades. The average number of annual farm employees dropped from 99 million in 1950 to 2.9 million in 1997.[10]

Like many other US households, farm households receive income from a variety of sources, one of which is farming. The 1996 average household income for farm operator households was $50,360, which is on par with the average US household. About 84 per cent of the average farm operator household income comes from off-farm sources, and many operators spend most of their work efforts in occupations other than farming. Off-farm income includes earned income such as wages and salaries from an off-farm job, and net income from off-farm business. Off-farm income also includes unearned income, such as interest and dividends and social security.[11]

A comprehensive and developed financial support system

The United States' agricultural sector can obtain financial support from commercial banks, the farm credit system, insurance companies, and government agencies which provide a wide range of insurance services such as crop insurance and revenue insurance. Farm business debts at the end of 1997 were $165.4 billion. Among them, farm real estate debt was $85.4, while farm business non-real estate debt was $80.1 billion.[12]

An overview of structural changes of American agriculture

Beginning in the late 1930s, the American agricultural structure has undergone rapid changes. This could be described by terms such as industrialization, consolidation and coordination. By 1920, the gasoline-engine tractor had been developed to the point where it was both efficient and convenient, and farmers began to substitute this form of power for horses and mules on a widespread basis. The direct result of farm mechanization in the United States was that the requirement for farm labour declined dramatically. In 1890, some 40 to 50 man-hours of labour were required to produce 100 bushels of wheat on five acres with a gangplough, seeder, binder, thresher, horses and wagons.[13] In 1930, some 15 to 20 man-hours of labour were required to produce 100 bushels of wheat on five acres with a three-bottom plough, tractor, tandem disk, combine and trucks. In 1975, only three to five man-hours of labour were required to produce 100 bushels of wheat on three acres with a tractor, 30-foot sweep disk, 2-foot seed drill, 22-foot self-propelled combine and truck.[14]

This great decrease in labour requirements combined with biological and chemical advances in this period resulted in great changes in the agricultural sector. The size of farm that an average family could operate efficiently grew dramatically (see Figure 5.1), and in a consolidation process farms grew by purchasing land and assets of other farms.

Consolidation is the necessary adjustment of the agricultural sector to changing technology. Farms with smaller sizes will not fully employ

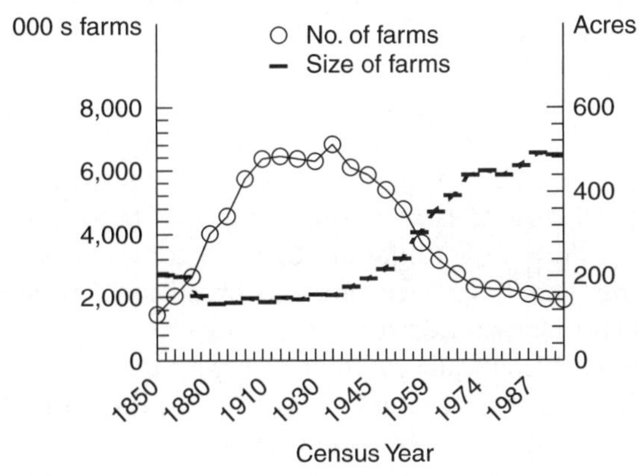

Figure 5.1 Number and size of farms in the United States[15]
Source: Data adapted from Harrington and Koenig, presentation at the Agricultural Outlook Forum, 2000.

Table 5.2 Indices of farm output, input and productivity, USA 1870–1990 (1967 = 100)

Year	Output	Input	Productivity	Year	Output	Input	Productivity
1870	17	43	40	1945	70	103	68
1880	26	56	47	1950	74	104	71
1890	31	66	43	1955	82	105	78
1900	40	77	53	1960	91	101	90
1910	43	86	50	1965	98	98	100
1915	49	92	53	1967	100	100	100
1920	50	98	52	1970	101	100	102
1925	41	99	51	1975	114	99	116
1930	52	101	51	1980	125	105	119
1935	52	91	57	1985	142	93	153
1940	60	100	60	1990	143	90	160

Source: United States Department of Agriculture, Economic Research Service.

their operators, and farms need to grow to at least a certain size to remain efficient and competitive. The agricultural sector realized industrialization of production through consolidation of farms, and combined with biological and chemical revolutions agriculture productivity increased dramatically (see Table 5.2). These changes in the 1930s to the early 1980s resulted in American agriculture developing into a bimodal distribution of farms – many small farms and a growing number of large farms, with few in between.

Since the 1980s, and especially in recent years, structural changes in American agriculture have told a different story. This could be described as a period of coordination, reflecting the fact that decisions on what, how and how much to produce are being made in agribusiness boardrooms instead of independent farming households. The production and distribution system has traditionally been coordinated through market mechanisms, with most farmers operating on a produce-and-then-sell basis. In the period of coordination, through contractual coordination, those open markets have been replaced by personal negotiations and often closed contractual linkages.

The emergence of vertically coordinated supply chains or value chains is a growing phenomenon of recent years. In 1997, the US broiler industry was dominated by vertical coordination with over 90 per cent of production occurring under production contracts.[16] These value chains may control the growing, processing and distribution of a product, sometimes all the way from the genetics of the agricultural commodity to the supermarket shelf.

In broiler contract production, the processing firm provides the young chicks, feed, poultry science and other technical supports, as well as delivery and collection of the chickens. Firms use field supervisors to oversee production units, with the supervisor typically visiting each unit once a week. The grower provides the physical structure in which the chickens are housed, the waste disposal facility, and the labour for the feeding, cleaning of the structure and other day-to-day care of the chickens. The grower is paid per pound of live broilers produced, and the contracting period is usually three years.[17]

A different type of contracting has emerged in rice production. Usually the processor provides the rice production technique, and the rice grower provides a guarantee of production practices and quality in exchange for a price premium. The reason why the coordination production system has prevailed is that the system can satisfy the needs of both firms and farmers. On the firm's side, contracted production is necessary for risk control and information transmission.

Risk has been a hallmark of the agricultural sector. One risk is in the prices of inputs, and a common strategy is to reduce the risk of high prices of inputs by contracting with suppliers. A second source of risk is related to the quantity and quality of production. Because of high fixed costs at all stages of processing and packaging, unit costs have become very sensitive to operating at full plant capacity. Thus, flow scheduling is critical to being cost competitive. Matching the physical capacity of various stages is critical to the overall efficiency of the system, and although such coordination is more difficult to attain in an open market, it can be guaranteed by contractual production.[18] The third type of risk is in the safety of food products, and here there are two dimensions. One is the health risk of food-borne disease and the other is the risk of polluting water, air and land resources in the food production process.[19]

Another reason for processing and packaging units to adopt coordinated contracted production is that the traditional open and spot market system cannot efficiently satisfy the need of greater diversity and exact quality and flow control. Open markets increasingly encounter difficulties in conveying the full message concerning attributes (e.g., quality, quantity, timing) of a product and characteristics of a transaction. The main difficulty of spot markets for conveying proper information is the speed of information flows and the rate of adoption. Negotiated coordination has resulted in rapid transmission of information between the various economic stages and has consequently enhanced the ability of the system to adjust to changing consumer demands, economic conditions or technological improvements. The ability of the production and distribution system to be more responsive and adjust rapidly to changing conditions is becoming more important with the increased rate of change in economic and social systems worldwide.[20]

From the standpoint of growers or farmers, risk control is also the main incentive to join a coordinated contract production system. By contract production, farms can reduce production and market risks. Other incentives for farms to join a coordinated production system include improved access to new technology, information and capital.

Factors affecting structural changes

Factors affecting structural changes in agricultural restructuring in the USA fall roughly into the following categories – economic opportunity factors, technology factors, and policy factors:

- *Economic opportunity factor.* In the USA, farming can be and largely is combined with other economic pursuits. So one of the strongest forces for structural change in farming has been the growth of non-farming economic opportunities attracting human resources from farming and allowing the remaining farmers to consolidate the assets of existing farms.
- *Technology factor.* Technological advances have been linked to farm structural changes for more than a generation. First, a technological advance is adopted by a few farms to increase production for more profit. The increased production causes prices to fall, forcing other farms to adopt technology to stay competitive. Besides, technological advances tend to help save labour and increase efficiency. Farms that adopt the new technology but do not expand find that they no longer fully employ their operators. Finally, many technological advances require a certain minimum size for farms to be utilized efficiently.
- *Policy factor.* Agricultural policies such as price and income support policies, credit policies and governmental research policies have contributed to structural change, as have macroeconomic policies. For example, the pre-1996 agricultural policies of the USA aimed at stabilizing and supplementing net farm income through supply management and direct payments based on the volume of production. These policies favoured large farms by distributing more risk-reduction benefits and directing payments to large farms rather than to small farms. The result was that large farms could safely take on more debt and financially leverage the acquisition of the assets of small farms. This accelerated the growth of large farms.

Comparison and implications

Because the situations of the two countries are different, the American approach cannot be simply transferred to Guangdong and the rest of China. However, the two countries share some basic principles related to agricultural restructuring.

Major differences between the agricultural practices of Guangdong and the United States

Through the above discussion it can be concluded that the major differences between the agricultural systems in the USA and Guangdong and the rest of China are as follows:

1 The United States has abundant land resources, and high-cost farm labour, while China has abundant farm labour but very scarce land resources.
2 The US agricultural system is one of large-scale, high-mechanization, high-productivity, high-specialization and high-industrialization, while Guangdong' is small-scale, intensive in labour, with a low-level of specialization, industrialization and productivity.
3 The contribution of science and technology is also different. In the United States, any available science and technology is transferred into the agriculture sector very quickly. In Guangdong, this is usually a time-consuming process.
4 The United States has developed a comprehensive financial and economic safety system to support and assist its agricultural sector, while Guangdong is poorly developed in its support system for farmers.

These differences, which expose the weakness of Guangdong's agricultural structure, will become the major causes of challenges facing Guangdong, especially after China enters into the WTO.

US experience appropriate to Guangdong

Although the situations of the United States and Guangdong are very different, some American agricultural experiences are appropriate for Guangdong's situation:

1 Factors that affect agriculture structural adjustment are applicable. For example, off-farm economic opportunities, science and technology and government policies will affect Guangdong's agricultural development in similar ways.

2 The development of a coordinated production system also has great implications for Guangdong. In order to further enlarge the scale of production, Guangdong, characterized by numerous small individual farms, has no choice but to develop a coordinated production structure in order to effectively obtain economies of scale.
3 The third experience that Guangdong's agricultural sector can learn from the United States is a comprehensively developed market economy. Agriculture restructuring is an auto-responce process; farmers respond to a changing socio-economic environment. It is a sustainable adjustment process driven by the maximum revenue principle, and the government needs to provide or create a favourable socio-economic environment for agricultural development.

US experience inappropriate for Guangdong

Consolidation is not an appropriate experience for Guangdong. In the United States, mechanization caused large-scale farm consolidation that played a major role in the development of US agriculture, especially in increasing agricultural productivity. However, Guangdong's agricultural sector cannot afford to use large-scale farm machinery to substitute for farm labour in order to increase agricultural productivity in the way America has.

Approaches to Guangdong's agricultural structuring

From the above analysis, it is obvious that Guangdong's agriculture restructuring should be focused at both the macro level – outside the agricultural sector – and the micro level – inside the agricultural sector.

Macro-level approaches

The economic system should be improved to provide a *favourable macroeconomic and social environment* for agricultural development. In a market economy, given a well-informed producer, production activities would be guided by market signals. The pursuit of maximum profit would force enterprises and farmers to arrange production activities according to the changing market environment. This has been proved by the US experience. Therefore, the fundamental approach of agricultural structuring is to establish a comprehensive market-oriented economic system as soon as possible. This includes establishing financial, credit, insurance and legal systems. In such a comprehensive market-oriented economy, farming is a business and a farm is a commodity production unit. Agriculture should enjoy not only the same rights as other industries, but also some preferential policy protection because it is such a crucial industry.

Development of small towns should be accelerated to provide more economic opportunities for farmers. According to the American experience, non-farm economic opportunities are an important element for changes in agriculture. The development of small towns will encourage the development of small enterprises, agribusinesses and the service industry, and will thus attract a lot of surplus labour from the farming sector. Only after a significant amount of farm labour is attracted away from farming can the agricultural structure achieve strategic adjustment.

Elimination of trade restrictions regarding foreign trade for agribusinesses is also imperative. Until now, most agribusinesses have no right to engage in foreign trade. The export and import of agricultural products mainly depends on foreign trade companies. However, if Chinese agribusinesses are still restricted from taking part in foreign trade after China enters the WTO, Chinese farmers or agribusiness companies will have their hands bound when fighting with giant multinational producers in global markets. Macro-level approaches are therefore fundamental in agricultural structural adjustment. Restructuring is a tough process and cannot be accomplished by any single industry; it is a national game.

Micro-level approaches

Agribusiness

Guangdong should foster the *development of agribusiness* and encourage the development of a *vertical contracted production system*. The most serious challenge facing Guangdong and the rest of China is that the numerous small farms equipped with old tools and farming methods will have a hard time competing against modern multinational agribusiness from developed countries. The market for most of Guangdong's farms is within the province, while many American farms are becoming increasingly involved in international activities.

In the present situation, with the high pressure of underemployment in the whole country, expanding farm sizes by merging is not a viable choice for getting rid of the disadvantages inherent in the present system. The alternative is to foster the development of agribusiness to increase the competitiveness of Guangdong's agriculture. Using vertically contracted production, agribusiness can increase a small farm's marketing ability and increase access to capital, information and advanced technology. Development of agribusiness will also attract a lot of farm labour out of the farming sector, thus laying down a foundation for further structural adjustment in agriculture. Finally, the development of agribusiness can help to realize industrialization of agricultural production. By contracted production, agribusinesses and farms form a production chain from farming, to processing and finally to distribution.

However, the issue of how to encourage the development of agribusiness remains a tough task for Guangdong. Agriculture, with its vulnerability, is most in need of government support at this moment. Guangdong's agriculture with its additional weaknesses such as small-scale production, poor financing, poor information and education and lack of assets is more vulnerable in a market economy. Governmental support should focus on financial support and management assistance to agribusinesses and farmers. Financial support should mainly focus on providing low-interest loans and favourable tax policies for agribusinesses, especially those that are interested in coordinated contractual production with farmers. Management assistance should focus on the support of developmental strategies for agribusinesses, the establishment of contracted production system and information about production techniques. To do so, agricultural administrative departments should provide relevant services to farmers in need.

No matter how developed the agribusinesses are, they cannot cover all of the small farms. Therefore, fostering the development of *agricultural cooperatives* to increase the marketing ability of individual small farms is very significant. Cooperatives were the byproducts of market economies and have prevailed in every industrial country for centuries. Their main function is to increase the bargaining power of farms by making them work together. Cooperatives are businesses-owned and controlled by the people who use them. They differ from other businesses in being member-owned and operating for the benefit of members, rather than for investors. Like other businesses, most cooperatives are incorporated under State laws. The farmer cooperatives in the USA are exempted from taxes and antitrust prosecutions.[21, 22]

In the United States, there were 4,006 farmer cooperatives in 1995,[23] falling into three major categories – marketing, purchasing (farm production supplies) and service. Marketing cooperatives market agricultural products for patrons in unprocessed and processed condition. Products typically include milk, fruits, vegetables, nuts, livestock, poultry, eggs, grain, wool and cotton. Purchasing cooperatives purchase, manufacture, distribute and provide feed, petroleum products, fertilizer, chemicals, farm supplies and service of various kinds to their patrons. Supply cooperatives range in size from very small local retail units to large regional manufacturing and wholesale organizations. Service cooperatives provide artificial insemination, breeding of livestock, data processing, equipment leasing, insurance, financing and other services to agricultural producers.[24]

The US government has fully recognized the important role of the agricultural cooperatives in promoting the development of rural communities and in improving the competitiveness of small farms. The government has established the Rural Business-cooperative Service under the US Department of Agriculture. RBS established several programmes to help rural residents form new cooperative business and improve the operations of existing cooperatives. For example, the Cooperative Services provides technical assistance to cooperatives and those thinking of forming cooperatives. It also conducts cooperative-related research and produces information products to promote public understanding of cooperatives.

Agricultural cooperatives are economic organizations tailored for agriculture in Guangdong and the rest of China. One of the disadvantages facing China's agriculture is that numerous farms of small scale are positioned in the huge domestic market and in the emerging global market. With poor marketing expertise, inadequate marketing capital and information and lack of economies of scale, such small farms have very poor ability to compete in the marketplace. If the farms are not organized properly to compete in the market, the situation will become more difficult after China enters the WTO. Therefore, another practical approach for Guangdong's agriculture is to help farmers to organize agricultural cooperatives to improve competitiveness.

In recent years, one kind of marketing cooperative has emerged in the Pearl River Delta Region. However, they have developed very slowly and the main obstacles include:

1 A lack of relevant laws or regulations about farmer cooperatives in China and thus no uniform principles for cooperative organization and operation management.
2 A lack of necessary knowledge about the establishment, management and business strategy of cooperatives.
3 A lack of awareness among farmers of the function of cooperatives.

To encourage the development of farmer cooperatives, the Guangdong government or agricultural administrative departments should at least provide the following support or assistance to farmers. First, relevant regulations or laws should be established as soon as possible. At present, there are no relevant regulations or laws about cooperatives; farmers do not understand what kind of organizations could be established and what the benefits in establishing such organizations might be. Second, agricultural departments should provide information and knowledge to promote understanding of cooperatives among farmers and offer technical assistance to those who are interested in forming cooperatives.

Investment in R&D and the agricultural extension system

In order to increase investment in R&D and improve the agricultural extension system, it is necessary to speed up the transfer of agricultural technology to farmers. This is a two-fold issue. First, technology development is the most crucial element to realizing agricultural structural adjustment and R&D investment is the guarantee of technology development. Second, technology itself is not productivity until it is transferred to users. The experience of American agricultural development has shown that technological development is not only one of the major factors that affects the course of agriculture adjustment, but it is also the major factor that affects agricultural productivity growth.[25]

At the same time, the present agricultural extension system must be reformed to speed up the transfer of research results to farmers. The present relationship of education, research and the extension system is not favourable for the transfer of advanced agricultural technology to farmers. On the one hand, agricultural technologists and experts are very important in the extension system, but because of the lack of funds and poor payment, very few college graduates are willing to work in extension stations. On the other hand, the research of postgraduates and professors is not combined very well with the current needs of agricultural production. The worse situation is that there are no effective and efficient channels for researchers to transfer their experimental results into the production field. The current situation is one in which farmers do not know what the academies are doing and the researchers do not know what the farmers need.

In the United States, it is mainly the land-grant agricultural colleges and universities, that conduct agricultural education, research and extension activities. The federal Department of Agriculture, through its Office of Experimental Stations, is involved in ongoing experiments of general importance. The extension service includes hundreds of specialists usually stationed at the State College of Agriculture and a much larger field force of county agents, home demonstration agents and others. It seems that both China and the USA have the same framework of education, research and an extension system. However, there are huge differences in operation. In America, everyone involved in teaching, research or extension activities all belong to the faculties of the Land-grant College. The whole system, including education, research and extension, is funded by the local, state and federal governments, or other agencies. In China, the extension stations survive mainly through revenues obtained from delivering services.

There is a close relationship between research, education, extension and farmers in the United States system. Most agricultural college professors spend their time in both education and research and in addition they also are the instructors of the extension agents. Most of the extension agents have a master's degree. Not only do the extension agents work closely with farmers, but the researchers and professors also contact farmers through phone calls, workshops and field visits. In China, professors mainly engage in education and research and there are no extension responsibilities. Researchers of the agricultural academy mainly focus on research and tests rather than working with outreach programmes. The extension agents have no fixed or regular channels to obtain updated scientific and technological information.

The functions of extension are different. In the USA, the agricultural extension is essentially an agricultural education offered to non-enrolled students – the farmers. This is why Land-grant Colleges offer extension services covering all kinds of agricultural knowledge from farming techniques to marketing skills. All of the services are offered free. In China, because of the limitation of extension agents, the agricultural extensions mainly focus on the use of new varieties of crops, pesticides, fertilizers and so on.

The methods of offering service are also significantly different. In the USA, the extension service combines both active and passive methods. Service is offered through workshops, field instruction and even the Internet (i.e., active offering), or consultation. In China, the extension service is mainly offered through selling new products (new varieties, new fertilizers or chemicals and other new supplies) and explaining how to use the new products. Alternatively, consultation services are also provided to the farmers who visit the extension stations.

To date, there are two essential issues related to extensions in Guangdong. The first is how to eliminate the unfavourable influence of the vertical management system to enhance cooperation between extensions with respect to education and research. Here the so-called vertical management system means that different administrative government departments respectively administer the extension service and education systems. The agricultural academy is also another relatively independent system. In this case, there are very clear boundaries between these three functional institutions. Because there are no laws or regulations to stipulate their interaction, although the combination of research and education with production activities is often encouraged or emphasized by the governments, the linkage between these three institutions is still very weak.

The second essential issue is how to solve the extension-financing problem. If the extension system relies on self-financing, it will be very difficult for the extension system to attract agricultural talents to engage in an extension career. The resolution of these two issues could be that governments, central and local, establish some research extension funds. Faculties, extension agents and researchers in agricultural universities, the extension system and academies would be qualified to apply for grants from these funds only when they collaborate on research with extension projects. Cooperation would need to be between faculties and extension agents, or researchers and agents. In order to avoid conflict and distinguish duties, the whole province could be divided into three responsibility areas allocated to the agricultural universities, colleges and the agricultural academies respectively. In addition, the evaluation of each professor or researcher could be combined with his/her achievements associated with extension-related activities. In this way, the financing problem of extensions can be partially resolved. Moreover, it creates a linkage between research and production while it does not need to break down the comprehensive institutional structure that has already been developed by the existing education and research system and can make better use of the system to serve the farming sector.

Conclusion

This chapter has compared the structure of the Guangdong and American agricultural sectors and analysed the American agriculture restructuring experience. The main differences between the United States and the Guangdong systems include the fact that US agriculture has abundant land resources and high-cost farm labour, while Guangdong has abundant labour resources and scarce land resources. In the USA, agriculture is a highly specialized, highly mechanized and large-scale production industry with high productivity, while Guangdong's agricultural sector is less specialized, less mechanized and small-scale in terms of production capacity with relatively low productivity. The US agricultural sector can respond to new science and technology promptly, while Guangdong's agricultural sector responds slowly because of the poor linkage between research and production. The US agricultural system has a comprehensive financial supporting system while that of its counterpart in Guangdong is still poorly developed. Most of these differences indicate structural weaknesses of Guangdong's agricultural sector which not only are the main cause of farm household income stagnation in recent years, but also the major cause of challenges facing Guangdong's agricultural sector, especially when China enters the WTO.

Because of the great difference in respect to the two countries' situations, the American experience cannot simply be transferred to Guangdong. Because of the tremendous pressure of underemployment in rural areas of China, the American agricultural development experience of consolidation is not appropriate to Guangdong's agricultural development. However, factors such as off-farm economic opportunities, technological advancement and so on, that affect agricultural structural adjustment can play a similar role in Guangdong's agriculture. The development of a coordinated production structure is also a useful experience to learn from. The other implication from the American experience is that in a market economy, agricultural adjustment is an auto-response process in which the agricultural sector adjusts its structure to the changing socio-economic environment. What the government needs to do is to establish or create a favourable socio-economic environment for agricultural development in order to optimize the agricultural structure.

In the current situation, when China is experiencing the transition from a planned economy to a market-driven economy, the proposed solutions for Guangdong include macro-level and micro-level approaches. The macro-level approaches are to establish a comprehensive market economic system as soon as possible, to speed up the development of small towns and to empower the agribusinesses in order for them to engage in foreign trade.

The micro-level approaches are to encourage the development of agribusinesses, to foster the development of farmer cooperatives, to increase investment in R&D and to improve the agricultural extension system in order to speed up the adoption of agricultural technology among farmers. The macro-level approaches are fundamental for long-term development, but they are also the most difficult to implement.

The micro-level approaches are practical and also essential in the current situation.

Notes

1 Liming Wang and John Davis (2000), *China's Grain Economy*, Ashgate.
2 Terry L. Roe and Munisamyth Gopinath, *'The "Miracle" of U.S. Agriculture'*, *Minnesota Agricultural Economist* University of Minnesota Press.
3 *Guangdong Agricultural Statistic Yearbook 1999.*
4 *Ibid.*
5 *Farm and Foreign Agricultural Service* (2000), http:/ /www.usda.gov/yourusda/fastext.htm.
6 United States Department of Agriculture (1999), *Agriculture Facts Book 1999.*
7 David H. Harrington and Steven R. Koenig (2000), 'Structural Charge: Farm and Financial Dimensions', *Agricultural Outlook Forum 2000*, Arlington, Virginia.
8 United States Department of Agriculture (1999), *Agriculture Facts Book 1999.*
9 *Ibid.*
10 Willard W. Cochrane (1993), *The Development of American agriculture*, 2nd edn, University of Minnesota Press.
11 United States Department of Agriculture (1999), *Agriculture Facts Book 1999.*
12 *Ibid.*
13 Willard W. Cochrane, *The Development of American Agriculture*, 2nd edn, *op. cit.*
14 *Ibid.*
15 David H. Harrington and Steven R. Koenig (2000), *Agricultural Outlook Forum 2000, op. cit.*
16 Patricia Aust (1997), *An Institutional Analysis of Vertical Coordination versus Vertical Integration: The Case of the U.S. Broiler Industry*, Michigan State University.
17 *Ibid.*
18 Lee F. Schrader and Michael Boehije (1996), *'Cooperative Coordination in The Hog-Pork System: Examples from Europe and the U.S.'*, *Agricultural Economics Staff Papers*, Purdue University.
19 *Ibid.*
20 *Ibid.*
21 Rural Cooperative Publications: *Cooperative Principle and Legal Foundation*, http:/ /www.rurdev.usda.gov/rbs/pub/cir4/cir4.htm.
22 Audits of Agricultural Producers and Agricultural Cooperatives (1995), *AICPA Audit and Accounting Guide*, New York, American Insitute of Certified Public Accountants.
23 *Rural Cooperative Publications: Farmer Cooperative Statistics*, http:/ /www.rurdev.usda.gov/rbs/pub/cir4/cir4.htm.
24 Audits of Agricultural Producers and Agricultural Cooperatives (1985), *AICPA Audit and Accounting Guide, 1985, op. cit.*
25 Terry L. Roe and Munisamyth, Gopinath, *The 'Miracle' of U.S. Agriculture, op. cit.*

6

Guangdong's State-Owned Enterprise Reform: Problems and Solutions

Biao Chen and Wayne Jones

Background of SOE reform

Prior to 1979, China maintained a centrally planned or command economy. A large share of the country's economic output was directed and controlled by the state, which set production goals, controlled prices and allocated resources.

During the 1950s, all of China's individual household farms were collectivized into large communes. To support rapid industrialization, the central government, in the 1960s and 1970s, invested a huge amount of monetary and human capital in SOEs. As a result, by 1978 nearly 87 per cent of government revenue was from state-owned enterprises (SOEs) and 78 per cent of the urban workforce was employed by SOEs according to centrally planned output targets.[1] Private enterprises and foreign-invested firms were almost non-existent. A central goal of the Chinese government was to make China's economy relatively self-sufficient. Foreign trade was generally limited to obtaining only those goods that could not be made or obtained in China. China's real GNP grew at an estimated average annual rate of about 6.1 per cent between 1970 and 1980.[2]

These government policies kept the Chinese economy relatively stagnant and inefficient, mainly due to few profit incentives for firms and farmers. Competition was virtually non-existent, and price and production controls caused widespread distortions in the economy. The Chinese standard of living was substantially lower than that of many other developing countries, but the Chinese government hoped that gradual reform would significantly increase economic growth and improve living standards.

Since 1979, China has launched several economic reforms, and industrial reform began to change the way SOEs operated in China. The central government initiated price and ownership incentives for farmers allowing them to sell a portion of their crops in the free market. In addition, the government established four special economic zones for the purpose of attracting foreign investment, boosting exports and importing high-tech products into China. More reforms followed to decentralize economic policy-making power in several economic sectors. Control of various enterprises was granted to governments at different levels. These enterprises were generally allowed to operate and compete based on free-market principles rather than under the direction and guidance of the state government.

Additional coastal regions and cities were designated as open cities and development zones. They were allowed to experiment with market-oriented economic reforms and to offer tax and trade incentives to attract foreign investment. State price controls on a wide range of products were gradually eliminated. Since the introduction of these economic reforms, China's economy has grown faster than in the pre-reform period and the result has been a quadrupling of GDP since 1979. Chinese statistics show that China's real GDP from 1980 to 2000 grew at an average annual rate of 10.2 per cent, making China one the world's fastest growing economies.[3]

Difficulties facing SOEs

In order to analyse the Chinese economy, two factors should be considered. The first is development. China is still a developing country, and to eliminate poverty and grow national wealth quickly is the top priority. The second priority is reform. In order to make the transformation from a planned economy, dominant for the past 30 years, to a market economy, almost everything had to be changed. The general economic situation in China is encouraging, but there are still some problems and some development strategies need to be adjusted. China is in a historic period of reforms and readjustment, and this period will last for the next 15 to 20 years. Reforms in technology, economic structure and social systems are among the major tasks, and the reforms are both encouraging and difficult.

One problem occurring in the reforms is the fact that development speed in recent years has been so high that supply has grown faster than demand. Consequently, deflation has appeared. Some enterprises have been producing as much as possible regardless of market demands. For instance, the number of VCD player manufacturers mushroomed in 1999 to become the world leader in VCD production in 2000 and more than 1000 factories producing VCD players came into existence. As a result, most of the companies in this industry went bankrupt.

The phenomenon of oversupply has expanded from limited regions of China to the whole country, and this has changed the original track of economic development. At the same time, it has hindered the economy from recovering from the Asian financial crisis. Under these circumstances, maintaining a high rate of economic development has become difficult. In recently years, oversupply has kept some products at a low level of quality. Profitability of businesses is going down, further limiting the growth of the economy, and hence the GDP growth has slowed down. The Chinese economy has entered a period of minimum profitability due to intense competition, with the number of enterprises making a profit being the same as those losing money. The main reason for the low profitability level has been high operating costs.

The residential consumption focus has changed from education to entertainment and cultural activities. Although consumption in certain products, such as information products, has increased quickly, consumer confidence has declined. Also, the price of production materials decreased continuously from 1997–1999.[4] From 1998–1999, individual income levels did not increase. At the same time, growth of the population has required more and more jobs, but there are only three million new jobs every year.[5] China needs more jobs and more wealth, but capital flow is relatively slow and there are huge amounts of unpaid debt among businesses. Credit, necessary for a healthy economy, is difficult to come by for both enterprises and individuals.

The fate of the new and traditional industries is completely different; but the economy is experiencing a complete shake-up. Resources switch among different industries and businesses and are effectively utilized, but these adjustments are far from enough. Initiatives and the flexibility of enterprises have increased, and SOEs enter the market competition actively but are facing serious debt problems. Financial instruments need to be modernized to meet the need of the SOEs and other companies. At the same time, China is becoming an assembly plant for the world since it lags behind in technology development. Many core technologies need to be imported, and investment in technology development is not adequate.

The state-owned sector is a dominant employer in China. Until 1999 there were 79.3 million SOEs in China, employing 70 per cent of the labour and capital used in China's industries.[5] However, the SOE sector only generates 40 per cent of the country's total output. At a news conference in March 1998, newly appointed Chinese Premier Zhu Rongji outlined a number of major new economic initiatives and goals to reform China's economy and maintain healthy economic growth.[6] Reforming and restructuring unprofitable medium- and large-sized SOEs to make them profitable was one of the initiatives. Another was to reorganize the banking system, increasing the regulatory and supervisory power of the central bank and allowing commercial banks to operate independently. A third initiative was to substantially reduce the size of government and reorganize governmental institutions. All these goals were to be achieved within three years. However, the economic slowdown in 1998 and early 1999 caused the government to slow the pace of SOE reform due to concerns that massive layoffs would result.[7]

As China attempts to adopt more modern technologies, the problem of relative inefficiency in the state sector will become more prominent. As other sectors of China's economy become more modernized, the SOE sector falls further behind. It is difficult for SOE managers to do more than refinance existing loans, as the approval of loan requests from SOEs by state banks is becoming less automatic. For many SOEs, the difficulties seem to be everywhere making the reforms very difficult to accomplish. The reform process cannot focus on just one issue since almost everything everywhere needs reforming to some extent. The following are highlights of the difficulties SOEs are experiencing in China, which also can apply to SOEs in Guangdong.

Lack of a guiding theory

The lack of a guiding theory in various policies and the frequently changing policies confuses SOE managers. Since 1984, many measures, such as reallocation of benefits and power and separation of ownership from operation, were implemented in the SOE sector, but the policies are not consistent and thus the general effect is not good. In the mid-1980s, in order to solve the problem that the central government had too much power over the operation of the SOEs, the Chinese central government decided to return the decision-making authority back to the SOEs. However, most of the power actually went to the local governments, which became very involved in the operation of the SOEs. To solve this dilemma, the central government took new measures to try to separate government ownership from the operation of the SOEs, but a new problem appeared.

Theoretically, the owners of the SOEs are the country and the people, which means that in effect there are no specific owners. Who should monitor the business of SOEs? Who should guarantee the interests of the people? There seemed to be no clear answers to these questions. At present, the reform of SOEs has taken the path of establishing a modern enterprise system, but consistent and clear guidance from the government is still lacking in many respects. The state's attitude towards business bankruptcy, the concern over loss of control on state property due to introduction of foreign capital to reform SOEs, and so on, remain ongoing issues in need of clarification from the central government.

Obstacles from the beneficiaries

The three major beneficiaries of SOEs are the employees, the management, and the different levels of government involved. During the reform period, these beneficiaries can sometimes become obstacles when their interests are affected.

Employees. In the traditional system, employees of SOEs have their 'iron bowls' – secured employment and guaranteed income. As long as the enterprise can continue its business, the employee will get a salary and other benefits. Most SOE employees do not want to lose this stability; they are not used to taking risks. So, it is very difficult for inefficient SOEs to break the 'stability' and take experimental steps towards reform. The central government is pressured to fully take into account the interests of employees in its efforts to reform SOEs. However, reform means the old system should be broken and a new system established. The result is that the interests of the stakeholders will be rearranged; some people will benefit from the reform and others will not. In order to decrease the pressure from the interest-losing employees, the central government has to take compensation measures before it proceeds with reform. Unfortunately, it is precisely these compensation measures that decrease the effect of the reform, increase costs of operation, and lead to the waste of resources. Therefore, to a certain extent the interests of employees becomes an obstacle to the SOE reform process.

Management. Under the traditional system, managers have very little decision-making power in the operations of their company. Without owning the firm's assets, managers do not have the inherent incentive to maximize the firm's value. At the beginning of the movement, the management of the SOEs was not an obstacle to reform, instead, the managers were actually in favour of it. This is because at that time they were facing many problems such as declining profits, interference from the local governments, and complaints from employees. Through the reform they hoped to gain more freedom and decision-making power and freedom in operating their businesses. However, as the reforms proceeded and the managers obtained more freedom to run their businesses, they themselves became an obstacle to further reform. One main problem is the lack of monitoring over management performance. Since the state, as owner of SOEs, or its representatives (e.g., the industrial bureaus), do not possess complete information on the daily operations of a venture, SOE managers can easily allocate the firm's internal resources to benefit themselves. This moral problem worsens when managers are given even greater managerial autonomy. Some managers just want to keep the situation as it is and do not welcome further reform which may change this status quo.

Government departments. Some government departments are also beneficiaries of SOEs, and to some degree they are obstacles to further reform. Under the planned economy, certain departments controlled some SOEs, but as the reform of SOEs continues different departments begin to share the power. Many government departments start to become involved in the running of the businesses and then want to benefit from them. The central government has decided to try to change this situation by setting up the State Owned Property Administrative Bureau to oversee SOE activities. This measure intends to keep all government departments out of the management of SOEs.

Lack of support of other social reforms

From the perspective of the Chinese government, most of the issues associated with SOEs are relatively clear and it knows how to solve those problems. However, many SOE reform measures face tremendous difficulty in implementation. The main reason is that there has not been enough social reform to support the SOE reform. For example, China has had its Bankruptcy Law for many years and the government is trying to apply it to many inefficient SOEs. However, dealing with laid-off workers, for example, has become an obstacle to SOE bankruptcy proceedings. Without a solid social security system to take care of the unemployed, the bankruptcies of the inefficient SOEs are just empty words on paper.

Theoretically, a firm should have the right to fire its employees. However, if a worker is laid off, who will care for him? The only possibility is for the government to take over this responsibility, but it needs to figure out a way to build a social welfare system to take care of these people. If this problem is not solved, the reform of SOEs will go nowhere. In a centrally-planned economy, the SOE is not just a business, but also a social machine. In a SOE, there is usually a kindergarten, a hospital and a school. Many compulsory education schools in China are SOE schools, and one-third of the hospital beds in China are in SOEs. That is why so many workers in SOEs try to firmly hold on to their present jobs. It is not just a job – it equals a house, welfare, medical insurance and many other things that come along with the job.

At the end of 1998, there were 699,570,000 employed in China, 90,580,000 of which worked in SOEs (down from a peak of 112,610,000 in 1995). Guangdong had a total of 37,370,000 workers, with 47,470,000 employed by SOEs.[8] These figures do not take into account the millions more retired employees which SOEs also have to care for. The older a SOE is, the more working and retired employees it has associated with it. Some old SOEs have more retired employees than working employees. The old system connects employment with social welfare, so one can imagine what an employee's attitude might be towards reforms if he or she has worked hard for 20 years and then finds that when laid off, their present and future social welfare is cut off, and that they are unable to support themselves far the rest of their lives.

Heavy tax and debt burdens

In 1995, SOEs contributed 444.1 billion RMB yuan (US$53.5 billion), or 71.1 percent, to total state revenues.[9] By the end of 1997, the balance of short-term loans to state industries was 1,652.7 billion RMB yuan (US$199.1 billion) and the interest was 1364 billion RMB yuan. The interest on long-term and short-term loans was 315.1 billion RMB yuan and 3,249 billion RMB yuan respectively. The interests were even higher than the tax rate. The average debt rates for SOEs is 78 per cent, and some go beyond 100 per cent.

High export costs

A large number of products are exported via Hong Kong. Most goods are sent to the USA via Hong Kong, where trade intermediaries raise the original prices by an average of 40 per cent. For some products, such as toys and clothing, the price hike will be as high as 100 per cent of the original price. Consequently, a significant part of the value created by SOEs goes to the Hong Kong middlemen.

Analysis of some policies of SOE reform

The source of SOEs' poor performance is complex and controversial, and the issues related to them have become a burden for the overall economic reform in China and Guangdong. The planned economic system causes the problems, and reform of SOEs has become a very urgent matter for the country. The SOE problem is connected with many issues such as payment for the creation of new jobs for millions of workers after the SOE shakeup, and social security for millions of retired state employees. The mission is not easy. The following is an analysis of the current SOE reform measures being taken by the central government.

Debt to equity transference

There are two types of transfer. In the first type, the loans of the SOEs are turned into shares held by banks or other creditors. The creditors become shareholders of the SOEs. Recently, banks have put aside substantial amounts of money for the transfer. In the second type, if a SOE is listed, the stated-owned shares of the company are turned into publicly traded shares. The capital from the sale of the state shares will be used to pay off loans. At the same time, banks made seven interest rate reductions on loans in 1998 and 1999 and this has reduced SOEs' loan interest. There are three main types of shares in SOEs:

- The first type is known as state shares. In most companies, the state owns most of the shares, 80 per cent or more.
- The second kind is those held by the enterprises' employees.
- The third type is those held by legal entities, including other enterprises, banks, non-bank financial institutions, insurance companies, pension funds, and so on.
- In some companies there is a fourth type of shares, that is the enterprise shares or collective shares. These shares are accumulated from investment of the enterprise's retained profits.

Many companies offer employee shareholders both fixed interests and dividends for the shares they own, and count the interest as part of the firm's costs. In contrast, state shares are not paid dividends.

The approach of having debt transferred to equity will mean that a large number of state-owned shares frozen for many years can then be bought and sold. Private firms are encouraged to buy the shares of SOEs, and through the sale of stocks, all or partially, combined with reorganization through bankruptcies, the debt ratio of SOEs will decrease significantly. The non-state-owned capital will have more growth space, and the internal structure of SOEs will also be improved. Unlike most SOE reform efforts in the past decade, which focused primarily on managerial factors within the enterprise itself, the approach of debt to equity transfer targets the relationship between firms and banks. Theoretically, this measure can eliminate financial risks and improve the operating efficiency of both the banks and the SOEs. The debt-to-equity approach is still in its infancy. The first swap took place in September 1999, and since then several hundred firms have undergone the process. It is too early to judge its effectiveness. Every approach needs to be tested in practice, and some managers of SOEs may regard the debt-to-equity transfer policy as another free lunch, and not feel the added pressure of bankruptcy. They do not believe the banks and the asset management companies set up by the state to supervise reorganization of SOEs will really reconstruct the SOEs. This mindset needs time to be corrected. Further reform measures include:

Reform of the salary system. One corrective measure is to raise the salary and bonus levels of managers. Salaries for managers will be, due to the reform process, five to eight times higher than the wages of workers. Currently, salaries for managers are relatively low, and low income affects the motivation and sense of responsibility of managers. Aside from increases in salary levels, the managers of a SOE can also own some shares of the company. The board of directors of some SOEs may set aside a bonus fund for managers which may be performance related.

Separation of business operation from government control. The functions of government departments involved in a SOE's operation will be replaced with those of the boards of directors, where the responsibilities of the directors and executives are clear. The board of directors is composed of representatives from the government, experts, and some executives.

Adjustment of product structures. Outdated technologies should be discarded. Enterprises whose products have no market, cause heavy pollution or are of low quality should have their operations suspended.

Separation of the social function from the SOE. China is trying to transfer the social function of SOEs from within the firms to society by establishing a complete social security system. This has the effect of turning SOEs back into businesses instead of social machines.

Effectiveness of reforms

In 2000, the National Bureau of Asian Research (NBR), the Luce Foundation and the National Science Foundation, along with the Chinese

Academy of Social Sciences, conducted a survey of SOEs and other types of business organizations in China.[10] Information was collected frrom 800 business organizations in four provinces, inducing 433 state-owned enterprises. Data was obtained on: (1) equity distribution after reorganization forced by changes in the law, (2) the organizational structure of firms, (3) management difficulties, and (4) financial and labour issues.

- *SOE reorganization regulations* China's 1994 Company Law was instrumental in creating a shareholding system for SOEs. Under this law, two types of business organization were created. Joint stock limited companies are analogous to publicly held firms in the West and have public share offerings. Limited liability companies are more akin to private firms with managers who report to a board of directors. The survey indicates that the national government went from having, on average, an 11.35 per cent controlling interest in SOEs to holding an 8.61 per cent equity share after the law was passed. On the other hand, provincial governments slightly increased their equity share in SOEs from 8.66 per cent to 9.13 per cent.[10]
- *Organizational structures* *Oiye jituan*, or business groups consisting of large SOEs along with some other types business, have gained in popularity since Chinese reforms were introduced in the 1980s. They were similar in nature to the Japanese *keiretsu* and Korean *chaebol* and often form to take advantage of economies of scale, marketing or production efficiencies, greater political clout, and synergies associated with having financing firms as members. Such groups resemble conglomerates and may even have cross-shareholding arrangements. The survey data indicates that approximately 66 per cent of SOEs are part of a business group, and that there are, on average, approximately eight firms associated with each group.[10]
- *Management difficulties* The survey data also shows that 66 per cent of firms encountered capital shortages, 60.25 per cent had difficulties finding reliable suppliers, 57.50 per cent had problems attracting customers, and 55.25 per cent perceived too much state interference.[10] These problems illustrate the many challenges that managers still face even though some reforms have been attempted.
- *Financial and labour issues* Finally, the survey data sheds light on significant trends that are permanently changing the characteristics of SOEs. The average number of workers per SOE declined from 2,525 in 1995 to a little over 1,130 in 1999. The percentage of workers who were permanent employees dropped from 84.29 to 14.96, while the percentage of temporary employees rose from 15.61 to 84.85 during

the same period.[11] These dramatic changes are partially explained by the massive layoffs that have occurred in SOEs as a result of their poor financial performance. Another important trend has been the change in financial strategies that firms have pursued. There has been a greater inclination to invest in other firms, particularly those in the same region. Firms have also somewhat decreased their dependence on funding from state sources (e.g., direct central budget allocations and indirect funding from state-owned banks).

Conclusion

Restructuring of SOEs will continue to play an important role in China's and Guangdong's reforms. The above discussion shows that the Chinese government has put into practice a series of major policies and measures to stimulate economic growth and improve the efficiency of SOEs, and through the concerted efforts of all parties involved, major progress has been made in the SOE reform process. The economic returns of SOEs have been improved, and at the same time SOEs have succeeded further in their efforts to transform their operational mechanisms and have reinforced internal management. There is great hope that SOEs, through these reform efforts, will become more efficient economic entities and continue to be the main powerhouse of China's and Guangdong's economy.

Notes

1 Edward S. Steinfeld (1998) *Forging Reform in China*, Cambridge University Press, Cambridge, pp. 16–7.
2 Robert Ash and Y. Kueh (1996) *The Chinese Economy under Deng Xiaoping*, Oxford University Press, Oxford, p. 12.
3 World Bank (2001), www.worldbank.org.
4 National Bureau of Statistics of China (2001).
5 *Ibid.*
6 'Can China Avert Crisis?' (1998) *Business Week*, 16 March, pp. 44–9.
7 *Ibid.*
8 *Chinese Statistical Yearbook* (1999) Government of China.
9 Edward S. Steinfeld (1998) *Forging Reform in China, op. cit.*
10 Lisa A. Keister and Jin Lu (2001) *NBR Analysis: The Transformation Continues – The Status of State-owned Enterprises at the Start of the Millennium*, Bureau of Asian Research, vol. 23, no. 3, pp. 5–31.
11 Lisa A. Keister and Jin Lu (2001) *NBR Analysis: The Transformation Continues – The Status of State-owned Enterprises at the Start of the Millennium, op. cit.*

7

Managing Growth of Township and Village Enterprises in Guangdong: Lessons Learned and Opportunities

Jingchao Geng

Introduction

Township and village enterprises (TVEs) have been an economic miracle in Guangdong since 1978. Their average annual income growth has been 31 per cent over the past 20 years. They have become the principal economic driving force of the rural economy and, as such, constitute an important pillar of the province's economy.[1] Indeed, the development of TVEs has played a critical role in the promotion of economic growth by gradually industrializing the economy, supporting agricultural development, increasing incomes in the agricultural sector, and bringing prosperity to the rural areas of Guangdong.

According to The People's Republic of China Township and Village Enterprises Law 1997, TVEs are defined as 'all kinds of enterprises, which are mainly invested in by the rural, collectively-owned economic organizations or peasants in the local township and village areas, that are needed to assume the obligation to subsidize the local agriculture.' The 'mainly invested' clause requires that the rural collective-owned economic organizations or peasants make over 50 per cent of the investment in the enterprise or, if the investing ratio is less than 50 per cent, that the collectively-owned economic organizations or peasants have real control of the TVEs.

It is important to note that this official legal definition of TVEs did not exist before the 1997 TVE law. Prior to this, the term TVEs actually referred to many types of venture (with the exception of state-owned enterprises) in the local township and village community, including township and village collectively-owned enterprises, privately-owned enterprises, self-employed labourers, peasants' cooperative enterprises and joint ventures with collective organizations. TVEs were originally known as 'Commune and Brigade Enterprises' (CBEs) as mentioned in a 1984 government document.[2]

Guangdong's rural areas, along with other parts of China, fostered CBEs from the late 1950s to the late 1970s as part of the peoples' commune system. Unfortunately, the state carried out a strategy of preferentially developing state-owned heavy industry and inhibiting the peasant's ability to set up enterprises during that period.[3] Therefore, the development of CBEs had a slow start and an erratic growth pattern. In 1978, CBEs accounted for only a small proportion of Guangdong's rural economy. There were approximately 81,000 CBEs in Guangdong Province which employed some 1.95 million people during this period. This was a mere 4.8 per cent of the total of agricultural workers, and 11.3 per cent of the total rural labour force in Guangdong.[4]

It is the economic system reforms set in place since 1978 that were responsible for the dramatic development of TVEs in Guangdong. It could be argued that if there had been no reform, then the TVEs as they appear today would not exist. Along with the reforms which initially made it possible for TVEs to gain access to critical resources, other factors including a shift to more of a market orientation, the introduction of flexible management mechanisms, and the low cost of entry into certain markets have also made the dramatic development of Guangdong TVEs possible.

Phases of the development of Guangdong's TVEs

There have been five distinct phases in the development of Guangdong's TVEs since 1978.

The initial development phase of TVEs: 1978 to 1983

The reform of the Chinese economic system started in rural areas in 1978. The strong unified management system of the peoples' communes was superseded by a new policy called the 'household responsibility system'. The essence of this reform allowed for the leasing of cultivatable land to rural households that pay rent and taxes and enjoy additional income and partial residual rights to the land. The new policy in effect gave authority over production and management (including responsibility for production, distribution, allocation of labour and the accumulation of household property) to peasant workers. The policy greatly liberated the rural workforce and provided the peasants with the incentive to work hard.[5] Just a few years after the reform, the agricultural output in Guangdong increased substantially. The success of the reform provided a rich environment for the development of non-agricultural industries. Increased agricultural efficiency led to lower labour requirements which displaced many workers who were eager to develop non-agricultural industries in order to obtain employment. At this point, the central government adjusted the policies for CBEs, allowing for greater development, which provided more opportunities for Guangdong's CBEs.[6]

In 1979, the central government offered Guangdong the opportunity to carry out special economic policies and flexible measures with regard to foreign affairs and economic cooperation. It also approved three special economic zones – Shenzhen City, Zhuhai City and Shantou City in Guangdong.[7] The Guangdong government simultaneously implemented a series of policies that were beneficial to CBEs. The township and village collective organizations took advantage of this opportunity to develop more CBEs, especially the township and village collective organizations located in the Pearl River Delta region and along the coast (Guangdong has 3,368 kilometers of coastline). They took advantage of their special geographic advantage that directly linked them with Hong Kong and Macao, as well as their connections with the large number of overseas Chinese (two-thirds of the 30 million overseas Chinese are from Guangdong) to develop CBE joint ventures. It was during this period between 1978 and 1984 that CBEs rapidly developed. The total income of CBEs increased from 2,936 million yuan to 8,008 million yuan between 1978 and 1983. The average annual increase was 34.6 per cent from 1978 to 1983 (see Tables 7.1 and 7.2).

The growth in the number of CBEs was unable keep up with the increasing rural labour surplus. Since the rural reform had established households' rights to own their own property, numerous peasants impulsively started their own businesses. Although the policy at that time still prohibited peasants from setting up private businesses, some began to operate covert ventures.

The dramatic development phase of TVEs: 1984 to 1988

The central government went a step further to adjust TVE policy in 1984. In the State Council document no. 4 of 1984, the term CBEs was formally changed to TVEs.[8] Furthermore, the document explicitly stated the important role of developing TVEs. In particular, it made several important changes to the restrictive policies which originally affected CBEs.

First, the policy cancelled the limitation of ownership. The new policy allowed not only the township and village organizations to set up

Table 7.1 General information on TVEs in Guangdong

Items	**1978**	**1983**	**1988**	**1991**	**1996**	**1999**
No. of TVEs (thousands)	80.9	126.8	1,158.2	1,235.2	1,450.8	1,411.5
No. of Employees (thousands)	1,946	2,474	6,450	7,079	11,186	11,785
Average no. of Employees per TVEs	24.1	19.5	5.6	5.7	7.7	8.3
Total revenue (million yuan)	2,936	8,008	65,555	100,822	533,512	792,900
Average revenue per TVEs (yuan)	36,292	63,155	56,601	81,624	367,736	561,743
Taxes paid (million yuan)	134	330	1,757	3,113	11,424	17,160
Total net profit (million yuan)	434	828	2,692	7,258	25,690	40,502
Average net profit per TVE (yuan)	5,364	6,529	2,324	5,876	17,707	28,694

Sources: Data adapted and compiled from *Guangdong Rural Economic Statistics Yearbook*, 1993–2000 editions; Guangdong Township and Village Enterprises Administrations, *Annual Statistical Information*, 1995–2000; and Jiang Pan (1998) 'Issues on the System Reform and Open Door Policy', Development Research Centre of Guangdong Province People's Government, Guangdong Provincial Economic Society, *Memorial Collected Works of Guangdong Reform and Open Door to the World over 20 years*, pp. 240–9.

collective-owned enterprises, but also allowed peasants to establish share-owned or self-owned enterprises.

Second, the policy negated the limitation of industries TVEs could be part of. Prior to 1984, the government only allowed TVEs to engage in industries that served agriculture, such as the processing industry or the repair of agricultural machines. The new policy lifted this requirement and allowed all TVEs to be engaged in not only the areas that served agriculture, but also all other industries including manufacturing, trade, construction, transportation and service.

Third, the policy also allowed TVEs to expand into other districts. Prior to 1984, TVEs were only allowed to operate in the 'three local districts', that is (1) the district where they sourced their processed raw material, (2) the actual district in which they were located, and (3) they could only sell their products within their district. Since this limitation was also lifted, TVEs could conduct business with other regions or even other countries.

In addition, the government implemented policies that supported TVEs by allowing state-owned banks to lend money to them and providing tax reductions for collective-owned TVEs.

Due to these policy changes and the huge shortage of industrial products at the time, Guangdong TVEs developed at a rapid pace. This was the fastest growth period for TVEs in Guangdong since the reform began. In the brief five-year period since the policy revisions, Guangdong gave birth to thousands of TVEs and a large number of modern towns grew throughout the province. During this period, the number, income and exports of TVEs each grew more than 100 per cent (see Tables 7.1 and 7.2).

Table 7.2 Guangdong TVEs' average annual per cent growth in five phases of development

	No. of TVEs	No. of employees	Total income	Tax	Profit	Export
1978–83 (5 years)	11.3	5.4	34.6	29.3	18.2	29.6
1984–88 (5 years)	162.7	32.1	143.7	86.5	45.0	215.2
1989–91 (3 years)	2.2	3.3	17.9	25.7	56.5	46.1
1992–96 (5 years)	3.5	11.6	85.8	53.4	50.8	68.9
1997–99 (3 years)	−0.9	1.8	16.2	16.7	19.2	9.0

Source: Calculations based on figures in the *Guangdong Rural Economic Statistics Yearbook*, 1993–2000 editions; Guangdong Township and Village Enterprises Administration, *Annual Statistical Information*.

The rectifying phase of TVEs: 1989 to 1991

This period in Guangdong coincided with the period of national economic realignment. Because supply and demand were becoming unbalanced (more supply than demand), the national government made some adjustments to the economic structure of the country. These modifications included taking such steps as reducing infrastructure investment and adjusting industry and product structures. During this period, TVEs were immediately affected since they operated under non-state ownership.

The state carried out an austerity policy towards TVEs; they were directed to 'adjust, rectify, remold and improve'. Accordingly, the support in the form of tax relief and loans for TVEs was cut; the state stipulated that 'the money needed for the development of TVEs must come mostly from the peasants' own money'.[9] In 1990, TVEs did not receive any loans from banks in China. Some TVEs had to close or combine with other TVEs and change their business, and millions of employees in TVEs were forced to return to agriculture.[10] During this three-year rectifying period, the development of Guangdong's TVEs slowed. The average annual growth of total income was only 17.9 per cent during this three-year period (1988 to 1991) (see Tables 7.1 and 7.2).

The overall development phase of TVEs: 1992 to 1996

This was the second peak period of TVE development. In 1992, Deng Xiaoping visited southern China and gave his famous speech regarding reform in China. He pointed out that TVEs were one of the three elements in constructing a socialist economy with uniquely Chinese features.[11] In the same year, the Chinese Communist Party and the State Council issued several documents concerning TVEs. They reversed the prejudicial policies that had adversely affected them in recent years and affirmed the important role that TVEs played in the economy. The new policies created an unprecedented positive external environment for the further development of TVEs.[12]

The Guangdong provincial government again started to pay more attention to TVEs by creating measures that would support their development.[13] Consequently, many were able to strengthen their management, paid attention to enhancing their use of technology and human resources, and did their best to increase their efficiency. In particular, TVEs in the Pearl River Delta region accelerated their development of export-oriented businesses. The average annual growth of total income, taxes paid, profits and exports were all over 50 per cent (see Table 7.2).

The adjustment and innovation phase of TVEs: 1997 to present

Since 1997, TVEs have faced greater pressure as competition both domestically and internationally has increased dramatically. In the domestic market, the supply and demand of most commodities have balanced, while in some situations supply far exceeds demand, creating a buyer's market. Internationally, Southeast Asia was hit by the financial crisis in 1997 which also affected the Chinese economy. This particularly hit Guangdong TVEs because one-third of them were export-orientated. In addition, after many years of management reform the state-owned enterprises (SOEs) were gradually increasing their vigour. At the same time, the township-owned and village-owned TVEs started facing the situation of unresolved ownership. Therefore, under increased market pressures and competition, the growth of Guangdong's TVEs once again slowed. In the years from 1997 to 1999, the main financial ratios of TVEs were less than 20 per cent (see Table 7.2).

In 1997, the National People's Representative Committee passed The Township and Village Enterprises Law, which is the first independent law involving just TVEs. It established their legal status and helped facilitate TVE development. As China makes the necessary changes to conform to WTO regulations, Guangdong's TVEs are entering a new development phase which will likely see further restructuring of the industrial sector and the greater use of innovation in technology and management.

Developmental trends and characteristics of Guangdong's TVEs

Four main trends have emerged over the 20-year rapid development period of Guangdong's TVEs.

Change in TVE ownership structure from sole collective-run to diversified

At the beginning of the economic reform in the late 1970s, only the collective-owned enterprises existed in Guangdong's rural areas. Since the early 1980s, more and more successful private businesses have been established while the collective-owned enterprises continued to grow. In the 1990s, the collective-owned TVEs, especially those that were township-owned, gradually came to realize the weakness of sole collective ownership and explored many possibilities to reform their ownership structures.

Table 7.3 Ratios of different ownerships by number of TVEs, number of employees, total income, and net profit in Guangdong

	Type of TVE	1980	1985	1990	1996	1999
Per cent of TVEs	Township-owned TVEs	19.6	3.1	2.0	1.9	1.6
	Village-owned TVEs	80.4	13.9	7.5	7.0	6.0
	Privately-run TVEs	0.0	7.0	4.9	4.4	11.9
	Self-employed labourers	0.0	76.0	85.6	86.7	80.5
Per cent of employees	Township-owned TVEs	38.9	27.2	23.5	20.7	17.2
	Village-owned TVEs	60.1	35.0	27.8	32.1	29.8
	Privately-run TVEs	0.0	9.6	8.5	6.4	22.9
	Self-employed labourers	0.0	28.2	40.2	40.8	30.1
Per cent of total income	Township-owned TVEs	51.9	44.2	42.3	33.3	30.0
	Village-owned TVEs	48.1	32.0	24.1	28.2	25.7
	Privately-run TVEs	0.0	6.7	7.8	7.3	28.0
	Self-employed labourers	0.0	17.1	25.7	30.3	16.3
Per cent of net profit	Township-owned TVEs	41.5	21.0	11.5	10.7	15.7
	Village-owned TVEs	58.5	41.0	33.7	31.9	28.5
	Privately-run TVEs	0.0	10.2	10.0	12.0	23.5
	Self-employed labourers	0.0	27.8	44.7	45.4	32.3

Note: The standard of privately run TVEs and self-employed labourers has changed since 1997. Some self-employed labourers were merged into the private-run TVEs.
Source: Calculations based on figures from the *Guangdong Rural Economic Statistics Yearbook*, 1993–2000 editions.

Over the past 20 years, the proportion of collective-owned TVEs has gradually decreased, while the proportion of private-run and self-employed TVEs has gradually risen. Table 7.3 shows that the proportion of collective-owned TVEs (including the township-owned and village-owned

TVEs), the number of employees, income and net profit declined from 100 per cent in 1980 to 7.6 per cent, 47.0 per cent, 55.7 per cent and 44.2 per cent respectively in 1999. Conversely, the proportion of privately-owned TVEs has seen their numbers ascend from 0.0 per cent to 92.4 per cent, 53.0 per cent, 44.3 per cent and 55.8 per cent respectively in 1999.

Change from small businesses to include small, medium and large TVEs

Generally speaking, the sizes of TVEs in 1999 were small and medium, with an average of only 8.3 employees per TVE (see Table 7.1). After 20 years of development, some TVEs have developed into large companies. For example, there were 1,278 TVEs whose income was over 50 million yuan in 1999, while the average income per TVE was only 560 thousand yuan. There were 8,686 TVEs with an annual income of over 5 million yuan in 1999 that accounted for a mere 0.06 per cent of the total number of TVEs; however, their combined income was 336.8 billion yuan which accounted for 42.5 per cent of the total income of the province's TVEs.

Township-owned TVEs employ the most people, and Table 7.4 indicates that the average employees per township-owned TVE in 1999 was 91.9. Although the number of township-owned TVEs was only 1.6 per cent of total TVEs, these enterprises produced 30.0 per cent of the total income for all TVEs during this period (see Table 7.3).

Market focus of TVEs has become more internationalized

At the beginning of the reform period, Guangdong's TVEs only concentrated on provincial and domestic markets. Since 1985, the collective organizations, particularly those located in the Pearl River Delta and the coastal areas, have utilized their geographical advantages and relationships with overseas Chinese to develop export-oriented TVEs and move

Table 7.4 Average employees per TVE in different ownership in Guangdong

Item	1980	1985	1990	1995	1999
Township-owned TVEs	41.8	52.1	64.8	81.8	91.1
Village-owned TVEs	16.0	14.8	20.4	32.4	41.5
Privately-owned TVEs	0.0	8.0	9.5	11.3	16.0
Self-employed labourers	0.0	2.2	2.6	3.5	3.1

Note: Some self-employed labourers were merged into privately-run TVEs by the new statistic standard of privately-run TVEs and self-employed labourers in use since 1997.
Source: Calculations based on figures from the *Guangdong Rural Economic Statistics Yearbook*, 1993–97 editions.

Table 7.5 Guangdong's provincial TVE exports

Item	1978	1985	1990	1995	1999
Export of TVEs (US$)	0.50	2.89	26.74	124.31	236.07
Export of Guangdong Province (US$)	13.88	29.53	105.60	556.67	776.82
Export of TVEs as per cent of total Guangdong exports	3.6	9.8	25.3	22.3	30.4

Sources: *Guangdong Yearbook* and *Guangdong Rural Economic Statistics Yearbook*, 1993–2000 editions.

into foreign markets. Until 1990, there had been only 1,667 export-orientated TVEs with 1.416 million employees and exports of 13,646 million yuan. After 1990, Guangdong TVEs strengthened their attractiveness to foreign investment and enlarged their export channels. This was due to the rapid development of export-oriented TVEs in the 1990s. At the end of 1998, there were 31,002 of these TVEs in Guangdong, which had 2.417 million employees and exports of 178,248 million yuan. They accounted for 24.1 per cent of the total exports of the export-oriented TVEs in the country, more than any other province. TVEs accounted for 30.4 per cent of Guangdong's total exports in 1999, up from 3.6 per cent in 1978 (see Table 7.5).

Changes in industry structure have affected TVEs

Since 1978, Guangdong's TVEs have placed greater emphasis on more fully utilizing their natural resources, low-cost labour and land to develop labour-intensive industries. Most of these TVEs have focused on manufacturing and agricultural output has declined relative to other types of industry. The manufacturing industry accounted for 82.0 per cent of the total output of TVEs, while agricultural output was responsible for only 0.9 per cent in 1999 (see Table 7.6).

TVEs have played an increasingly greater role in Guangdong's economy

After more than 20 years of reform, Guangdong has made remarkable achievements in social and economic development. It has developed from a backwater province whose economy had been dominated by agriculture, having a low standard of living and slow economic development, into a province with a robust economy, relatively high productivity levels and

Table 7.6 Output of Guangdong's TVEs by industry type (all numerical entries in per cent)

	Industry type	1980	1985	1990	1995	1999
First industry	Agriculture	7.0	3.3	1.6	1.0	0.9
Second group of industries	Manufacturing	72.2	60.4	71.5	78.3	82.0
	Construction	8.0	17.3	9.9	7.5	5.0
	Transportation	4.1	5.5	6.0	4.2	3.0
Later industries	Commerce, catering trade, etc.	8.7	13.5	11.0	9.0	9.1

Source: Calculations based on the *Guangdong Rural Economic Statistics Yearbook*, 1993–2000 editions.

advanced export-oriented activities. Guangdong Province has been ranked first among China's provinces in terms of GDP, total investment in fixed assets, total retail sales of consumer goods, total exports and imports, foreign investment, power generation, and privatization efforts of postal services and telecommunications for many consecutive years.[14]

A number of business entities have contributed to the remarkable achievements of Guangdong's economy – joint ventures, stated-owned and collective-owned enterprises, and private businesses. However, there is no doubt that TVEs were the main engine driving Guangdong's growth.

TVEs have been important to the economic development of Guangdong over the past 20 years

In 1999, the added value of TVEs was 196,795 million yuan, which accounted for 23.2 per cent of Guangdong's GDP. The taxes paid by TVEs amounted to 17,160 million yuan, which was equal to 22.4 per cent of the province's financial revenue in 1999, a 19 per cent increase from 1978 (see Table 7.7). The development of TVEs has also increased social efficiency since the economic reform. Production and management of TVEs have involved almost every part of the economy, and the output level of many products has greatly increased. Some TVE-produced products have dominated the provincial market. For example, TVEs produced 95 per cent of brick and tile lines, and small- and medium-sized agricultural machinery; 80 per cent of iron ore, food, cloth, clothing, shoes, aluminum materials, ceramics, leather products, plastic products and toys were made by TVEs. Moreover, 50 per cent of machine-made paper, paper mould, appliances (e.g., refrigerators, and

Table 7.7 Taxes paid by Guangdong's TVEs

	1978	1985	1990	1997	1999
TVE taxes (million yuan)	134	830	2,516	11,693	17,160
Provincial revenue (million yuan)	3,946	6,546	13,102	54,395	76,619
TVEs' tax as a per cent of provincial revenue	3.4	12.7	19.2	21.5	22.4

Sources: *Guangdong Statistics Yearbook*, 1993–2000 editions; *Guangdong Rural Economic Statistics Yearbook*, 1993–2000 editions.

room air-conditioners), cement and mix-feed were the products of TVEs.[15]

Some products of Guangdong TVEs account for the highest market share in the nation. For instance, the largest producers of Chinese air conditioners, refrigerators, automatic rice cookers, electric fans, microwave ovens and facial tissues are TVEs in Guangdong.[16]

TVEs are the driving force of Guangdong's rural economy

The rural economy in Guangdong was mostly based on the agricultural industry in 1978, and TVEs produced less than one-quarter of the rural provincial output in that year. The output of other TVE industry types surpassed the output of agriculture for the first time in 1986, indicating that Guangdong's rural economy had entered a new stage in its history. In 1997, the output of TVEs was 608,380 million yuan, which accounted for 82 per cent of the total output of the provincial rural economy.[17]

While TVEs took advantage of local natural resources, they also made significant contributions to communities. TVEs helped set up the agricultural byproducts, processing, storage and transportation industries so as further to develop the agricultural economy. As TVEs focus on their own growth, they also subsidize the farming sector with their profits.[18] This has been one of the main investment sources for the agricultural infrastructure and has speeded up the course of agricultural modernization. In 1997, Guangdong's collective TVEs contributed 1,008 million yuan in subsidies towards the agricultural infrastructure. This investment was mainly used in roads, bridges, irrigation and small reservoirs, and was more than the government invested in agricultural fixed assets in the same year.[19] In addition, TVEs also provide money to support rural welfare affairs, such as education, hospitals, culture, electric power and telecommunications. These efforts greatly promote the further development of not only the economy, but of society itself.

TVEs widen employment opportunities in rural areas and increase the income of rural residents

The development of TVEs has employed much of the rural labour surplus. Peasants have relatively steady work and income in the rural areas, due to a reduction of the pressure that forced peasant influx to the cities. In 1997, there were 10.059 million employees in Guangdong TVEs, which was 38.9 per cent of the provincial rural labour supply. In 1978 there had been only 1.95 million employees in TVEs, which accounted for 11.0 per cent of the total rural labour force. Since 1978, TVEs have eased the employment problem of about 10 million rural labourers in Guangdong, and this has helped optimize the labour structure in the countryside.[20]

In addition, TVEs also help increase the incomes of farmers. From 1978 to 1997, the average income per agricultural worker (including the farmers themselves and their families) increased from 193 yuan to 3,468 yuan. TVEs contributed 33 per cent towards farm incomes in 1997, as compared to 9 per cent in 1978.[21, 22]

Development of TVEs promotes the industrialization and building of modern towns in Guangdong's rural areas

For a long time before 1978, there existed a model of 'dualist social and economic structure' in China that stated that the cities develop industry while the rural areas develop agriculture. It has been the TVEs that have broken away from this rigid structure. Numerous peasants have worked together to develop their TVEs in rural areas. This is what is meant by 'leaving the cultivated land without leaving the community' and 'working in the enterprises without entering the cities'. Guangdong has embarked on a successful industrialization path with uniquely Chinese characteristics in which the urban and rural industries rely on and promote each other.

In 1999, the industrial output of Guangdong TVEs was 650,693 million yuan, which was 47 per cent of the industrial output of the province.[23, 24] This indicates that the TVEs have become an important pillar in the industrial economy of Guangdong; their development has led to the establishment of industrial regions and groups.

On the other hand, TVEs create wealth for rural areas and increase the ability of the local township governments to build infrastructure due to the strength of the local economy. As a result, a group of modern townships has arisen in Guangdong's rural areas to lead in the further development of TVEs. There were only about 120 administrative townships in 1978, but 1,596 townships were created by 1997.[25]

The development of TVEs has trained peasant entrepreneurs and industrial workers

TVEs have experienced strong market competition in the past. Many went bankrupt but many others became extremely successful, and the survivors of the shakeout had the strongest abilities to survive. After surviving fierce competition, the surviving TVEs have been able to bring industrial know-how to the rural areas, thereby increasing employees' scientific knowledge, technological skills and managerial abilities. The limited knowledge and closed-minded attitudes of peasants were broken and modern information and market concepts introduced. This has helped redefine the peasants in a single generation. Because of this, a group of peasant entrepreneurs who are market-orientated and good at management has emerged.

Reasons why TVEs did not emerge in rural areas before 1978

The emergence of TVEs is closely linked to the 'dualistic economy development model' that existed before 1978, which separated the city from the countryside and industry from agriculture. When the People's Republic of China was established in 1949, the central government set up the planned economy system that was mostly oriented to satisfy and protect the state-owned heavy industries in an effort to speed the process of industrialization. As discussed, the central government dictated that cities oversee industrial development, and that rural areas specialize in agriculture.[26] This led to the formation of a 'dualistic structure' between the cities and the countryside. The government also established what was known as the 'strongly cumulating system'[27] which was a special planning system that concentrated the limited resources of the nation on heavy industries and city economies.

The 'strongly cumulating system' was really implemented by three separate systems. The first was concerned with the 'unified purchase and sale of grain'.[28] This system enabled the government to control food transactions among peasants by closing the grain market.[29] The state unilaterally determined the price of the grain and made purchases accordingly. Then, grain sales were made to the city dwellers and the non-farming citizens living in the towns. Through this system, the government could help city industries accumulate capital with a mechanism known as the 'gap of price scissors', which essentially referred to the unequal exchange between industrial and agricultural products.

The second system was the so-called 'People's Commune System', which referred to the strongly unified and centralized control of resources. Natural resources including land, forest and other resources in rural areas were said to belong to the collective organization – the commune or the production brigade. The law prohibited selling the land, hence the peasants were not allowed to have their own property. The brigade arranged for the peasant's employment, food and other basic necessities.

The third system was the household registration system. This system was separated into two different management subsystems; one for the citizens who lived in the city, and the other for the peasants who lived in rural areas. Based on this arrangement, peasants were not allowed freely to move to cities and were physically restricted to remain within their designated local residential areas. These social economic policies forced the peasants, who made up the majority of the population of Guangdong, to remain in the countryside.

As the economy developed and the agricultural labour productivity level increased, it was certain that the agricultural sector would be altered and the industrial sector would emerge. The process of rural industrial development, subsequent adjustment and optimization followed the agricultural changes. The procedure led to a reduction in the number of agricultural projects and culminated in a mass migration of the agricultural labour force into the manufacturing, commerce and service sectors. Due to the government's severe household registration policy for peasants, the land could not freely be sold, nor could the peasants capitalize on their efforts. This led to the separation of surplus labour from the agricultural sector, but these workers were still only allowed to work in other areas of the same commune. For this reason, the CBEs eventually emerged in the late 1950s. Affected by the government policy of focusing on developing state-owned heavy industries from the 1950s to 1978, the CBEs did not have a good opportunity to develop; they were only able to survive in industries that served the agricultural sector, such as in the food processing and agricultural machinery repair industries.

Since China implemented the reform of the economic system in 1978, the rural area gradually abolished the strong unified and centralized system of the commune. The peasants gained greater enthusiasm to produce more agricultural products (the more the peasants produced, the more they stood to gain). Grain harvests became much larger in the years after the 1978 changes were put in place and the productivity of the agricultural labour force also increased. These factors greatly contributed to the development of non-agricultural industries in rural areas. During this period, the central government softened its restrictive policies on CBEs by gradually allowing them to develop their businesses; however, the household registration policy and the land-ownership restrictions were not immediately changed. Consequently, CBEs could only be set up and developed in the same community.

The dualistic economic development model created the distinctive industrialization route that rural China took. This is different from the dualistic economic phenomenon generally found in developing countries. The trend of peasants leaving the agricultural sector to engage in manufacturing, commerce and services is no different in China than in most other developing countries; what is different, however, is the unique phenomenon of some members of the rural labour force not migrating to the city, but instead staying and continuing to work in their local communities and performing new non-agricultural tasks. This activity was ultimately caused by the planned economic system and the people's commune system.

Reasons for TVE's dramatic development after the 1978 reform

There are four main factors that contributed to the dramatic development of TVEs in Guangdong since 1978.

1 Economic system resources were influenced by development

The initial restructuring of the social and economic systems caused a significant effect on economic growth and efficiency.[30] If the structure of an economy is unable to change and only allows for a single sector to survive and develop, then the success of the economy is dependant on the viability of the industries within that sector. On the other hand, if the original structure could be altered to remove the unequal distribution of resources between sectors, then the restructuring activities could create a more viable economic system. As the economic and social structures change, the system can continue to restructure.

Thus, the type of economic system in place can also be viewed as a kind of resource.

Since China began reforming its economic system, it has gradually changed from a planned economy to a socialist market economy; it has started to allow a variety of resources to be regulated by the market. The national government has changed the initial policy of allocating system resources; that is, it has altered the economic system of only having cities developing industries and the rural areas developing agriculture, to allowing every region to develop the industries they want to. It also cancelled the policy of discrimination against peasants from entering industries. Now, government policy allows rural collective organizations and peasants to enter industries that used to be monopolized by the SOEs. As mentioned, the government abolished the 'three limitations' for farmers that led to restructuring labour and other resources. The market is not only a type of economic system which causes the redistribution of resources and restructuring of the factors of production, but it also leads to changes in values and behaviours. From this, the TVEs acquire the system resources that are of critical importance for promoting their dramatic development.

2 Continual expansion of demand provides a vast market for TVEs

Supply shortages were commonplace under the old planned economic system in China. It was a structural problem that caused a shortage of investment funds – excess funds were available, but they were not available where they were needed. There were other problems associated with the structure of the economy that caused supplies of some items to be limited, and the government had to purchase other products that were made in excess.[31]

For example, the state purchased 118 varieties of agricultural products and 96 types of industrial products for daily use before 1980. There were 46 varieties of commodities for which citizens in the cities of Guangdong needed special government permission to purchase in 1981.[32] After the reform policy began, demand for goods and services continually expanded, in sharp contrast to the shortages in supply. This led to a huge sellers' market in China in the early 1980s, creating a great opportunity for all enterprises. TVEs seized the opportunity better than the SOEs did, which made their dramatic development possible.

Compared to the ability of SOEs to capture the market, TVEs had two competitive advantages: first, the management system of TVEs was flexible, while SOEs had a difficult time avoiding overcoming the lasting effects of the old planned economic system. SOEs were unable to increase their capacity to meet the consumer demand. This great gap between supply and demand became the market niche of TVEs; it also was an economic driver for their continued growth. Second, TVEs did not have significant financial problems since most of them were newcomers. SOEs, on the other hand, had existing deficits caused by their systems and policies that seriously impaired their operations; and their decreasing market shares exacerbated the problem. TVEs and joint ventures, on the contrary were able to attain more market share in an economy where there was a strong demand for consumer goods.

3 The changing of objectives of the central government and the township and village governments influenced TVE development

The Chinese Communist Party and the central government have gradually changed their core objective from focusing on class struggle to economic development since the reform of the economic system began. The state withdrew its pervasive control of the rural economy with the hope of obtaining steady tax revenues from agriculture, controlling costs in the rural areas, and gaining the political support of the peasants.[33] The government negotiated with the peasants to change the decision-making system from a centralized decision model to a decentralized one in order to lower the cost of transactions and to generate greater enthusiasm on the part of local governments.

Since the lifting of the 'household responsibility system' in the countryside, township and village governments (TVGs) were extricated from the heavy-handedness imposed by the central government of having to direct agricultural production, and began to develop local economies involved in all industries. Local government officials responsible for implementing these changes now have their performance measured not only by how effectively they carry out the policy dictated by the central government, but also based on how the local economy develops. This provides a strong incentive for local officials in that they could receive promotions if they do a better job fostering local economic growth. Because the time it takes to make changes in the agricultural sector is quite long and the term of office of the officials is limited, the main focus for local government in terms of economic reform is the development of rural industries. During the early period of economic reform, the distribution of the factors of production was still under the centrally-planned system. It was difficult for many organizations and individuals to obtain the limited resources, technology and capital they needed. For TVGs involved in the development of TVEs, there is no doubt that this situation helped to promote and increase the power of TVEs.

TVGs use their power to help each other. First, they provide financing support through the collective accumulation of capital and they guarantee bank loans for TVEs. Second, they allocate land to TVEs free or at low cost. In addition, TVGs also help TVEs to find basic resources, give workers greater social status, and share the political risk with managers. The rapid development of Guangdong's TVEs cannot be separated from the support provided by the TVGs. Jean C. Oi (1992) considers the critical reason for rural development in China as being the cooperation between the government and the enterprises based on collective ownership.[34] For example, in 1985 88 per cent of the amount of the fixed fund and the circulating fund bank loan for the township-owned industrial enterprises that was guaranteed by the local government in Shunde county was repaid.[35]

4 Low-cost entrance to the market and low-cost operation increased TVE profits

The cost of initial market entrance is a critical factor for the success of enterprises. It affects not only whether or not a venture is able to enter a particular market, but also the profit level earned by the firms. In the early 1980s, there were three factors that determined whether TVEs could enter the low-cost commerce and service sectors monopolized by SOEs.

First, TVEs have access to a low-cost labour force. As discussed, this labour supply came from the separation of workers from the agriculture sector, which was partially due to the increase in agricultural production resulting from greater efficiencies. The wages for workers in the traditional agricultural sector are comparably lower than those found in other sectors, which means that the opportunity cost is low for agricultural labourers to change jobs. This is especially true for workers who are unemployed and no longer have jobs in agriculture. This change in the agricultural sector is the critical factor that provided a low-cost labour supply for TVEs.

Second, TVEs can often use the collectively owned land and natural resources for free. The land and other resources in the rural areas of China are owned collectively. For the township and village and the brigade-set-up enterprises, there were no costs associated with utilizing these important resources. Furthermore, because some TVEs that were collectively owned actually emerged from existing CBEs, those that contracted with the TVEs did not need to make the initial investments

Table 7.8 Financial ratio comparison between TVEs and SOEs in Guangdong (all numerical entries in per cent)

Item		1990	1992	1994	1996	1998
Profit on year-end fixed assets	TVEs	17.9	20.1	18.8	14.4	15.3
	SOEs	3.8	6.8	5.6	4.2	2.2
Profit on total income	TVEs	7.0	7.6	6.6	4.8	5.2
	SOEs	2.7	4.8	4.3	1.6	2.4
Total income on year-end fixed assets	TVEs	256.4	263.7	283.2	299.0	272.1
	SOEs	141.3	142.9	130.1	124.1	90.3

Source: Calculations based on data from the *Guangdong Statistical Yearbook*, 1991–99 editions and the *Guangdong Rural Economic Statistical Yearbook*, 1993–99 editions.

that the CBEs needed to. Contracting with TVEs was a very common management system in the 1980s. In this system, overseers of the TVEs contracted with the management of the TVEs to set certain financial targets. If the managers exceeded the targets, they received a bonus. They could also change CBEs into governable assets. All of these things were due to greatly reducing the cost structure in TVEs and the cost per product.

Third, the existence of a sellers' market in the early 1980s decreased the initial expenditures associated with bringing products to market and offset the initial cost of innovations in technology. In other words, as long as TVEs could produce the products, they did not have to worry about the products not being sold. Since there was a very good relationship between the management and employees in TVEs, government costs related to the enterprises were decreased.[36] In the initial period of the reform of the economic system, the state laws, especially the market economic laws, were not perfect. There were not many economic regulations that governed the market and citizens' working knowledge of the laws was not very strong. They were not familiar with the laws and how to use them. At this time, since citizens' behaviour was based on tradition, the effect of the new laws on the operating costs under the different systems was not the same. Table 7.8 indicates that the efficiency of TVEs was better than that of SOEs from 1990 to 1998.

Revitalized management systems help spur rapid development

As TVEs are considered to be outside the planned economic system, their resources have had to be allocated and adjusted by market forces. TVEs directly face the competitive market, assume sole responsibility for their profit or loss, and have much tighter budget constraints. They are really profit-seeking enterprises.[37] In the TVE sector, there are no guaranteed positions for either managers or workers. If losses are continuous, TVEs must either go bankrupt or be taken over. In fact, TVEs broke out of the 'cage' created by the traditional planned economy, carved out a market-oriented road that was based on the demand of the market, and became pioneers in the socialist market economy.[38]

Although the market was easy to enter when TVEs first experienced rapid growth, strong market competition in recent years has made the average lifetime of the competitive advantage of TVEs very short. After experiencing market competition, the surviving TVEs have set up a series of management systems that are market-oriented and follow market principles. These TVE management systems are more effective for a market economy than those used by the SOEs.

Although SOEs have also been exposed to the reform process of the economic system since 1978, they are still affected by the old planned system. They are operated using non-market principles, especially in the area of human resources management practices. The People's Congress passed a bankruptcy law in 1986, but its implementation has never gone beyond the experimental stage.[39] An interesting comparison between peasant entrepreneurs and managers in SOEs is presented in Table 7.9.

Challenges and recommendations

Although Guangdong's TVEs have achieved great progress, they still face a number of challenges. First, TVEs are facing stronger competitive pressures than have existed in the past. As reforms spread throughout the economic system, SOEs are gradually adjusting to competing in the market and the initial advantage of the TVE system is comparably weakened. More and more joint ventures are entering the Chinese market and new enterprises are emerging. Competitive pressures will likely increase further with a greater number of foreign companies entering China and the removal of domestic protective measures resulting from WTO admittance.

Second, there are problems resulting from collective-owned TVEs having no clear ownership and no clear lines of responsibility within the enterprises, which is similar to the situation facing SOEs. The owners, that is the general members of the collective economic organization, do not have direct access to monitor the activities of the venture and managers of TVEs do not need to be responsible for the losses incurred by

Table 7.9 A comparison between peasant entrepreneurs and managers in SOEs

	Peasant entrepreneur	**Managers in SOEs**
Identity	Peasant living in rural area	City dweller
Status	Manager, owner-manager	State cadre
Motivation	Survival in the early days, business success	Moving up the hierarchy
Background	Town and village leader, craftsman, ex-serviceman, etc.	Engineer (38 per cent), Manager (35 per cent), Party official (24 per cent)
Education	Generally lower	Higher, 77 per cent with higher education
Business orientation	Market-oriented	Production or sales-oriented
Autonomy	High	Still limited
Risk-taking	Medium to high	Low
Initiative	High	Little
Management style	Paternalistic, by instinct	Bureaucratic, by rules
Organizational structure	Informal, family link	Formal and hierarchical
Decision-making	Quick	Slow
Entrepreneurship	Plays a role	Not exercised

Source: Fan, Chen and Kirby (1996).[40]

the enterprises. Furthermore, the local township and village government interferes with the management activities of collective-owned TVEs.

Third, the production system of TVEs is not well-planned because it has resulted in the creation of too many factories producing the same goods for a market that does not want all of them. This leads to the waste of resources and overcompetition. There is an 80 per cent production overlap of products between TVEs and other general industrial enterprises in China, while only 0.46 per cent of TVE products are related to the agricultural sector.[41] This means that TVEs mainly compete with other enterprises in the industrial sector but neglect to fully utilize the local agricultural resources and other natural resource advantages that may be available to them.

Finally, the size of the majority of TVEs is small. Based on the 1999 China Planning Committee, China Statistics Bureau, China Economic and Trade Committee and China Treasury document, *The Standard Size of Big, Medium-size and Small Business*, both annual sales income and total assets were less than 50 million yuan for small businesses. Therefore, 99.9 per cent of Guangdong's TVEs in that year would be categorized as small businesses. Because of the lesser scale of operations of these businesses, small TVEs have some disadvantages in areas such as technology, labour skills, education levels of staff, access to bank loans, government assistance and information.

In the near future, Guangdong's TVEs should have better opportunities for development. First of all, as the Chinese socialist market economic system gradually establishes itself, TVEs will benefit because they are market-oriented and follow market principles. Second, as a result of China's entry into the WTO there will be more chances for TVEs to do business internationally. This will increase the exporting activities and innovation of TVEs. Third, while the central government proceeds with its strategy for developing western China, Guangdong's TVEs will have more market opportunities, which will help develop their businesses.

Facing these challenges and opportunities, Guangdong's TVEs must keep doing business in a market-oriented fashion and stick to market principles if they want to avert failure. Following on the success of TVEs, it is necessary for China to allow other kinds of ownership and all scales of enterprises to exist in order more fully to develop the economy while China is still in the reform stage.

It is also necessary for the government to study the successful experiences of other countries, such as the United States, when assisting small businesses. US policy is to 'aid, counsel, assist and protect' small businesses.[42] For the collective-owned TVEs, the emerging issue is how more meaningfully to reform their ownership structure. It is first necessary to identify who the real owners of the TVEs are. This can be done in many ways, such as through 'joint stock cooperative' reform (i.e., the employer and employees in TVEs purchase the enterprises and become the shareholders), or by having the businesses rented, sold to or combined by a third party in the private sector. The objective of the reform should be to reinvigorate the collective TVEs and pay attention to who owns and controls them. For instance, if the private sector purchases the collective TVEs, it will change their ownership arrangements.

Conclusion

TVEs in Guangdong have grown dramatically since the 1978 reform of the economic system, but their development has not gone smoothly. They have undergone an evolution following a market orientation. The dramatic development of TVEs is a result of factors such as the reform of the economic system, new market-oriented policies, flexible management mechanisms, and the low costs associated with market entrance. TVEs represent the pioneers of the reformation from the planned economic system to the social market economic system in China.

The development of TVEs breaks the 'dualist social and economic structure' that separated the cities from the rural areas, and industry from agriculture. It establishes the modern economic model – allowing a TVE industrial sector to exist in rural areas. The development has undergone a unique transformation with Chinese features, in a way that is different from economic changes found in other developing countries. As many TVEs and groups of townships emerge in rural areas, a change from the traditional agricultural countryside to more modern townships, villages and 'urban areas' results. This in turn has the effect of gradually reducing the huge differences between the cities and rural areas.

TVEs are facing markets with more and stronger competition in the twenty-first century. As the reform of the economic system deepens, SOEs will gradually get used to the competition in the market. A greater number of joint ventures are entering the Chinese market and other enterprises are continually emerging. The low-cost market entrance that many TVEs first experienced does not seem to exist anymore, and the factors that have helped TVEs continually to develop will soon disappear. The collective-owned TVEs, as with the SOEs, have the additional problem of having no clearly defined owners; they need to reform their ownership structures to clearly identify who the real owners of the collective TVEs are. The majority of TVEs are small businesses that need the government to not only offer them equal opportunities, but also to carry out assistance policies. Facing these challenges and opportunities, Guangdong's TVEs can only keep doing business in a market-oriented fashion if they want to survive and prosper.

Notes

The statistics not referenced in this paper are from the Guangdong Township and Village Enterprises Administration, *Annual Statistical Information*, 1978–99 Guangdong Provincial Government, China.

1 Jiang Pan (1998) 'Issues on the System Reform and Open Door Policy', Development Research Centre of Guangdong Province Peoples' Government, Guangdong Provincial Economic Society, *Memorial Collected Works of Guangdong Reform and Open Door to the World over 20 Years*, pp. 240–9.

2 CDA (China Department of Agriculture) (1999), *50 Years of Development in Chinese Rural Economy*, Information Centre of the China Department of Agriculture.
3 Yifu Lin (1994) *The Miracle of China: Development Strategy and Economic Reform*, Shanghai Sanlian bookstore.
4 GDRESY (*Guangdong Rural Economic Statistics Yearbook*), 1993–2000 editions.
5 Jingchao Geng (1998) 'The Law Issues Research in Agricultural Management Systems', in Cunxue Wang (ed.), *The Law Issues Research of Rural Economy*, Law Press.
6 CDA (China Department of Agriculture) (2000).
7 Jiang Pan (1998), *op. cit.*
8 CDA (China Department of Agriculture) (2000).
9 *Ibid.*
10 Yongtao Jiang (1998) 'The Difficult and Bumpy Road but Brilliant 20 years: The Review and Prospect of Township and Village Enterprises since the Reform and Open Door to the World', *Chinese Township and Village Enterprises* vol. 10, pp. 4–7.
11 CDA (China Department of Agriculture) (2000).
12 *Ibid.*
13 Jiang Pan (1998), *op. cit.*
14 GDY (*Guangdong Yearbook*), 2000 edition, Guangdong People's Press.
15 GDTVEA (Guangdong Township and Village Enterprises Administration), *Annual Statistic Information* (2000).
16 Jiang Pan (1998), *op. cit.*
17 *Ibid.*
18 James Guanzhong Wen and Gene Hsin Zhang (1999) 'Communal Duality: Agricultural Subsidies from TVEs', *Contemporary Economic Policy*, vol. 17, pp. 79–86.
19 Jiang Pan (1998), *op. cit.*
20 GDRESY (*Guangdong Rural Economic Statistic Yearbook*), 1993, 1998, 2000 editions.
21 Jiang Pan (1998), *op. cit.*
22 GDRESY (*Guangdong Rural Economic Statistic Yearbook*), 1993, 1998 editions.
23 *Ibid.*, 2000 editions.
24 GDY (*Guangdong Yearbook*), *2000 edition*, Guangdong People's Press.
25 Jiang Pan (1998), *op. cit.*
26 Jirui Yang (1999) 'Township and Village Enterprises: Thinking of Supporting, Reform and Adjustment', *Rural Economic Research*, vol. 1, pp. 7–10.
27 Zhen Wang (1998) 'Summary of Theoretic Research in the Township and Village Enterprises' Development', *Chinese Countryside Survey*, vol. 6, pp. 32–7.
28 *Ibid.*
29 Terry Sicular (1998) 'Agricultural Planning and Pricing in the Post-Mao Period', *China Quarterly*, pp. 116, 671–705.
30 Lei Shi (1999) 'The Increasing Factors of Township and Village Enterprises in the Past 20 Years', *Social Science*, vol. 2, pp. 18–19.
31 *Ibid.*
32 Lingguang Liang (1998) 'Issues on the System Reform and Open Door Policy', Development Research Center of Guangdong Province Peoples' Government,

Guangdong Provincial Economic Society, *Memorial Collected Works of Guandong Reform and Open Door to the World over 20 Years*, pp. 4–8.

33 Binlong Jiao and Huafeng Qi (1999) 'Nation and Ownership: The Growth Research of Township and Village Enterprises Organization', *Productivity Research*, vol. 4, pp. 43–5, 59.

34 Jean C. Oi (1992) 'Fiscal Reform and the Economic Foundations of Local State Corporatism in China', *World Politics*, vol. 45, no. 1 (Oct), pp. 99–126.

35 Erlin Zhou and Yulin Zhang (1991) *Research on the Coordinating Development between Cities and Rural Areas*, Jiangsu People's Press.

36 Martin L. Weitzman and Chenggang Xu (1994) 'Chinese Township-Village Enterprises as Vaguely Defined Cooperatives', *Journal of Comparative Economics*, 18 April.

37 Bert Willian and Ning Zhu (1989) 'Market Effects and Industrial Structure', in Q. Lin, and B. Willian (eds), *Chinese Rural Industry-Structure, Development and Policy*, Economic Science Press.

38 Jiang Pan (1998), *op. cit.*

39 C. Goodhart and C. Xu (1996) 'The Rise of China as an Economic Power', *National Institute Economic Review*, (February) pp. 56–82.

40 Y. Fan, N. Chen and D. A. Kirby (1996) 'Global Perspectives: Chinese Peasant Entrepreneurs: An Examination of Township and Village Enterprises in Rural China', *Journal of Small Business Management*.

41 Minghua Yang (1999) 'Analyzing the Problems in Township and Village Enterprises Development', *Southeast China University Learned Journal*, pp. 30–4.

42 Sandra M. Anglund (2000) *Small Business Policy and the American Creed*, Praeger Publishers.

8

The Current Status and Future Strategy of Guangdong's Human Resource Development

Minsheng Chen

Introduction

Over the past 20 years, China's economic reform movement has made a great deal of progress and been widely praised around the world. Human resource development (HRD) has marked the most significant changes since the founding of the People's Republic of China in 1949. The Chinese have realized that human resources are a main contributing factor in the creation of material wealth, exploitation of natural resources, and enhancement of social reforms. Human resource development has promoted the development of society and economy. Benefits include growth of the macro-economy, enhancement of education and improvement of the environment and social moral standards. As investment in HRD has grown, the market has been enriched and the standard of living has improved.

Since the beginning of economic reform, China's education system has made significant improvements. While primary education has gradually improved, higher education has also shown progress. By August 1998, China had produced 430,000 graduates with master's degrees and 43,000 with PhD degrees. More than 200,000 graduate students will graduate and enter society in the coming years. The ratio of undergraduate to graduate students is approximately 11:1. These achievements have greatly changed the hierarchy of Chinese higher education and formed a more appropriate structure in which three levels of education, namely professional, undergraduate and graduate, complement each other. Many graduates have joined the forefront of teaching and research, and are devoting themselves to further promoting economic development.[1,2]

In the last 20 years, another important reform has attempted to change the planned economic system into a socialist market system.

This reform has not only liberated productive forces, but also greatly changed people's perceptions. Due to the introduction of a market competition mechanism, there has been strong consensus that human resources need to be further developed. Competition has also resulted in increased efficiency in the utilization of human resources. However, in comparison with developed countries, the quality of China's human resources still has much room for improvement, as does Guangdong's. The following discussion, though based on China as a whole, also applies to Guangdong.[1,3]

Current status of human resource development

The quality of China's human resources needs improvement

Currently, there is serious shortage of high-tech, modern and international management professionals. China has a large pool of human resources, but the quality is considerably lower than that found in more developed nations. First, the illiteracy or semi-literacy rates are still relatively high. 1997 statistics indicate that 12.1 per cent of adults over the age of 15 are illiterate. Second, the average education level of the citizen is still very low. Only 2.53 per cent of the Chinese population were enrolled in universities and 9.95 per cent in high school. The average education level of the national population was only 5.42 years.[1,3]

Statistics from the Personnel Ministry of China show that due to the disruption in the education system caused by the Cultural Revolution, 41.3 per cent of professionals in advanced technology areas are over 55 years old. Furthermore, many professionals have reached retirement age. China will be facing a shortage of replacements, and this will seriously affect scientific and technological development.[4]

Aside from having a shortage of professionals in advanced technology, China is in great need of modern business management professionals. Research conducted by The International Institute for Management Development, Lausanne, Switzerland (IMD), in 1997 indicated that the comprehensive quality of innovation in Chinese enterprises was ranked 41st, the availability of competent senior managers in the labour market 46th (in last place), and international management experience 40th. The study also showed that the time needed for new products to enter the market ranked 46th, the competitiveness of product price over quality ratio was 44th and the flow of personnel and their adaptability to competitive challenge 46th. Additionally, the ability of the educational system to meet the needs of a competitive economy was ranked 40th and the economic literacy rate 41st.[4,5]

Due to the influence of traditional thinking, some Chinese enterprise management professionals lack knowledge of modern management practices and how to successfully formulate international strategies, which seriously obstructs the progress of enterprise development. China's World Trade Organization (WTO) membership will force Chinese enterprises to develop more global strategies. The shortage of international management professionals has been and will continue to be a bottleneck for China's competing in the international arena.

The underdeveloped education system affects human resource quality

National development and modernization efforts depend on high-quality human resources, and qualified human resources in turn result from an educational system that meets the needs of the market economy. An underdeveloped education system inevitably affects the quality of human resources.

Human capital is undercapitalized

According to the United Nations Educational, Scientific and Cultural Organization (UNESCO), the average educational expenditures of the world were 5.7 per cent of the gross domestic product (GDP). The figure was 6.1 per cent in developed countries and 4.1 per cent in developing countries. China is one of the developing countries. Its educational foundation is quite fragile and expenditures in education are very limited; the government has invested only a limited amount on education and educational infrastructure. Since the 1980s, Chinese educational expenditures have been under 3 per cent of GDP, far below the world average (see Figure 8.1).[6,7] The average per person educational expenditure is

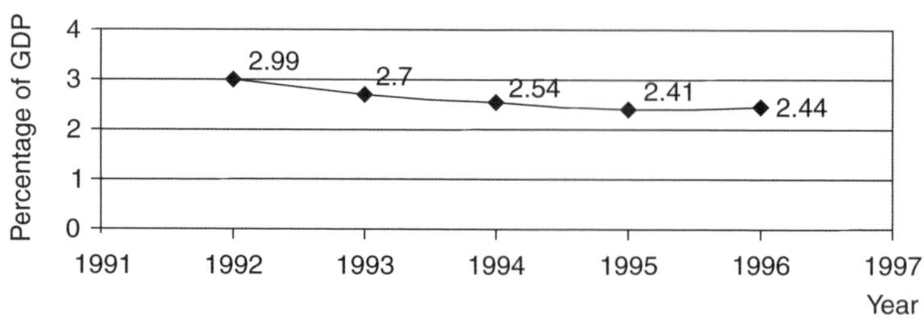

Figure 8.1 China's educational expenditures[6,7]
Sources: Data compiled from Wang. 'The key to Vigorously Develop a Country's Technology and Education' Popular Tribure (1999) and Zhao, 'To Increase Technology Investment is Government's Realistic Alternative', The Management of Science and Technology, January 2000.

only 0.6 per cent of that of the United States and Japan, and 66 per cent of that in India. According to the Education Reform and Development Project of China promulgated in 1993, educational expenditures would reach 4 per cent of GPD in the year 2000. Inadequate investment in education has become an important factor that limits the advancement of human resource quality.

The elementary and secondary education system is still exam-oriented

In elementary and secondary schools, teaching is still based on exams with too much homework. Teaching materials are dull and inflexible, and the teaching materials and teaching programmes, which are almost uniform nationwide, are not consistent with the development of a knowledge-based economy. For instance, the maths textbooks still use teaching concepts from the early twentieth century. Language and literature teaching methods are full of stereotypical writing with analysis of characters, words and sentences. Writing training is done by rote, with a focus on exams. Teaching methods are uniform and standardized and seriously limit the development of students' personalities and abilities to think creatively.

With regard to the exam-driven teaching model, Professor Samuel C.C. Ting, a winner of the Nobel Prize in physics, pointed out that getting the highest score in exams was not the most important thing when he stated, 'The well-known scientists are usually not the number one students in school, including myself.' Professor Steven Chu at Stanford University also pointed out that the Chinese educational system over-emphasized a knowledge of books and exams, but failed to motivate students' innovative thinking. 'The majority of Chinese students are smart and good at basic knowledge, mathematic inference and written exams. However, they may lack enough practical, imaginary and creative abilities,' he said. These comments clearly indicate the defects in traditional Chinese educational methods.[8,9]

Higher education training is not fully consistent with the establishment of a market economy

Reform of the education model and curriculum is a key to accelerating the development of human capital. In the past, due to the influence of former Soviet educational theories, higher education became a place that introduced knowledge and emphasized memorization, imitation and repetition of knowledge. The result was very narrow knowledge and rigid educational methods, which affected promotion of human resource quality and limited creativity. Narrowly defined knowledge not only causes students to lack a wide enough perspective, but also affects job alternatives after graduation.

Additionally, the course structure in higher education does not provide students with enough practical experience. Some courses deviate from the needs of the market, and students often lack sufficient opportunities to practice the skills they are developing. In developed countries, on the contrary, schools put a great deal of stress on practical teaching to train competent professionals. Schools frequently offer various practical opportunities for students, such as field trips and factory tours off campus, laboratory facilities, internships with companies, and so on. Students are required to finish a certain number of relevant practice assignments. Through these activities it may be possible for students to, on the one hand, accumulate practical experience, and on the other to make money to support their study and improve their lives.[9,10]

Career education and training need to be improved

In the last 20 years, China's career education and training programmes have been developing. However, due to weak national policies and insufficient understanding of the economic essence of career education and training, the development of these disciplines has been seriously limited. In most enterprises, especially state-owned organizations, there are no effective strategies for human resource development. The skills of the workforce, especially of management, cannot keep up with the needs of international competition and therefore organizations lack the ability to compete effectively.

Misperceptions lead to a lack of investment

Based on traditional thinking, some decision-makers tend to neglect 'non-productive investments', that is investments in human resources. They believe that investing adequate funds to set up more large-sized enterprises can rapidly speed up new and high-tech industries. Some even think that it is easy to develop high-tech industries by simply introducing more new products and establishing more factories. Noble Prize-winning economist Theodore Schultz, speaking about the economy of developing countries stated:

> It seems to be the public impression that the primary factor in poor countries is lack of enough capital, and increasing capital is key to economic blast-off. They usually do not invest those capitals from foreign sources in human resources, but utilize them in construction and equipment, even in stocks. The result is that the abilities of

human beings cannot progress alongside material capitals, and become a limiting factor of economic development.[11]

The future strategy of human resource development

The level of economic development restricts the improvement of human resources, and as a developing country, China has not had enough capital to invest in this area. Therefore, it is difficult to form a positive cycle between economic and human resource development. China is in an inferior position in international competition for human resources, especially for advanced professionals. Since the implementation of the reform and open-door policy, China has sent about 20,000 students to study abroad each year. The total number of overseas Chinese students is currently around 400,000, but only 33 per cent of this amount will be returnees. This is far from the two-to-one ratio which is thought to be the 'best proportion' by international standards. The ideal ratio would have two-thirds of students return to work in their country and the remaining one-third stay abroad for continued study and to help communicate information during the early stages of economic development in their home countries. Well-known universities in China, such as Tsinghua University and Beijing University, have many high-tech graduates going to the United States; in the past 20 years, one-third of Beijing University's physics graduates have gone abroad, and currently there are more than 500 in the United States.[12]

Since the early 1990s, Western countries, especially the United States, have been soliciting internationally a large number of talented high-tech professionals. As a result, developing countries are facing an increasingly serious situation in terms of a shortage of professionals in advanced technology. As the United States Department of Labour has pointed out, one million new positions in the United States will require skills in computer software development, and in the period 2000–5 the United States will need 100,000 computer professionals. Universities of the United States can only meet about one-third of this demand, so the United States has paid greater attention to educating more professionals. At the same time, it is also adopting strategies to attract the needed human resources, especially high-tech professionals from around the world. While the international exchange of human resources is becoming more popular, it has also created an increasingly serious situation for China regarding its own needs for technology professionals to meet the demands of its own economic development.[12] The brain-drain of human capital will continue to plague China unless measures are taken to remedy the situation.

Human resource development has become one of most important strategies in China's reform. As a result of China's ascension into the World Trade Organization, foreign capital will increase the pillaging of China's professionals and further halt the advancement of human resource development. To meet international requirements, it is imperative that a set of human resource policies that can motivate enterprises, families and individuals be established. The following are some measures designed to accomplish this.

Increasing human resource investment

Human resources require initial investments that are accumulated and eventually expanded. It is important for nations, organizations and individuals to be able to continue to develop qualified human resource talent. The modern theory of human resource management advocates that human beings are one of the most important forms of capital, having the ability to learn and the potential to make significant contributions; whereas other forms of capital are only 'goods' that can be bought and sold – once they are purchased, they become assets of inertia and ceaseless devaluation. Theodore Schultz believed that human capital was a main power and definitive factor in modern economic development. He said that the benefit of investing in this capital was far more than that in others. Obviously, development of qualified human resources is a necessary measure for China to increase overall national strength and achieve modernization.

Supporting improvements in education is an important form of human capital investment. Due to its current limitations in this area, China must first show that it values human capital by promoting investment in it as a rational proportion of its GDP. It is thought that one of the main contributions to the rapid recovery of the Japanese economy after the Second World War was the Japanese government's focus on education at all times. Even during the worst period of the 1950s, Japan still considered education a priority.

However, educational investment should not only rely on the government but also on businesses and individuals. Educational investment should gradually achieve a condition such that government expenditures will focus on primary education, while private and individual investment will focus on higher education. Likewise, enterprises would mainly invest in vocational and professional training, and ensure education consistent with the needs of a market economy. Human resource development, technological research and economic development, in this way, will become integrated.

In recent years, the enthusiasm for running private schools and investing in education has been growing. All levels of schools, especially higher educational institutions, are increasing the proportion of commoners enrolled in their programmes. In China, a commoner in the education system refers to a student whose education is not funded by the government. It is estimated that if the number of commoners in China's higher education institutions increases from two million per year to four million, it will result in an investment of about $12 billion. However, the majority of schools have an adequate supply of instructors to support increasing the number of students. For example, in Chinese universities the ratio of undergraduate students to teachers is 7:1, far lower than the 20:1 to 30:1 ratios of the United States, Japan and Korea.[13]

Having better-educated and more qualified commoners may not only foster a larger variety of talents, it may also help to solve the insufficiency of education expenditures. In many countries, paying for school has become a trend. In Japan, only 15.5 per cent of universities belong to the national or local governments, while in the United States about 50 per cent of the 4,000 universities are private. With the increasing number of commoners, governments and schools must set up corresponding support systems. For example, they must set up a structure to decide how much tuition is appropriate and who can get free or partly free education. At the same time, banks should be able to supply qualified students with loans guaranteed by the government.[13]

Now that education has come to be regarded as an industry, the government, enterprises and individuals can run it. Private secondary education also has great potential. At present, there are about 20,000 secondary schools owned by businesses, with 900,000 students. In recent years, as business profits have decreased, the quality of some schools has, to a certain extent, fallen as well. If the government can provide these schools with relevant support and promote their continual development, it may greatly decrease the pressure for government to invest in new educational facilities.[13]

Meeting the requirements of a knowledge-based economy

Educational reform needs to change traditional concepts to establish an innovative educational system

Studies show that the factors that have great influence on human creativity include intelligence, motivation and personality. Creative skills are certainly a significant influence, but having a passion is even more important. As Einstein pointed out, 'it is a serious mistake to think that the delight of observation and exploration can be inspired by enforcement and responsibility.'[14]

To establish innovative educational concepts, schools have to enlighten and encourage students' creativity, protect their curiosity, and train their creative thinking. Schools have to simultaneously pay attention to the humanities and natural science education. The California Institute of Technology in the United States, which has created several Nobel Prize winners, believes that natural science can only offer knowledge, but not intelligence, and an institute of technology cannot neglect education in the humanities. Harvard University demands that all students select eight credits hours of courses from the five major curriculums of history, philosophy, literature, social analysis and ethnics. At the University of Tsukuba, Japan, humanity courses have occupied more than 30 per cent of credit hours in basic subjects.

The advancement of culture diathesis and human spirit allows citizens to become modernists with vivid personalities aggressive philosophies and earnest moralities, enabling them to incorporate mission and social duty with a broad view of culture. Only if personality is given free rein can schools foster their students' creativity. While necessary basic courses will still be required, schools should form a system for students to have more course selection and development by themselves, allowing for individual interests, thinking abilities, spirit, imagination and innovative consciousness to develop. In addition:

Universities should give students more flexibility by increasing the number of elective courses while decreasing the number of required courses. Students should have the freedom to choose their courses, change their specialties, and even have classes outside of university. Upon passing required exams, schools should give students credit hours. Universities should allow students to go to work for a period of time, and then come back to continue their education. A time limit for completing a degree could be raised from three to five years or longer. As long as the students have earned enough credits and fulfilled all requirements they should be permitted to graduate.

Establishment of specialty universities will further broaden the extent of specialties, extend the boundaries of knowledge, emphasize the wholeness of knowledge, and train students to use comprehensive knowledge to creatively solve problems. In terms of the curriculum, universities have been setting up more courses that help improve students' social abilities tolerance and skills of expression and organization. Subjects such as public relations, organizational behaviour, information technology and foreign languages all raise students' international adaptive capacities and competitiveness.

In order to improve the role of educational institutions, higher education must further optimize its structure. Based on the basic disposal of educational resources driven by market mechanisms, higher education must reform its structure to harmonize relations between the system of education and society, and thus better match long-term human resource training with the needs of the market.

Higher education institutions should foster an open system. In order to gain more understanding and support from society, higher education should be open to all members of the populace and serve as a base for producing and communicating knowledge. In favour of exchanging, developing and fostering creative human resources, different departments, specialties and subjects should compete and at the same time cooperate with each other. Institutions of higher learning should provide resources for enrolling more foreign students, so that an understanding of different cultures and customs can help to improve students' international abilities.

If diathetic and creative education is the goal of future educational models, high efficiency and definitive duties, as well as the establishment of rights and interests of modern enterprises, should be the objectives for reforming the managerial system of higher education institutions. To simplify the administrative structure, some related departments may be merged, unnecessary departments closed, and excessive administrative staff moved to the forefront of teaching, research and service. To carry out employee contract policies, all positions should be assigned by contracts and competition. Administrative personnel should receive a higher or lower position based on their individual abilities and the particular needs of their jobs. To establish a system of job responsibility directly linked with benefits, bonuses should be paid according to performance appraisals. To socialize the support system of schools, the operational mechanism must be linked with the needs of the economy so that an environment is created for the training of creative teachers and administrative staff.

Perfecting the training system in favour of improving workforce quality. In a modern society, basic education is a major approach to human resource development. However, basic education only provides the foundation of skills and qualifications; professional skills come from continuous career education and training. In the face of increasingly severe competition, many American companies regard training of employees as a key to creating and maintaining the competitive advantage of their firms. In the early 1950s in the United States, only 20 per cent of the workforce were professionals including teachers, medical doctors and other management professionals. About 20 per cent were technical workers including engineers and technicians. The other 60 per cent were unskilled workers, mainly physical workers. In 1997, the percentage of professional workers remained the same, while that of technical workers increased from 20 per cent to 60 per cent, and of physical workers decreased from 60 per cent to 20 per cent.[15]

In the United States, the improvement of the quality of employees has become a very important factor in enabling businesses to maintain their competitive advantage in today's global market. Many corporations view the skill level of their workforce as the top priority for strategic implementation and they worry that advancing technology is de-skilling 75 per cent of the population. Their suggestion is continual training for employees.

Chuck Nielson, Vice-President of Human Resources at Texas Instruments, has noted, 'our challenge is creating an environment in which people love to learn'. The company mandates a minimum of 40 hours of training per year. Peter Drucker, the well-known management author, predicts that the fastest growing industry in the United States will be the continuing education and training of adults because things are changing so fast in every field and occupation. Furthermore, Stanford Professor Jeffrey Pfeffer cites training as a major source of sustained advantage.[16,17]

In 1991, it was estimated that United States companies spent more than US$633 billion on employee training, an increase of 59.26 per cent from US$397 billion in 1983. The total training cost was 3.2 per cent of total employee salaries. Some companies spent even more. For instance, Xerox spends about 2.5 per cent of its revenue annually on training, which equals about US$2,500 per employee per year. In addition, Hewlett-Packard spends 5 per cent of its revenue annually on job training for employees. Organizations offer a variety of training programmes to meet their needs, and training content deals with every sector of the workflow. In the early 1990s, a remarkable strategy of enterprises in the United States was universal training of employees in computer usage, which greatly increased efficiency, labour productivity and competitiveness of organizations.[18,19]

Training programmes could be carried out by an in-house training staff or by outside consulting firms. In the past decade, one important trend has been that an increasing number of leading companies have created in-house universities. By centralizing training under one umbrella, companies can ensure that their employees have the skills to give them a competitive edge and state-of-the-art knowledge about the firm's products and services. They view corporate universities as profit centres rather than cost centres.

In the process of enterprise reformation, managers play a very important role. First, they are the organizers and the pioneers of reformation. For the development of enterprises, they must be responsible for a series of tasks including use of new technology, improvement of management mechanisms, and increasing the skill level of employees. Second, managers are also the objects of reformation and adjustment. Their knowledge and skills become easily outdated in the acutely changing competitive environment. In the last 20 years, managers have always been the main objects of training in American companies. According to data from the United States Department of Education, the participation rate in training of management personnel during the 1990s was 52.2 per cent, 2.5 times higher than the average participation rate in the past.[17,18,19]

Training or retraining is an important approach to human resource development

A key to perfecting the training system is the reconstruction of knowledge at various levels of the workforce. This includes training in job skills that meet job requirements and improving the integrative qualities and abilities of enterprises, especially state-owned enterprises, which strengthen the firms' capacities for globalization.

At present, China is in a key stage of economic reform. National and local governments must put limited financial investments into many important projects. It is unrealistic to expect a large amount of capital to be invested in various training programmes. However, the importance of training cannot be downplayed, otherwise enterprises will experience a lack of competitive advantage. Organizations must reasonably increase their training budgets and make the training and retraining of employees a development strategy. At the same time, organizations must have corresponding measures to ensure that their workforce is motivated and able to take on future challenges.

Enacting administrative support to normalize human resource development

Government human resource departments must enact administrative support to normalize human resource development that is currently still very incomplete. The government should support human resource associations by encouraging the establishment of various management or consultant firms for human resources. The government may appoint relevant organizations to establish a uniform standard to encourage competition and flow of human resources, and it should also require those businesses that have reached a certain size to set up human resource management departments. The performance of human resource development should become one of the evaluating criteria for enterprises or organizations.

Including human resource management in strategic management

Human resource management should be a process of strategic implementation and an indivisible part of an organization's management strategy. Human resource skill development should become a coveted ability of top managers, and training and retraining should be considered a part of an organization's culture. Organizations must have corresponding measures to provide incentives for training to inspire employees to have a positive attitude towards it. In the United States, it is estimated that employees who receive training are not only more valuable to their firms, but also earn 30 per cent more than those who have not received training.[17]

Improving the labour market, reorganizing and consolidating human resources

Studies show that only if the labour market becomes the basic form of human resource arrangement will the structure of human resources be optimized. In this way, human resources are optimally combined with productive materials. Society is thus effectively retrenching labour consumption and reaching a result that fully and reasonably utilizes human resources and other resources. Establishing and perfecting the labour market is a basic condition for increasing the utilization level of human resources. The system of a human resource market should include:

1 *A human resource development policy.* Human resource development should be based on market rules and principles of maximizing investment returns. The establishment of development policies should reflect both the social and the economic benefits of human capital.
2 *A human resource circulation policy.* In a market economy, the key to socialization and marketability of human resources is definitely the proprietary right of a privatized workforce and observation of labour

behaviour. In other words, the proprietary right of the workforce is the private possession of labour. The circulation of the workforce is a form in which workers seek to maximize their investment returns, and therefore human resource circulation policies should be based on protecting such investment behaviour so that top results can be achieved through the marketplace.

3 *A human resource employment policy*. The value of human resources is that they can be translated into capital through labour. In the process of human resource development, investment of human capital forms the value of human capital. Generally, there is a direct relation between the investment in human resources and the value that it forms. Therefore, employment policies should be based on the magnitude of the human resource value and its transferable capital. Meanwhile, organizations should have the right to employ and fire their staff, and may optimize employment structures as a way to maximize profits. The risk of unemployment and competition will greatly motivate and stimulate employees to progress by themselves. Obviously, the establishment of policies of a human resource market is a comprehensive process; unemployment insurance and social welfare should also be included.

Establishing a reasonable mechanism for human resource investment and return

In terms of the condition of the market economy, investment is an economic behaviour that can bring returns to investors through economic benefits. Economists from developed countries have illustrated that human resource investment has a higher rate of payback. Statistics also show that human resource investments cost more than material investments. Especially when simultaneous investment takes place in both, human resource investment will be the essential guarantee for returns of material investment. Therefore, in order to motivate investors, the government and enterprises must establish a set of reasonable policies about human resource investment and return. As with material investment, it is reasonable for investors, either an individual or a group, to ask for returns from their investment in human resources. Investors' benefits have to be legally governed and protected.[20,21]

In order to motivate the interest of investors, contracts must be used to reflect the relationship between employing units and employees; the contract contents should be aptly based on the capital intensity and service length. Because the individual is like an investor, when dealing with the relation between employing units and employees, employing units must admit to the capital characteristics of human resources and make human capital comply with surplus distribution of enterprises together with material capital. While learning or renewing knowledge and technology, employees must pay direct or indirect costs, such as in the investment of materials. Since investment of materials capital can produce capital benefits based on the principle of capital equality, investment of human capital should also attend the distribution of surplus:[22]

> On the market economy condition, labourers select their development form according to the principle of maximized benefits. If the opportunity provided by society is not able to motivate workers to learn knowledge, skills or technology, or workers are able to get more benefit without advancing themselves, indeed they will give up on the investment of learning. Therefore, in terms of the need to define the proprietary property of labour in the market economy, the government and enterprises must set up a series of policies concerning the labour proprietary of socialism to strengthen the motivation system for increasing technology and skill. It is a fundamental requirement to set up a series of pay systems that can approximately reflect the changing trend toward the value of human resources.[23,24]

Establishing a corresponding human resource service system

Human resource development needs to have a corresponding social service system, which includes labour agency services, personnel appraisal, file management, training and intellectual development. As emerging entities that serve human resource development, labour agencies are a breakthrough in reforming the traditional model of personnel management. They are also a key to improving human resource circulation in the labour market. Research shows it is very significant to set up human resource intermediaries to allow the market of human resources to operate efficiently.[25] Functions of human resource intermediaries include:

1. Providing human resource information about the supply and demand of the workforce.
2. Coordinating relationships between organizations, including universities and enterprises.
3. Providing business diagnosis and consulting services for enterprises.
4. Providing qualification evaluations for institutes of human resource development.

Another important significance of intermediary agencies is to help separate the government from many administrative tasks and enable it to focus on guiding human resource development and imposing macro control. Departments related to human resource development should analyse and predict supply and demand, and formulate future development plans based on developmental goals. In this way, the government will be able to further reduce wasteful use of its own human resources.

Summary

The issues associated with developing human resources and their quality cannot be ignored in China. If they do not receive adequate attention, they will become a new bottleneck of China's economic development. First of all, with increasing international competition, China, as a developing country, is not only understaffed in terms of professionals knowledgeable in advanced technology and management practices, but it also has a shortage of human resources in general. China's businesses, and state-owned enterprises in particular, lack creativity and international competitiveness. Secondly, an underdeveloped education system makes it difficult to foster high-quality human resources that meet the demands of the market. The conflict between the developed society and the underdeveloped educational system has seriously limited China's continuing development of society, the economy and international competitiveness.

The status of China's human resources represents an insufficiency in human resource development. Improving the quality of the labour force is a key to sustaining China's development. The strategy of human resource development should become one of the most important parts of China's reform. Firstly, education investment is a primary form of investment in human capital. Due to limited national resources, investment in education should be the primary focus and become a rational proportion of GDP. Secondly, China has thoroughly to reform the educational system in order to foster innovative human resources to meet the requirements of a knowledge-based economy. Thirdly, because of the fast pace of technological advancement, the quality of human resources that a market economy requires becomes increasingly high. Human beings have already entered into the new era of lifelong study. Similarly, training and retraining have become an approach to human resource development. Perfecting the training system and raising workforce quality are important guarantees in creating competitive advantage. Fourthly, only if the workforce market becomes the basic form of human resource distribution will the structure of human resources be optimized and their development be associated with the improvement of production. Lastly, a relevant human resource service system is an important component in the establishment of a positive cycle of human resource development.

Notes

1 Wenda Huo (1998) 'The Exploration of Human Resource Development', *Journal of Jianhan University*, May.

2 Jingwen Li and Guochu, Zhang (1997) 'Modern Human Resource Economy: Analysis of Chinese Entrepreneurs', *Journal of Enterprise Management Theory-Mode-Application*, Social Science Publishing House, Beijing, pp. 12–20.

3 Wenwu Wu, (1996) *Systems Theory of Human Resource Development in China*, China Construction Industry Publishing House, Beijing, pp. 56–62.

4 Yanyun Zhao and Xiaoliang Ding (1998) *International Evaluations of the Current Condition in Human Resource Development*, Unpublished Working Paper (in Chinese), Guangdong, China.

5 Huixiang Chen (1998) *China Enterprise Criticism*, Beijing University Publishing House, Beijing.

6 Xiancai Wang (1999) 'The Key to Vigorously Develop a Country's Technology and Education', *Popular Tribune*, June.

7 Lanxiang Zhao (2000) 'To Increase Technology Investment is Government's Realistic Alternative', *The Management of Science and Technology*, January.

8 Keyong Cai (1999) 'To Change the Traditional Education System and foster Education', *Creative Professionals*, 2 February.

9 Liansheng Frang (1999) 'Education Should be Focused on Students' Creativeness', *Popular Tribune*, September.

10 Shu Hua Dou (1999) 'To Strengthen National Power, the Foundation is to Improve People's Quality', *The Strategy of Chinese Social Development*, March.

11 Theodore W. Schultz (1992) *Human Resource Investment*, Beijing Economic University Publishing House, Beijing, pp. 45–52.

12 Zhenguo Zhu (1992) 'New China Graduate Degree Education and Development', *Guang Ming Daily*, 14 October.

13 Shijie Yi (1999) 'Education Will Become the Largest Industry', *People Forum*, 29 October.

14 Zhide Hu (1999) 'Meet the Challenge of Knowledge–based Economy to Promote Creative Professionals', *Journal of Development*, April (in Chinese).

15 Zhuang Yang (1999) 'Developing a Strategy of Human Resources in the United States and Japan, and the Inspiration to China', *Economy Social System Comparison*, January, pp. 32–41.

16 Peter F. Drucker (1987) *The Frontiers of Management: Where Tomorrow's Decisions are Being Shaped Today*, William Heinemann, London, pp. 48–56.

17 H. J. Bernardin and J.E.A. Russell (1998) *Human Resource Management: An Experimential Approach*, 2nd edn, Irwin McGraw-Hill, Boston, pp. 186–96.

18 P. Galagan and K. Wulf (1996) 'Signs of the Times', *Training and Development*, February, pp. 32–6.

19 Srota Consulting Corporation (1989) *Report to respondents: Survey of Views Toward Corporate Education and Training Practice*, 1 Manhattan Road, New York, NY 10577.

20 C. M. Cummings (1994) 'Incentives that Really do Motivate', *Compensation and Benefits Review*, May–June, pp. 38–40.

21 R. L. Heinemann (1995) 'Survey of Merit Pay System', *Compensation and Benefits Review*, May–June, pp. 41–4.

22 A. Kahn (1993) 'Why Incentive Plans Cannot Work', *Harvard Business Review*, September–October, pp. 54–63.

23 J. A. Byrne (1996) 'How high can CEO Pay Go?', *Business Week*, 22 April.

24 Kaiguo Wang and Taochang Zong (1999) 'About the Origin and Development of Properties and Characteristics of Human Resource', *Journal of Chinese Social Science*, June.

25 Yue Wang (1999) 'Development and Analysis of Human Resources in the Conversion Period of Guangdong', *Journal of Teachers University of South China*, February.

9
Improving HRM Practices in Guangdong's SOEs

Yongling Zhu

Introduction

In 1998, less than two months after Shen, general manager of Xinyue M&E Engineering Co. Ltd – a subsidiary of Xinyue Company Ltd – left his job, Liu, deputy general manager of the company submitted his resignation to the board of directors. The reason they gave for relinquishing their positions was that the interpersonal relationships they had to deal with were too complex. As a matter of fact, complex interpersonal relationships were not the only problem related to human resource management (HRM) that the Xinyue Company (Xinyue) was facing.

Xinyue was established in 1980 with the approval of the State Council of China and registered in Hong Kong. In 1996 it was approved by the Chinese authorities to reorganize and become a financing vehicle for the Guangdong Provincial Communications Holding Group (originally Guangdong Provincial Communications Department) in Hong Kong. The leading shareholding companies are the backbone enterprises of the communications system. Their main fields of business are to raise foreign capital for investment purposes; to develop, construct and operate expressways in Guangdong Province along with their mechanical, electrical, service and safety facilities; to act as purchasing agent for machinery, equipment, materials and other goods that the Guangdong provincial communications system needs to import; and to make use of the advantageous conditions of Hong Kong as an international financial and information centre to channel Western management practices to Guangdong Province. The organizational chart of the company shown in Figures 9.1 and 9.2 illustrates its structure.

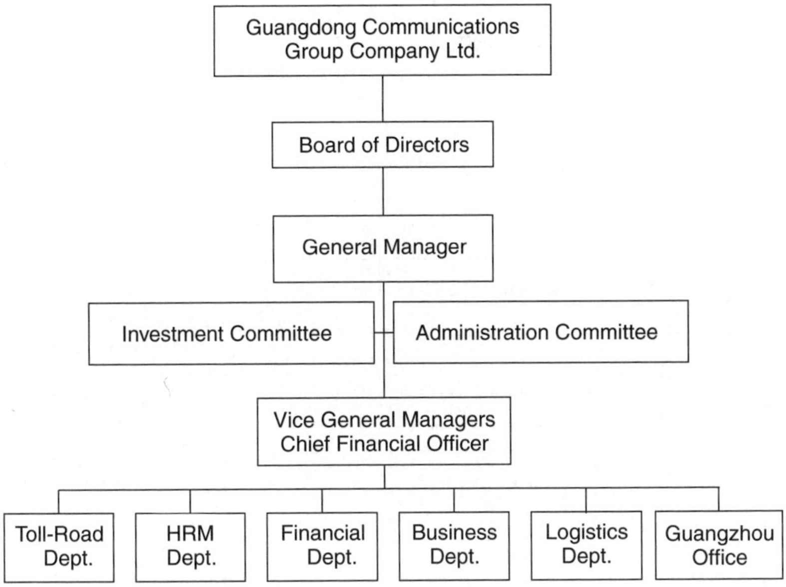

Figure 9.1 Organizational chart of Xinyue Co. Ltd
Source: Xinue Company Limited, *Annual Report*.

At the beginning of the reorganization, the company's goals and objectives were very clear. That is, to utilize the company's existing ownership interests in certain toll-road projects to take advantage of the buoyant financial markets in Hong Kong to raise as much foreign capital as possible for further investments in other attractive toll-road projects and to develop accessory facilities (including mechanical and electrical facilities, safety facilities and service facilities). The company intends to apply for listing on the Hong Kong Stock Exchange at an appropriate time when it matures and meets the listing requirements, including size and profitability. In order to make sure the goals and proposed strategy are realistic and feasible, the company engaged 15 world-renowned consulting firms to review its plans from different viewpoints. The company also invited government officials, legal experts and economists to identify potential problems that may occur during implementation of the plan. A lot of time and energy were spent on designing, reviewing and refining the proposed strategy. With the correct strategy and appropriate human resources, the company made remarkable achievements in the first two years. By 1998, it had acquired ownership interests in eight toll-road projects for RMB 2.3 billion, purchased a 35 per cent

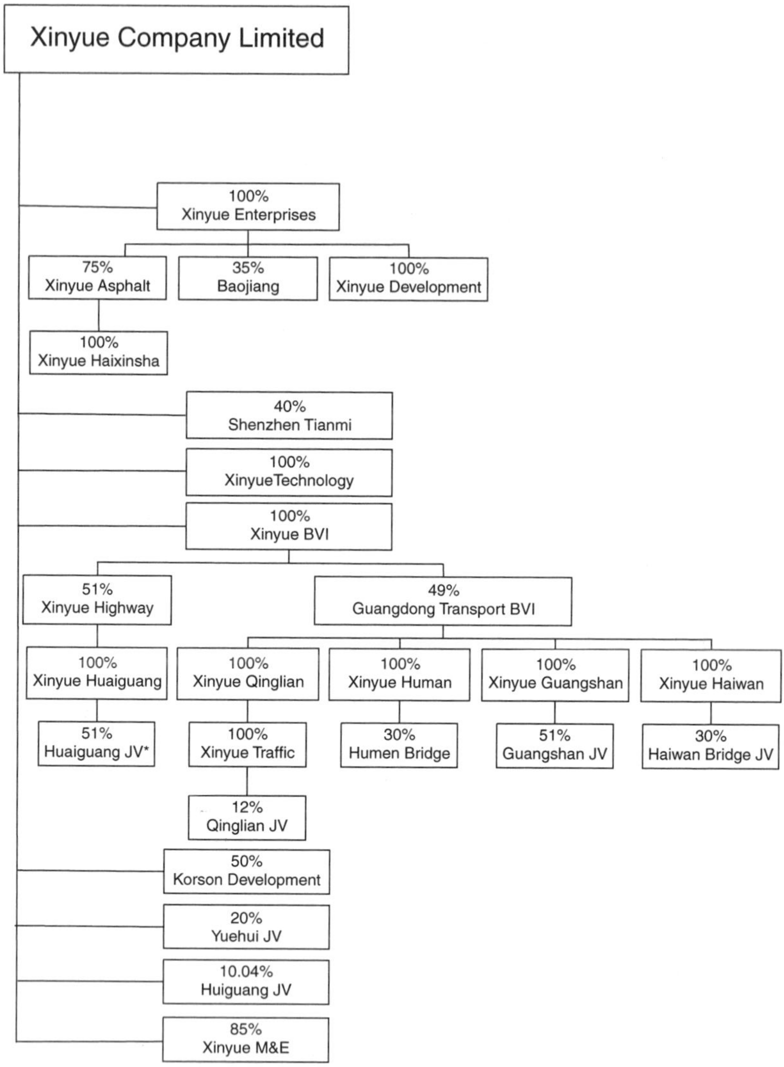

Figure 9.2 Structure of Xinyue Co. Ltd human resource management functions[2]
Note: JV means joint venture.
Source: Xinue Company Limited, *Annual Report*.

interest in Baojiang Metal Products Co. Ltd, which manufactures dazzle-proof webs and wave-shaped steel protection fences for use on expressways, and acquired a 40 per cent interest in Shenzhen Tianmi.

The first time it entered into the mechanical and electrical fields for highway projects, Xinyue came out the winner following a fiercely competitive tender for the mechanical and electrical project of the western section of the Shenzhen–Shantou Expressway. Since the project was partially financed by the World Bank, the tender process was strictly in accordance with international standards. In only two years, the company's net assets grew from HK$100 million to HK$890 million, with total assets of HK$1.3 billion.[1]

However, since the end of 1997, business conditions in Hong Kong changed considerably following the Asian financial crisis, and, as a result, the company had continuously to adjust its structure to adapt to the new environment. The adjustment process was not easy, because to a large extent the company's human resources had a hard time keeping pace with the rapidly changing business development. External interference also affected the human resources management of the company.

HRM has traditionally been referred to as personnel management with the basic tasks being record-keeping, regulatory compliance, and payroll. In fact, HR departments in many Chinese companies today are still configured according to these basic tasks. Most personnel managers know little about the underlying business and strategy of their company. Without any systematic HR plan linked closely with the strategy of the company, they have no idea about future demands in terms of human resources. They simply execute decisions made by others and handle the paperwork involved in hiring and firing, compensation, and so on. When the company expands into other businesses or when the company needs to be restructured, the HR managers do not know what to do. This is the reason why HR departments are often beleaguered.

However, today's human resource management differs from traditional personnel management. Besides covering the traditional functions of organizational design, recruiting and selecting, training and development, performance appraisal and management, compensation and benefits, employee and community relations, health and safety and productivity improvement programmes, more important HR roles are becoming those of being a strategic partner, administrative expert, employee champion and change agent. A growing number of organizations consider HRM functions and systems as a cornerstone for accomplishing an organization's mission and achieving organizational capability.

How is it possible to motivate employees to meet customer needs and broaden the customer base? How can one create a positive working environment and achieve high productivity? Facing a turbulent business environment that is increasingly competitive, how can a competitive advantage be attained and prevented from being undermined? What impact will the incredible pace of change in markets and technology have on an enterprise? All of these issues are what contemporary management is most concerned about, and HRM is playing an indispensable role in finding appropriate solutions to these issues.

Major trends and challenges related to HRM

The importance of HRM is increasingly recognized due to certain major trends in the business environment. Bernardin and Russell present five trends related to HRM:[3]

1 *More attention to productivity.* History shows that a nation that is the productivity leader eventually becomes the dominant world leader – economically, militarily, and politically. A close connection between HRM activities and productivity is perceived, and many companies try to control labour costs in order to increase productivity. For example, in 1996, Chrysler made 1.8 million cars, slightly more than it made in 1988, but with 9,000 fewer workers.[4] The reform of the state-owned enterprises (SOEs) in China is focused on enhancing productivity. In addition, many companies increase profitability through attracting new customers and developing new products or through mergers, acquisitions and joint-ventures. They encourage employees to learn new skills and share information, and motivate their creative and innovative spirit.

2 *More flexibility in response to changing business environments.* Organizations do not exist in isolation and are not self-sufficient. Rather, they exist as elements in a complex ecosystem.[5] A company must always pay close attention to its external environment and achieve congruence with it. Considerable flexibility is required in response to changing business environments, and more companies are focusing on their core competencies, outsourcing other work and using temporary or contract employees. A 1996 American Management Association survey found that 77 per cent of firms surveyed outsourced some of their HR activities, up from 60 per cent in 1994.[6] One HR executive stated that outsourcing and staff reductions made his department 'look less bloated and more like a real business partner.'[7] Moreover, technology advancement has made the world smaller and its pace faster, changing the way in which work gets done. For example, the Internet is being used to provide employees with access to

information regarding HR programmes and services. At the same time, technology advancement also requires companies that want to survive to learn rapidly and continuously.

3 *More intense international competition.* While many large firms such as Exxon, Ford and Procter & Gamble have become multinational corporations that span the globe, many medium-sized and small businesses are becoming increasingly involved in international business.[8] It is very common for German companies to move into the United States or for American businesses to move into Japan. Labour-intensive industries are migrating from developed countries with high labour costs to developing countries where the labour costs are low. Over the past two decades, just within the province of Guangdong, 30,283 Sino-foreign joint-ventures, 26,814 joint management enterprises and 19,407 wholly foreign-owned enterprises have been established.[9] It is expected that more investors will enter China since it has become a member of the World Trade Organization (WTO). Understanding the similarities and differences between domestic and international HRM in the context of particular HRM activities and domains becomes more and more important, and globalization is forcing multinational companies to increase their capability to learn and collaborate, and to manage diversity, complexity and ambiguity.

4 *More legal problems related to HRM.* Another important trend affecting the status of HRM is the proliferation of regulations and lawsuits concerning human resource issues. In a market-driven economy, competition is orderly and is regulated by laws accepted by all participants. The WTO has its own regulations, and the EU has also created its own set rules. Each country has established a set of regulations and laws related to HRM. For example, in the United States there is the Equal Employment Opportunity Act (EEO), Americans with Disabilities Act (ADA), Equal Pay Act, and so on. Violation of these laws may be costly. For instance, Texaco settled a race discrimination lawsuit for $176 million in 1996; and Baker and McKenzie, the largest law firm in the United States, was assessed $3.5 million in punitive damages for sexual harassment committed by one partner in the firm.[10] Some experts from Western countries are not confident that China will observe WTO regulations after being admitted. In fact, it is really not easy for China to do so.

5 *More diversified workforce.* In the United States, the composition of the workforce is changing drastically and these changes are affecting HRM policies and practices. More minorities and women have

entered the workforce and are beginning to move into previously white, male-dominated positions, and more workers are acquiring an advanced education. Educated workers tend to be more vocal and are demanding more involvement in corporate decision-making, and how to meet their needs represents a challenge to HRM. China is undergoing the same process. Women are challenging traditionally male-dominated posts in China. In addition, surplus labour in rural areas will crowd into urban districts to find jobs. Most workers are unskilled and need to be trained, but on the other hand, with the development of education, more educated workers will improve the knowledge structure of the current workforce. HR departments must be responsive to the changing characteristics of the workforce and be able to find, assimilate, develop and retain skilled and talented individuals.

In accordance with the business trends mentioned above, the biggest challenge facing HRM is how to help a company gain and sustain its competitive advantage that may be derived from organizational capability. As Professor Dave Ulrich of the University of Michigan stated:

> In the new economy, winning will spring from organizational capabilities such as speed, responsiveness, agility, learning capacity, and employee competence. Successful organizations will be those that are able quickly to turn strategy into action; to manage processes intelligently and efficiently; to maximize employee contribution and commitment; and to create the conditions for seamless change.[11]

Because traditional forms of competitiveness such as cost, technology, distribution, manufacturing and product features can be copied sooner or later, companies must build unique organizational capabilities that differentiate themselves from competitors and that cannot be duplicated by others. It is HRM that is responsible for developing these capabilities. This is the reason why HR managers are becoming strategic partners, administrative experts, employee champions and change agents.

However, changing the role of HR is not easy and it will depend heavily on the support of top management and line managers. It is essential that HR managers are integrally involved in the organization's strategic and policy-making activities, and there are signs that this is happening in many organizations. In the majority of Fortune 500 companies, the head of the human resource department reports directly to the chief executive officer (CEO) and there is a seat for him on the board of directors, the planning committee, or both. A 1992 survey of top human resource executives at 151 Fortune 500 companies found that a majority of these executives have significant input in corporate policy decision-making.[12] Seventy-one per cent of these same executives reported that their human resource functions were currently more involved in implementing business strategy than in past years.

To meet the challenges of the future, HR managers must earn the respect of their colleagues and of top management, and strive to overcome certain negative impressions and biases sometimes associated with HRM. Byars and Rue presented three ways to do so.[13] First, HR managers should become well-rounded business people, and need to understand the business complexities of the company.[14] Second, they have to become fully knowledgeable about present and future trends and challenges. Third, they must also promote effective human resource utilization within the organization, and demonstrate how they can contribute to the bottom line of the firm.

In order to help HR managers become more familiar with their businesses, Byars and Rue suggested that HR managers know the company strategy and business plan, know the industry, support business needs, keep their hand on the pulse of the organization, and learn to calculate costs and solutions in hard numbers.[15] In general, effective HRM is a critical success factor for companies to meet competitive challenges. In the next decade, the importance of HRM will be even greater.

Key HRM problems of Xinyue

As a state-owned-enterprise in Guangdong, besides having complex interpersonal relationships, Xinyue is facing more serious problems, as noted below, which will undermine its competitive advantages.

Human resource planning is not closely linked with company strategy

The company made a mistake in ignoring its HR planning (HRP). HRP has been defined as the process of 'getting the right number of qualified people into the right job at the right time.'[16] When the company reorganization was initiated, its business combination was simple – it emphasised raising money for toll-road projects. Each employee, with appropriate talents and skills, knew what he or she should do. At that time the general manager directly controlled the HR function of the company, and HRM was totally aligned with the company's strategy so that the efficiency and morale of the company was very high. It may be said that the company had the right people in the right positions during the early stages.

As the company expanded into other business areas, the organizational structure became more complex with a lot more employees. However, the top management simply asked the HR department to manage HRP and did not give any detailed guidelines. Unfortunately, the HR manager was not involved in the discussion and formulation of the company's development strategy; he did not know exactly what the business strategy was. When he discussed employee requirements with line managers, they thought that HRP was the HR manager's responsibility and it was none of their business. The department heads did not give the HR manager any specific details as to what sort of skill sets and experience were required in order to achieve the goals of their respective departments. Nor was the HR manager, who had little knowledge of the company's underlying business, able to anticipate changes in the business environment. As a result, the HR manager did not have the necessary information to prepare for effective HRP to bring in sufficient new recruits with the right skill sets and background. Therefore, the HR plan he prepared failed to match the company's strategic plans and the estimated human resource requirements were off the mark.

The poor HRP caused problems for the company. For example, after the Asian financial crisis, raising money in Hong Kong became very difficult. The top management of the company decided to modify the business focus, and was determined that the company should shift its focus from investment in toll-road projects to becoming a provider of accessory mechanical and electrical facilities for highway projects. The company then realized it had a serious problem in terms of human resources. It did not have enough experienced staff with the necessary skills and abilities to develop this business. Another example also shows the disconnection between its HRP and business strategy. When the company decided to enter into the market of expressway protection fences by acquiring a partial equity interest in Baojiang Metal Products Co. Ltd (Baojiang), it did not plan for a competent executive to manage its investment in that company. As it turned out, although Baojiang's market share has improved in the last few years, its profitability has not been satisfactory. There is no doubt that HRP should be an ongoing process that must be continuously reviewed and revised in light of the available resources and changes in the company's strategic initiatives.

The company did not focus on its core competencies

Under the current system, it is difficult for the company to focus on its core competencies. It cannot out-source its HR functions, as even these functions are not deemed core competencies of the HR department. There are two reasons for this problem. First, at present there are few employment agencies and consulting firms that specialize in HR activities in China. Second, personnel management policies in China were developed during the period when the country was essentially a planned economy. These policies emphasize control of behaviour instead of encouraging creativity and innovation.

In addition, the company was viewed as a subsidiary of the government and its personnel management was almost the same as that of the government sector. Although, recently, the Guangdong provincial government issued 'Implementation Measures as to Deep Reform of the Management System of Leaders of the SOEs'[17], which called for the establishment of a new management system for senior executives of the SOEs and integration of personnel management with asset management of the SOEs belonging to Guangdong provincial government, in essence the provincial government intends to 'commercialize' the SOEs by changing the ownership structure and management system. Central to the initiatives is to set up certain flagship holding companies which will take over the ownership interests in large-sized SOEs from the provincial government. Once separated from the direct control from the government, it is hoped that the SOEs will operate more on a commercial basis as opposed to being an arm of the government.

However, the HRM practices may remain the same as those found in government bodies. These measures do not separate HRM of enterprises from HRM of the government sectors; the only change made is that enterprises no long belong to government departments, but to enterprise groups that are also controlled by the provincial government. According to the same reform principle, county and town governments will have command of many medium and small-sized enterprises. There is no question that enterprises are still subsidiaries of all levels of government, so it is unavoidable for governments to interfere with enterprise management. At the same time, non-SOEs will unwittingly be discriminated against. The reality is that the government wants to control the SOEs, and control of the HR of the enterprises is an important tool. The HR department of a company becomes the mechanism that delivers government policies. HR staff are busy attending meetings, writing reports and coping with inspections, especially since it is an age of reforms and government policies quickly change. When policy changes do occur, the HR manager must do many things; he or she has no time or energy to become familiar with the business strategy of the company. It is impossible at this point to create a HR plan that can meet the needs of the organization.

Performance does not affect remuneration

In spite of the fact that the company's top management has been expected to manage the behaviour and outcomes of employees, there is no pay for performance, and many employees have begun to connect pay with responsibility and contribution, in the end a successful pay-for-performance (PFP) system has not yet been implemented. It is very hard to put such a system into action, because it is very complicated to find a solution. There are at least four factors that make it difficult to implement PFP programmes. First, PFP systems tend to increase the income differential between employees, although they are accustomed to egalitarianism. Any significant income differential may result in internal competition and conflicts between staff, affecting cooperation and teamwork. Managers are tired of solving these conflicts, which may affect the company performance in areas such as productivity or cost reduction. Internal resistance to any change in employee pay is often strong enough to discourage managers from implementing any PFP.

Second, the income level of employees is relatively low, and they are naturally very concerned about any change in their pay. Also, many employees cannot face their own weaknesses and poor performance objectively and fairly, so they would not be willing to improve their skills and level of performance. If their pay were reduced under a PFP, they would usually attribute the reduction of income to unfairness on the part of management. When their living standard is affected by a PFP, their complaints can attract some sympathy from customers who have no idea about the real story. This may also damage the image of the company. Third, because the company is owned by the government, there are too many things that need to be approved by it, and, hence the firm is forced to rely on it. Some government officials require a company to take on their friends and relatives as employees; some employees gain promotion opportunities and other privileges because they have close ties to certain government officials, who have the power to control important resources of the company. Although there are few such employees, they do have a tremendous negative effect on the company. Management is usually reluctant to treat these 'special ones' as normal employees because of their special relationships with someone in power. This leads to unfair treatment of employees, and naturally employees doubt the professionalism of the management.

Finally, many managers who are the source of performance information see the performance appraisal process only as a necessary evil they must go through to fulfil their job requirements. They feel uncomfortable evaluating others and feeding any negative comments back to their subordinates. Thus, they tend to rate everyone high or the same, making the performance appraisal useless. As one manager succinctly put it:

> There is really no getting around the fact that whenever I evaluate one of my people, I stop and think about the impact – the ramifications of my decisions on my relationship with the guy and his future here... Call it being politically minded, or using managerial discretion, or fine-tuning the guy's ratings, but in the end, I've got to live with him, and I'm not going to rate a guy without thinking about the fallout.[18]

HRM issues related to SOEs in China

The problems mentioned above are common to other SOEs. They partially derive from the unique characteristics of Chinese culture and the management systems that China has adopted over past decades. From 1949 until the late 1970s, China remained a planned economy; all management systems, including personnel management, were based on a planned economy. Young Chinese workers were allocated jobs by local labour bureaus and then assigned to work-units, which registered their citizenship status. Most of them were given permanent jobs. This 'iron-rice-bowl' employment policy was from the Soviet model in the early 1950s[19], which was originally intended to protect skilled workers, but eventually spread to cover the majority of urban industrial workers. The lifelong employment policy fostered loyalty of workers to their enterprises, but at the same time it made employees heavily dependent on their organizations. Chinese culture encourages collectivism and egalitarianism, and emphasizes compliance with tradition and obedience to authority. Most Chinese workers do not like risk-taking initiatives and are accustomed to just waiting for instructions from their superiors. But there is also a strong sense of hierarchical authority in Chinese societies. These characteristics of Chinese culture cause HRM in China to differ somewhat from that in Western societies.

In addition, with China's entry into the WTO, HR managers of the SOEs will encounter more challenges. The regulations of the WTO are based on free-market principles, but China is still in the process of transforming from a planned economy into a market-driven one. It has a shortage of talented individuals who are familiar with international market norms and business customs. Entry into the WTO implies that Chinese enterprises have the right to enter the markets of member nations with few restrictions and vice versa. Chinese SOEs are being forced to compete in a global economy.

Human resource capital is one of the most important factors in deciding whether to enter foreign markets, and it is likely that SOEs will face the following HR issues when China becomes a member of the WTO.

Job losses and arbitrary assignment of workers

As market barriers come down under the terms of the WTO, more foreign companies and products will crowd into China. Many multinational corporations will build operations in China, competing with local SOEs with abundant capital, advanced technology and management expertise, and acquiring a significant share of the markets they enter. Under WTO regulations, the Chinese government cannot provide the SOEs with special protection, and it is expected that a number of them will go bankrupt and thousands of unskilled or low-skilled workers will lose their jobs. The Chinese social security system will be burdened by a high rate of unemployment. At the same time the government will need to spend more to retrain the unemployed, otherwise social stability might be threatened. If this happens, the government might force some SOEs to employ the workers from the enterprises that go bankrupt in order to maintain social stability. The SOEs that are forced to take on excess staff will obviously become less competitive, which in turn might lead to even more SOE bankruptcies and closures.

The loss of skilled and talented staff

Today, China has a shortage of skilled workers with a talent for commerce. If a large number of multinational firms enter into or grow their businesses in China within a short period of time, the labour market will become very tight and the SOEs will have difficulty retaining skilled and experienced staff. Compared to the SOEs, foreign companies have several advantages. First, large multinational corporations are in a position to offer good pay packages and substantial incentive programmes to attract and retain talent. Second, many foreign companies can provide their employees with a clear development path and significant training opportunities. For example, the Gillette Company offers an international training programme where promising executives are sent to the corporate office in Boston for 18 months. This programme costs between $40,000 and $55,000 depending upon whether the employee is single or married,[20] but it is considered worthwhile to the company. This is because it impresses on employees that the firm is concerned with their future development.

Third, foreign firms often make use of contemporary HRM concepts to foster corporate culture and increase employees' commitment to the company. As Bob Wilner, home office director of international HR of McDonald's said,

> We want our company to be part of our workers' families and lives. When we open a restaurant, we invite the families of our workers to eat there first – even before the local dignitaries. People really get a sense of pride, and it pays off.

Finally, nepotism is not a big problem with most large multinational corporations and interpersonal relationships tend to be simpler than those found in a typical SOE. This is one of the reasons why many skilled workers hope to stay in foreign companies. If the SOEs don't improve their HRM practices and establish effective incentive systems as soon as possible, more and more valuable employees will leave the SOEs for foreign companies. The SOEs will be fighting an uphill battle if they cannot retain experienced and skilled staff.

A shortage of employees who understand international markets

As a result of China's entry into the WTO, some excellent SOEs with competitive products by international standards will go abroad to set up marketing offices, plants and other facilities in foreign countries. However, companies that enter global markets will find these places different from their home country in a number of dimensions. These differences may determine the economic viability of establishing an operation in a foreign location, and they have a strong impact on HRM in that operation. There are four primary factors affecting HRM in international markets: culture, human capital, the economic system, and the political-legal system. Among these, culture is the most important factor. It is a reflection of the values that the members of a community share, and often determines the other three factors and the effectiveness of various HRM practices in the host country.

Human capital is an important factor that must be taken into account in order to find and maintain a qualified workforce when a company attempts to expand into a foreign market. Economic systems influence

HRM through investment in human capital and the tax system. Political-legal systems often impose regulations on certain HRM practices, such as training, compensation, hiring, firing and layoffs. For example, the EEC's Community Charter of 9 December 1989 provides for the fundamental social rights of workers. These rights include freedom of movement, freedom to choose one's occupation and be fairly compensated, a guarantee of social protection via social security benefits, freedom of association and collective bargaining, equal treatment for men and women, and a safe and healthy work environment, among others.[21] In fact, there is a huge difference between China and the United States in terms of culture, human capital, the economic system and the political-legal system. This is one of the main reasons why many SOEs in Guangdong Province, such as Guangdong International Trust and Investment Co., Guangdong Enterprise Group, and so on, did not succeed in the United States.

Although China has opened the door to the outside for more than 20 years, many Chinese people are still wary of being in contact with Western culture. The significant differences in social systems between China and Western countries often causes uneasiness among Chinese people towards Western culture. Some SOE managers are deeply affected by this mind-set, and when they are sent to a foreign country for business purposes it is difficult for them to integrate with the local culture or market. Without the necessary ability to understand foreign culture and markets, the SOEs will find it difficult to compete successfully in the international arena.

There is still a long way to go to become learning organizations

As Gareth Morgan stated:

> In this world, where rapid change and transformation are becoming the norm, organizations face new challenges. In addition to planning and executing tasks in an efficient, rational way, they face the challenge of constant learning and, perhaps even more important, of learning to learn.[22]

Chinese tradition emphasizes learning. The senior leaders in China encourage people to learn new knowledge, new skills and new ideas. There is a saying in China – learn, learn, and learn again. As a matter of fact, if Chinese decision-makers did not learn international norms, they could not enter global markets in the first place. This is the reason why the government has spent a considerable amount of money sending executives and policy-makers abroad for training.

As we move into a knowledge-based economy, information, knowledge and learning ability are becoming key resources. We have seen how information technology can be used to develop decentralized organizations that are simultaneously global and local. The Internet and other methods of electronic information exchange break the old assumption that the structure and capacities of organizations are limited by constrained information processing. During this development, human intelligence is the main driving force. Today many organizational researchers are interested in creating learning organizations. Cybernetics suggests that learning organizations must develop capacities that allow them to do the following:[23]

1 Scan and anticipate change in the greater environment to detect significant variations.
2 Develop an ability to question, challenge and change operating norms and assumptions.
3 Allow an appropriate strategic direction and pattern of organization to emerge.

Most Chinese enterprises lack such capacities. What is worse is that they are unaware of the importance of learning ability and creativity. Many managers are content resting on their laurels and are only interested in holding on to their current positions. They have no idea how technology in their business sector is developing and how globalization may change their future. They seem very busy having unproductive meetings, making business visits, playing golf and mahjong, and pleasing their superiors. They have no time to scan and analyse what changes have occurred in their industry. In fact, most SOE executives with a sense of responsibility do see this problem, but it is difficult to change it. This is because it is actually the current management system of the SOEs that brings about these problems. First, the current management system does not establish any effective incentive system for senior executives of SOEs. Excessive government interference often renders SOE senior executives powerless in making commercial decisions to maximize profit. Actually, few SOE executives have been dismissed for failing to meet budget targets or for creating losses. Therefore, SOE executives do not need to be responsive to customer needs, market conditions and new technology. The only thing they need to do is to wait for instructions from their superiors and to maintain a good relationship with them. They became skilled in making things for which they are responsible look better than they actually are. They often ignore or fail to report deep-seated problems and often withhold or underplay bad news, giving their superiors rosy pictures of a situation or telling them what they would like to hear.

Second, learning is not rewarded, and sometimes even punished. But Learning can stimulate creativity and spring forth ideas, and people are eager to practise what they have learned. They would like to reform irrational systems and practices for the advancement of society at large. However, in China, sometimes when an individual challenges conventional norms and assumptions with new ideas, he might be considered a radical. At the extreme, he might be criticized or even fired. If he achieves any success, it is deemed as a result of the support from the organization and colleagues instead of through his individual effort. On the other hand, if he makes any mistakes, it is considered his own fault; he will be criticized and reprimanded and may even lose his job.

These problems concerning organizational learning in SOEs are deep-rooted and will take time to remedy. However, they must be addressed as soon as possible, otherwise if solutions are not found in time the SOEs will never attain any competitive advantages through HRM in today's increasingly globalized and competitive business environment.

As a matter of fact, the biggest threat the SOEs will face after China's entry into the WTO is a shortage of talented people who have a good command of advanced technology, management skills, a knowledge of WTO regulations, and familiarity with the culture of relevant countries. Up until now, China has mostly focused on reorganization of SOE structures rather than training and development the workforce. The news media are one-sided in reporting the imminent accession into the WTO, emphasizing only the benefits associated with it; the challenges that it will bring about are largely ignored. It will be very helpful if those affected learn more about the WTO and how to be better prepared for it.

Role of the government in the global economy

There is much room for the Chinese government to improve the external environment of its SOEs. SOEs in general are less efficient than the private sector in most countries including China, and following China's entry into the WTO the government will be forced to abandon discriminatory policies against foreign businesses. What should the government do when the domestic economy opens up? As the owner of the SOEs, how should the government manage them? Experience from developed countries has provided possible solutions to these questions. The Chinese government should focus on creating a fair social environment for healthy competition. Specifically, the government should regulate the market, encourage competition, protect the interests of weaker groups, and create equal employment opportunity by strengthening the laws. At the same time, it should maintain a good social security system, reduce crime, protect the natural environment and develop human capital, instead of directly interfering in the commercial operation of the SOEs. Thus, the functions of the government can be described as follows:

The government should review the whole legal system based on the requirements of a market-driven economy

Revising and perfecting the legal system is necessary to regulate the domestic market, manage the SOEs, and enable them to compete successfully in the global economy. The legal environment is one of the most important components of the external environment for HRM, and legal considerations are a primary force shaping employment policies. For example, in the United States there are many federal, state and local laws and regulations that affect HRM. Bernardin and Russell provide a list of important Laws and regulations since 1866 affecting HRM in the United States (see Table 9.1).[24] In particular, these legal measures seek to enforce fair labour, equal opportunities, and attack age, gender, and race discrimination.

The main goal of these laws and regulations is to eliminate discrimination based on race, colour, religion, sex or national origin. The laws and regulations effectively define the relationship between employer and employee, and between union and management. Each individual basically has an equal opportunity in employment and career development. Competition in all walks of life is fierce, but people do feel the system is fair to a large extent. Even if they fail in their business endeavours, they usually would not attribute the failure to being unfairly discriminated against. Thus, social stability is maintained, and economic development continues. However, China is used to managing society by 'red-title documents' from the administration departments. These documents are actually the policies for handling social affairs, but they are usually not available to the general public and foreign investors. Many people don't know how these policies are established, nor do they know which policies may affect their interests. So there are complaints about social equity in China, which may threaten social stability and hinder economic development. The government should urgently seek solutions to these problems by improving the legal framework and creating a fairer social environment.

Table 9.1 Laws and regulations affecting HRM in the United States

Laws and Regulations	Purpose	Administration
Civil Rights Act 1866	To establish the right of all citizens to make and enforce contracts	Federal courts
Civil Rights Act 1871	To make citizens liable for suits	Federal courts
Fair Labour Standards Act 1938	To set minimum wages, hours of work, child-labour conditions	Federal courts
Equal Pay Act 1963	To prohibit sex discrimination in wages and salary: equal pay for equal work	EEOC and federal courts
Civil Rights Act 1964 (Title VII), As Amended in 1991	In 703 (a) and (b), to declare all discriminatory employment practices unlawful	EEOC and federal courts
Age Discrimination in Employment Act 1967, As Amended in 1978 and 1986	To prohibit discrimination against persons age 40 and older	EEOC and Federal courts
Equal Employment Opportunity Act 1972	To extend coverage of the 1964 Civil Rights Act to include both public and private sectors, educational institutions, labour organizations, and employment agencies	EEOC and Federal courts
Rehabilitation Act 1973	To protect persons with disabilities against discrimination (public sector)	Department of Labour
Americans with Disabilities Act 1990	To prohibit discrimination against persons with disabilities	EEOC and federal courts

Source: H. John Bernardin and Joyce E.A. Russell (1998) *Human Resource Management: An Experiential Approach*, 2nd edn, The McGraw-Hill Companies, Inc., p. 48.

Protecting the environment, and improving public health and safety are important functions of the government

According to reports from the Occupational Safety and Health Administration (OSHA), in the United States, work-related accidents and illnesses cost an estimated 56,000 American lives each year. On an average day, 17 people are killed in safety accidents, 16,000 are injured, and 137 die from occupational disease. Each year, 700,000 days are lost to injuries and illnesses related to musculoskeletal disorders because of overuse of particular parts of the body. It is estimated that safety accidents alone cost the American economy over $100 billion a year.[25] Therefore, improving employee safety and health became an important task of United States government. It created OSHA in 1970 within the Department of Labour. OSHA covers virtually all employers and their employees in the United States, and its responsibility includes developing safety standards and enforcing them. It is authorized to conduct workplace inspections, and if an employer does not comply with OSHA's standards the penalty can be very substantial.

With improvements in the investment environment, more multinational corporations and foreign investors will enter China and establish factories, plants and other facilities. They will bring in not only capital, but also technology, create new jobs and relieve the pressure of employment, thereby contributing to the domestic economy. However, the arrival of multinational corporations also brings about negative effects in the country. As some critics of multinationals have noted, they (multinationals) are often not accountable to anyone but themselves. Their effect on the economies of host nations is basically exploitative. They exploit local populations, using them as wage slaves, often as a substitute for unionized Western labour.[26] In fact, over the past several years local newspapers have reported many industrial accidents that took place in foreign-funded enterprises in Guangdong Province. To maximize profit, these foreign-funded companies usually force their employees to work overtime, use chemicals whose long-term health effects are unknown, and cut use of safety equipment and health facilities.

Lastly, serious problems such as work related hazards, occupational diseases, environment pollution and so on do exist. Aside from private companies, SOEs in pursuit of efficiency and profit have also become less attentive to the safety and health conditions of their workers than before. Recently, a fire broke out in a theatre of Jiaozuo City, Henan Province, that resulted in more than 70 deaths. This theatre was run by a private owner. People questioned why the theatre was allowed to operate without passing fire-control inspections as stipulated by the relevant laws. Moreover, the pollution resulting from industrial waste is threatening the public health and quality of life. All major rivers in Guangdong province are more or less polluted, but many employers will only address the issues of work hazards and environmental pollution if and when required to by law. Therefore, the government has a great deal of work ahead of it to protect the natural environment and to improve public safety and health.

Developing human capital is a main responsibility of the government

A country's human capital may profoundly affect a foreign company's desire to invest there or enter its market. A country with low human capital can only attract facilities that require low skills and low wage levels, while the ones with high human capital are attractive to investment that creates high-skill jobs. This is why third-world countries are usually unable to attract foreign investments in hi-tech industries. They often attract investments in labour-intensive sectors, such as manufacturing and assembly lines with low-skill work, because of their relatively low levels of human capital.

Human capital refers to the knowledge, skills and experience of the labour force. A crucial factor that determines the level of a country's human capital is its level of education, that is, the educational opportunities available to the public. Low investment in education results in low human capital, and the only way to improve human capital is through better education. China, as the largest country in terms of population, must place greater emphasis on and increase investment in education. According to data from the Education Department of China, as of 1997, the people having completed college education make up only 1.2 per cent of its population;[27] only 4 per cent of young people are able to attend college[28]; while in Ireland over 25 per cent of 18-year-olds attend college.[29] In rural areas there are many children who do not complete elementary school. Moreover, the current wages system in China is not conducive to education development and does not encourage individuals to invest in education. Because investment in education does not always result in better career development, many people choose instead to cultivate '*guanxi*' (that is, close relationships) with those ones who have authority to offer them good positions. In China, as far as job opportunities are concerned, '*guanxi*' is often more important than skill and knowledge. By comparison, the educated workforce in developed countries tends to have better job opportunities than less educated people, so there is incentive to seek higher education. In the United States, for example, an individual's salary usually reflects his education level and experience. Research estimates that an individual's wages increase by between 10 and 16 per cent for each additional year of schooling.[30]

Two years ago, the Chinese government put forward a slogan: 'revitalizing China through science, technology, and education', but more practicable measures must be taken to achieve the government's strategic objective. Increasing the education budget, encouraging individuals' investment in education, reforming the current compensation system, and preventing nepotism and corruption in personnel management are measures the government should take to enhance human capital and improve the quality of its workforce.

As owner of the SOEs, the government should only exercise its rights as a shareholder in accordance with the charter of the SOEs, and should not interfere with their business activities and internal management

It is high time the situation in which the government is both a player and arbiter is changed. The government should separate its regulatory functions from management of commercial entities. The laws and regulations with respect to business management should cover all types of enterprises in China, no matter whether they are SOEs, or private companies, or foreign-funded businesses. Current laws and policies are not conducive to the further development of SOEs. Indeed, SOEs are often inadvertently put in disadvantageous positions *vis-à-vis* private companies, which may lead to reduction in the value of state-owned assets. There is no doubt that the government must protect national assets; the question is how to increase the value of national assets without excessive interference with the internal management of the SOEs.

The most important issue is how to select and motivate senior officers of the SOEs, including members of the boards of directors, chief executive officers and chief financial officers. Selection of these executives should be based on merit and conducted in an open, fair and just fashion. The government only needs to set up a special department responsible for establishing guidelines and procedures for recruitment and selection of senior executives of SOEs, and to monitor the outcomes of the SOEs. Independent professional consultants should undertake audits and detailed evaluations of their financial performance. In addition, the government should provide all of the venture types with information services, and give them help when they expand into international markets, or when they are unfairly treated in a foreign market. The awareness of service quality, sense of responsibility and efficiency of the government sector are also a source of competitive advantage with which the enterprises compete in the global market.

Suggestions for improving HRM practices

The government department in charge of enterprise affairs must be held responsible for its decisions and actions. If a company suffers any economic loss due to a wrong decision by, or an unjustified interference from, government officials, the government should compensate the company and investigate those officials to see if the situation involved corruption. From the serious corruption cases involving government officials that were recently revealed, such as those involving Chen Kejie, former vice chairman of the National Congress Commission, and Hu Changqing, formal vice-governor of Jiangxi Province, it has been demonstrated that corruption is usually behind the unjustified interference with SOE management. Corruption of government officials damages the business environment and depresses the morale of society. It also affects HRM of the SOEs.

On the other hand, the SOEs should stop relying on the government for protection. They should find and develop their own competitive advantages. Over the past several decades, SOEs have received so much protection from the government that many of them are totally dependent on the government, without any awareness of the need for sound marketing programmes and long-term strategy. The SOEs must be more careful in the selection of top management and recognize the importance of continuous training and development. Senior management should have strategic foresight and a strong sense of responsibility. To this end, Guangdong provincial government is taking proactive measures by sending senior managers abroad for further study and international exposure. In addition, top management should be kept relatively stable. Frequent changes in top management personnel make it difficult for SOEs to formulate and execute long-term strategic plans. If executives are not sure if they will be with the company on a long-term basis, they will not be as committed to the company. In fact, the leaders of many businesses, such as Bill Gates of Microsoft, Henry Ford of Ford Motor, Alfred P. Slogan of General Motors, among others, ran their organizations for more than 20 years.

The SOEs should allow capital investment from the private sector

Theoretically, SOEs are national assets that belong to the general public, and thus every citizen should have a vested interest to see that they are well run. However, in reality very few people take an active interest in the SOEs because they do not see the link between their personal interest and the fortune of the SOEs. They do not care whether the SOEs make money or not. Thus, SOEs (except for those enterprises that are of strategic importance to the national economy and defence) should allow capital investment from the private sector, including foreign investors, as much as possible through share transfer or by becoming publicly listed companies. Based on the experience of more developed countries, public companies are more transparent with proper corporate governance. In addition, it is easier for public companies to raise money, attract talent and gain competitive advantages. In effect, when top management is under the watchful eyes of shareholders whose interest is closely tied to the company, senior executives will be more prudent in decision-making. Recently, Guangdong Enterprise, a SOE registered in Hong Kong, succeeded in attracting a strategic partner and investor – an investment bank based in the United States – as part of its restructuring. This is really an effective way for the SOEs to enhance their competitive advantages and to improve productivity.

HR departments of SOEs should out-source some HR activities that are not core competencies, and focus on core areas

HR staff and employees should use human resource information systems (HRIS). Outsourcing some HR activities and using HRIS helps HR departments increase efficiency and reduce costs. As a partner in executing strategy, an administrative expert, an employee champion and a change agent, HR departments must address the following questions:[31]

1. To what extent does our company have the right shared values to reach its goals?
2. To what extent does our company have the required knowledge, skills and abilities?
3. To what extent does our company have the appropriate measures, rewards and incentives?
4. To what extent does our company have the right organizational structure, communications systems and policies?
5. To what extent does our company have the ability to improve work processes, to change and to learn?
6. To what extent does our company have the leadership to achieve its goals?

HR managers must be skilled at figuring out the potential problems the company faces, and, in terms of business strategy, manage to obtain and develop what is missing. The HR departments of SOEs should not be viewed as a convenient place for the government to dump veterans or laid-off officials. Also, we should stop stereotyping HR personnel as incompetent support staff. On the other hand, HR professionals also need to possess adequate knowledge about strategy, the market and the economy in order to carry out responsibilities properly. To gain competitive advantages through HRM practices, SOEs need to outsource HR activities that are not core competencies of their inhouse HR department and provide HR personnel with necessary training and development programmes.

Rational remuneration systems and effective incentive systems are the keys for effective HRM

According to a regulation from the Labour Department, the income of senior executives of SOEs is limited to four times the average worker's income. Managers and staff are generally not allowed to hold shared interest in SOEs. Even when an enterprise makes a considerable profit, the supervising official or the board of directors is often only allowed a small portion of the profit to be spent for the benefit of employees, and bonuses are usually disbursed based on a predetermined formula in accordance with seniority, instead of performance. Hence both management and staff are not motivated to improve productivity. Some managers have even abused their positions for personal interest. *Prosecution Daily*, on 28 August 2000, disclosed that 51 per cent of criminals, former high-ranked officers (above the level of deputy county manager), who committed serious crimes of corruption in Hubei Province in 2000, were senior executives of SOEs. The exposure in 2000 of a series of corruption-related incidents committed by senior executives of SOEs has tarnished their public image.

The morale of senior executives of SOEs is at a low point. Although the government has taken many measures to help SOEs overcome their difficulties, many SOE managers worry about the future of the SOEs. They believe that the current compensation and incentive systems fail to motivate the management of SOEs to work hard and maximize profits. Under the current system, SOE management might be tempted to commit corruption because their pay levels are relatively low, and in the absence of a sensible PFP system, some senior executives of SOEs have lost interest in company performance. If directors and managers have personal monetary interests in the SOEs they work for, the situation would be much better.

This is consistent with *agency theory*, which states that problems arise in corporations because the agents (top management) are not willing to bear responsibility for their decisions unless they own a substantial amount of stock in the corporation. What needs to be done right away is to improve the morale of managers of SOEs, and establish compensation and incentive systems that can tie their own interests with interests of the company. Some incentives can be offered for managerial personnel that have already been widely used in the United States (for example annual bonuses, long-term performance plans and stock options for managerial personnel). The main idea behind these incentives is to link pay to performance. According to Pearl Meyer, an executive pay consultant in New York, in 1997 the typical US CEO pay package comprised 20 per cent salary, 27 per cent short-term (annual) incentives, 16 per cent long-term incentives, and 36 per cent stock-based pay.[32] It is not unusual for CEOs to be awarded bonuses and stock options that reach eight digits. In 1997, even the median total compensation for CEOs of Forbes 200 Best Small Companies reached US$500,000.[33]

According to trends in corporate governance, shareholders are demanding that directors and top managers own more than token amounts of stock in the corporation, and stock is increasingly being used as part of a director's compensation.[34] Actually, several years ago some collective enterprises in China attempted to transfer certain shares from the company to individuals. For example, Holley Group tried to transfer 30 per cent of shares to managers since 1994.[35] The 'Implementation Measures as to Deep Reform of Management System of Leaders of SOEs' recently issued by Guangdong's provincial government stipulated that chairmen of the boards of directors and general managers who have made substantial contributions to the SOEs could be granted certain amounts of stock or stock options. However, the government must set up detailed procedures and guidelines for granting stock or stock options; otherwise, it will result in corruption or cancellation of this provision. As with the Holley Group, in spite of strong support from the local government it was unable to achieve its goal, because the granting or transfer of shares encountered too many legal and political problems. Of course, besides the need for material rewards, SOE managers usually expect spiritual encouragement from their superiors, peers and subordinates, especially from their direct supervisors. Their achievements and contributions should be recognized and respected.

To be competitive in a dynamic, complex environment, SOEs have to become less bureaucratic and more flexible

SOEs need to develop strategic flexibility – the ability to shift from one dominant strategy to another – and also need to become learning organizations skilled at acquiring and transforming knowledge, information and experience quickly and efficiently throughout the organizations, while improving their behaviour to reflect new knowledge and insights. Learning organizations seek continuous improvement through regular self-examination and experimentation. People at all levels, not just top management, are expected to be involved in scanning the environment for critical information, suggesting changes to strategies and programmes to take advantage of environmental shifts, and working with others continuously to improve work methods, procedures and evaluation techniques.

Research indicates that organizations that are willing to experiment and able to learn from their experiences are more successful than those that do not.[36] Currently, the lack of creativity and flexibility is a main disadvantage of SOEs. Over past decades, SOEs have been managed in the same way as the government sector, and their organizational structure became very rigid and bureaucratic. The creativity of employees was not encouraged, and many workers were satisfied with just following instructions. However, reform of the SOEs has been developing for many years, and some SOEs have introduced more flexible management systems. For example, Baiyunshan Enterprise Group, based in Guangzhou, built up a new incentive system which had a positive effect on workers' morale.[37] However, creativity cannot be fostered in only a short period of time; it requires the company to develop the kind of culture that supports change and risk-taking, to admit that problems and errors are inevitable and to promote an openness that encourages dialogue and expression of conflicting viewpoints, and to recognize that legitimate error can be used as a resource for new learning. Therefore, SOE executives should scrutinize their organizational structure, management systems and corporate culture. If they are not sensitive to the change in the environment and not responsive to the demands of customers and markets, or if they hinder creativity and innovation, it will be necessary to reform them as soon as possible. Although the Chinese culture favours collectivism, and it is necessary to encourage individualism properly to foster creativity. In addition, some measures that are used to enhance creativity and flexibility in American companies, such as teamwork, flexible work schedules, decentralization of decision-making, information systems, and so on, can be experimented with by SOEs.

Steps for Xinyue to improve HRM practices

Although the SOEs as a whole are faced with a number of difficulties, Xinyue is a promising company. Its biggest advantage lies in its human resources. Its employees have good professional qualities and a strong work ethic. The average age is just 32 and more than 80 per cent of employees have completed their college education. The top management team is energetic and open to suggestions from both inside and outside the firm, and the organization is able to learn from past experience. Most of the employees make an effort to contribute to the company, which is the main reason why it has survived the Asian financial crisis which led to the collapse of a number of SOEs in Hong Kong and China. However, while the company has a competent team, its HRM practices need to be strengthened to prepare for the increasingly competitive environment. In order to maintain Xinyue's competitive advantage, the company should take the following steps to improve its HRM practices.

Link HRM with the company's strategy

Recently some significant changes have taken place. For example, the Hong Kong economy has been recovering from the Asian financial crisis, China is amending a number of laws and regulations for entering into the WTO, and the government's new round of institutional reform is underway. Xinyue has also changed from a subsidiary of the Guangdong Provincial Communications Department to a subsidiary of Guangdong Provincial Communications Holding Group. In light of these changes, the company should review its strategy and make any modifications accordingly. It needs to identify what opportunities or threats these changes will bring and what its strengths or weaknesses are under the current environment. It is important to make sure that it is not tempted to move into areas that require skills that it does not currently have and is unable to acquire. Based on external and internal environment analysis, adjustment of the strategic plan and organizational structure should be taken into account. During the process of adjustment, the HR department must determine the impact of the company's objectives on each department or unit, and define the skills, expertise and total number of employees required to achieve the company's and departments' objectives. If the company's current human resources cannot meet these requirements, an appropriate action plan should be developed to meet the anticipated human resource needs.

Take detailed job analysis seriously

After the company's strategy and objectives are determined, the HR department can estimate which tasks and activities are necessary to achieve the company's objectives. The HR manager should make a detailed job analysis, not only analysing job content but also reporting the results of the analysis in the form of a job description and a job specification. A job description focuses on the job as it is currently being performed, whereas a job specification concentrates on the characteristics required to perform the job. In fact, job analysis is a cornerstone of all human resource functions, and there has been some confusion in the company during the recruitment process because it did not have a detailed job analysis. In addition, job analysis can reveal if the current method of performing a job is efficient or contains unnecessary tasks. With the help of job descriptions and job specifications, it can appraise present human resources through a skill inventory and make a reasonable prediction of its net human resource requirements for a specified time period in future. Another purpose of job analysis is to identify what the core competencies of the company are. Non-core business activities can be outsourced with cost savings which can help the company focus on its core business.

Pay more attention to training and development of employees

As previously mentioned, environmental changes may significantly influence the objectives and strategies of all organizations. These changes can make the skills learned today obsolete in the future. Business expansion of a company often requires employees to update their skills or acquire new ones. In effect, Xinyue's core business has expanded from investment in toll-roads to international trade, electronic and mechanical engineering projects, and safety and service facilities for highways. Neither the management team nor the staff was well-prepared for this growth, and some individuals do not yet know how to operate a computer or get useful information from the Internet. Also, office automation systems have not been used across the company. Moreover, new information on policies and laws or hi-tech concepts needs to be delivered to its workforce as soon as possible so that employees can capitalize on opportunities that are available. All of these examples show that training is of critical importance to the company.

Training is a prerequisite for maintaining a high-quality workforce, while career development is indispensable to retain talented people. Although career development is a new concept in Guangdong, more and more employees are increasingly concerned about their career prospects in the company. From the organization's viewpoint, career development can reduce costs due to employee turnover, meet the immediate and future human resource needs of the company on a timely basis, and better inform the company and the individual about potential career paths within the company. Xinyue has a succession plan for dealing with transfers, promotions, retirements, resignations and discharges, but it has no career development plans yet. It should assist its employees in developing their career plans, and communicate career options within the company to employees. The HR department should carefully advise employees regarding possible career paths to achieve their career goals.

Create a fair competitive environment and establish a practicable PFP system

In China, educated individuals are always concerned about whether or not they are treated equally; they hope to have equal opportunities for development. A fair environment can boost morale, improve productivity, and help the company become more efficient; it also has a positive effect on the way in which employees view their jobs and the management team. Thus, management vacancies in the company should be filled through fair and open competition. The HR department should design appropriate procedures for recruitment, selection, and promotion based on fair, just and open principles. Each employee should have an equal opportunity to obtain management positions based on merit and performance. HRM should foster a company culture of fairness, equity and healthy competition, and at the same time it should motivate employees to contribute as much as possible to the company through establishing a practicable PFP system. Although it is impossible to have a perfect PFP from the beginning, the company has to take the first steps in the right direction. Initially it must introduce a performance management system, and in order to soften objections and pay could be partially linked to performance within a given time period.

Generally, competing firms cannot readily imitate the human resources of a company. Whether or not an enterprise can gain competitive advantages in fierce international competition depends on whether it can make use of its human resources effectively. SOEs in China are facing a number of problems related to HRM, but as long as China continues its reform and open-door policies, these problems can be solved. Managers of SOEs should pay attention to the critical changes in the external environment, and at the same time take actions to improve the internal management situation within the firm and make the most of the human resources available.

Notes

1 Xinyue Co. Ltd, *Annual Report* (1998).
2 *Ibid.*
3 H. John Bernardin and Joyce E. A. Russell (1998) *Human Resource Management: An Experiential Approach*, 2nd edn, McGraw-Hill, pp. 9–11.
4 *Ibid.*, p. 10.
5 Gareth Morgan (1998) *Images of Organization: The Executive Edition*, Sage Publications, p. 61ff.
6 Charles R. Greer, Stuart A. Youngblood and David A. Gray (1999) 'Human Resource Management Outsourcing: The Make or Buy Decision', *Academy of Management Executive*, vol. 13, no. 3, pp. 85–96.

7 H. John Bernardin and Joyce E. A. Russell (1998) *Human Resource Management: An Experiential Approach, ibid.*

8 Raymond A. Noe, John R. Hollenbeck, Barry Gerhart and Patric M. Wright (2000) *Human Resource Management*, 3rd edn, McGraw-Hill, p. 11ff.

9 Guangdong Commission of Foreign Trade and Economic Cooperation, *Outstanding 50 Years, Marching Forward to the New Century* (1999), p. 15.

10 See note 3, p. 15.

11 Dave Ulrich (1998) 'A New Mandate for Human Resource', *Harvard Business Review*, pp. 1–2.

12 Stan Caudron (1994) 'HR Professionals Become Strategic Business Partners', *Personnel Journal*, vol. 8, p. 58ff.

13 Lloyd L. Byars and Leslie W. Rue (2000) *Human Resource Management*, 6th edn, McGraw-Hill, p. 11.

14 Charlene Marmer Solomon (1994) 'Managing the HR Career of the 90's', *Personnel Journal*, vol. 6, p. 66.

15 See note 11, p. 11.

16 C. F. Russ Jr. (1982) 'Manpower Planning System: Part I', *Personnel Journal*, vol. 1, p. 41.

17 Guangdong Provincial Government (1999), 'Implementation Measures as to Deep Reform of Management System of Leaders of SOEs', *Guangdong Political Journal*.

18 C. Longenecker (1987) 'Behind the Mask: The Politics of Employee Appraisal', *Academy of Management Executive*, vol. 1, p. 183.

19 A. Takahara (1992) *The Politics of Wage Policy in Post-Revolutionary China*, Macmillan – now Palgrave Macmillan.

20 R. Grossman (1997) HR in Asia, *HR Magazine*, p. 105.

21 See note 7, p. 543.

22 See note 5, p. 76.

23 See note 5, p. 82.

24 See note 3, p. 48.

25 See note 5, p. 272.

26 See note 5, pp. 283–90.

27 Zhili Chen (1998) *Our Education after 20 Years Reforming and Opening*, China's Ministry of Education, Beijing.

28 Xuewei Yang (1998) *20 Years after Recovery of College Entry Examination*, Unpublished Working Paper, Guangdong.

29 See note 7, p. 542.

30 R. Solow (1988) 'Growth with Equity through Investment in Human Capital.', *The George Seltzer Distinguished Lecture*, University of Minnesota.

31 See note 10.

32 T. A. Stewart (1997) 'CEO Pay: Mom Wouldn't Approve', *Fortune*, pp. 119–20, 31 March.

33 T. G. Condon and B. Zajac (1998) 'Feeling Your Pain', *Forbes*, pp. 280–92, 2 November.

34 Thomas L. Wheelen and David J. Hunger (2000) *Strategic Management and Business Policy*, 7th edn, Prentice Hall, p. 34ff.

35 S. V. Lawrence (2000) 'Privatization: Back-door Takeover', *Far Eastern Economic Review*, 17 August.

36 W. Mitchell, J. M. Shaver and B. Yeung (1992) 'Getting There in a Global Industry: Impacts on Performance of Changing International Presence', *Strategic Management Journal*, pp. 419–32.

37 Wu Xiaopan (2000) 'Control Big Companies and Deregulate Small Ones, Distinguish between Reward and Punishment', *Yangcheng Evening*, Guangzhou, 30 March.

10
To Be a Visionary Executive: A Perspective from a Guangdong Executive

Linhai Fang

Introduction

Since the late 1970s, China has instituted an open-door policy which has led to the profound transformation of China's economic system and structure. A socialist market economy that is much more market-driven has replaced the traditional planned economy. Furthermore, China is working rigorously to expedite the process of integrating with the world economy, by taking such actions as joining the World Trade Organization. The advent of the Internet and electronic technology has given rise to the new economy, speeding up the process of globalization. Internal reform and external push have completely altered China's business environment and competitive landscape. Chinese businesses are not domestic any more, but becoming truly global. As a result, Chinese corporate executives confront the toughest challenge ever to battle against the competition. At the same time, with the help of new technologies they enjoy a rare opportunity to catch up with their counterparts in the more developed countries.

In order to lead their corporations into the new era and into the twenty-first century, Guangdong's corporate executives definitely need to acquire new skill sets, perspectives and knowledge bases. This chapter will focus on only the theoretical framework of how to become a visionary corporate executive, targeting the areas that will be instrumental in helping Guangdong's executives to acquire strategic thinking skills and become visionary executives.

An overview of vision is discussed first, followed by a framework built on the knowledge dimensions essential to becoming a visionary corporate executive – such as strategic management, change and uncertainty, information technologies, globalization, culture and leadership. During the discussion of the above-mentioned dimensions, some Guangdong issues related to becoming a visionary executive are presented. Lastly, some basic qualities of a visionary executive are recommended and discussed. Indeed, in light of today's rapid technological revolution and business transformation, along with the tremendous ambiguity, uncertainty and complexity involved in the business decision-making process, a sound organizational vision is extremely crucial for a corporation to succeed in the competitive business environment. A corporate executive's visionary ability will be extremely critical for any companies to develop a winning strategy and stay on the right course. This chapter attempts to give Guangdong executives some help in becoming visionary corporate executives.

Vision

Almost every successful corporation shares a common attribute, in that a visionary leader guides it. Successful executives always give vision one of the highest priorities. Carly Fiorina, CEO of Hewlett-Packard (HP), in an extensive *Business Week* interview just one day after the announcement of her appointment, mapped out a set of priorities for herself.[1] Among them, she placed the first priority on creating a compelling vision for HP.

Indeed, vision, literally defined as power of imagination and expression and wisdom in understanding the true meaning of facts, especially with regard to the future, is like the rudder of a ship, a roadmap on the march, or a guiding light in the darkness. In terms of business, it particularly reflects a sense of direction and provides a systematic view to the growing complexities of the internal and external environment of a corporation. It is a realistic, credible and attractive future for a corporation.

Vision is even regarded as one of the essential elements for corporate success. This is well-illustrated by the stories of HP and IBM. If Carly Fiorina had not envisioned transforming HP into an Internet company, it is inconceivable that HP would have successfully increased its sales by 10 per cent and its profitability by 8 per cent in 1999. This was much more than the 2.1 per cent increase in both sales and profit in the previous three years. The success helped rank the company 44th among the Fortune 500 companies in 1999.[2]

Similarly, if Lou Gerstner had not identified the changing environment and mapped out the plan to reconstruct the blue-chip giant, it would have been hard to imagine that IBM could step out of its difficult slough and become one of the most important leaders among today's revolutionary e-businesses so quickly. It would also be quite impossible for the company to rank 67th in *Business Week*'s Annual Performance Rankings in 2000.[3]

However, to optimize the benefit of a vision, only having it is not enough. A vision should be understood. Some argue that vision has now become one of the most overused and least understood concepts. Successful visionary executives are those who do not just keep the vision in mind as a concept or theory; instead they can almost see and touch the vision and, more importantly, express it in a vivid statement of words. One study of the common characteristics of successful people found that many were able to picture themselves vividly. After identifying their goals, they retained that image in their minds constantly, assuring themselves repeatedly that they knew they would succeed.

This ability to visualize and verbalize a vision is a very important quality of a corporate executive because he/she can thus provide clear guidance on what future to stimulate progress towards. He/she can then use this guideline to challenge and motivate employees to achieve the goals of the corporation.

An important finding of a research study conducted by some Harvard University professors was that successful corporations were those that could articulate a coherent vision.[4] John T. Chambers, CEO of networking giant Cisco Systems Inc., now the third most valuable company in the world, very clearly described his goal as changing the way people 'live, work, play, and learn' through Internet technology.[5] In addition, he wants to build Cisco into a $50-billion company within five years. Motivated by these clear and specific targets, Cisco performed quite a feat of 130 per cent increase of its stock price and around 44 per cent sales growth in 1999.[6]

In Guangdong, it is a fact that there are not many visionary managers. Few executives can clearly express their visions and effectively direct employees to achieve the goals of their corporations. This is understandable because Guangdong has only a short history of opening up to the world and a true market economy has not yet taken shape. Consequently, executives have not accumulated enough knowledge, experience and understanding about the context or rules of a market economy. In a planned economy, vision was meaningless for Chinese executives because they did not need to be concerned with the future of their corporations. They just did everything according to the mandatory plan of the government. Concepts of market and competition did not exist at all, and executives had no profit and loss responsibilities for their corporations. The government made important decisions for them. As a result, there was neither incentive nor necessity for executives to be visionary. The centrally-planned structure and the state-owned system took its toll on the development of visionary executives in today's business world.

Social and economic systems that are much more market-oriented have been gradually forming in Guangdong since the early 1980s. The present state policy of deepening reform emphasizes empowering state-owned enterprises. Inevitably, there will be many new issues confronting Guangdong's executives when transformation of China's economic structure continues in the future. It has become imperative for Guangdong's executives clearly to identify pivotal events and recognize the significance of a corporate vision. There are no engines more powerful in driving an organization towards excellence and long-range success than a realistic, farsighted and achievable vision of the future. A well-thought-out vision is the primary vehicle by which corporations are able to renew and transform themselves. To be visionary, though, is a challenging task, and a definite must for executives if they want to lead their corporations to prosperity.

Framework for acquiring visionary ability

The following framework for acquiring visionary ability is especially recommended for Guangdong's executives. Western executives probably think that the framework is extremely basic and too much like common sense. However, due to the lack of business education and training, and experience in operating in a market-driven environment, Chinese executives are not familiar with the strategy formulation process and business planning. Even though the dimensions discussed in the framework are very basic concepts, it will still be a challenge for many executives fully to comprehend these dimensions. It is hoped that the discussion of the framework will help to achieve the purpose of this chapter – that is, to facilitate executives, especially Guangdong's executives, to think strategically about how to better become a visionary executive.

Strategic management

Vision and strategic management can supplement each other as they are interrelated; strategic management skills will enhance executives' visionary abilities. Strategic management refers to a set of managerial decisions and actions that determine the long-run performance of a corporation. Obviously, strategic management aims at the long-term development and prosperity of corporations, and requires executives to have enough foresight and insight regarding the internal and external environments on which corporate survival depends. Therefore, vision is usually regarded as one of the fundamental concepts in strategic management.

Corporate strategy should begin with a vision, and a vision should play a key role in the formulation and implementation of a corporate strategy. In other words, the purpose of a vision is to guide and facilitate the strategic management process. Strategic management, as an important concept of business administration, has been broadly applied in business practice, academic research and executive education. It covers the whole spectrum of business management, integrating all kinds of managerial knowledge such as general management, marketing management, human resource management, organizational behaviour, accounting, finance, and so on.

Undoubtedly, strategic management will enable executives to take a strategic and systematic view, to broaden their horizons and truly to understand and diagnose appropriately situations in their corporations. Moreover, executives can use a series of valuable tools learned in strategic management, such as the Strengths/Weaknesses/Opportunities/Threats (SWOT) analysis, the Value Chain, Five-Force Model, Boston Consulting Group Growth-Share Matrix, GE's Business Screen, and so on, to help fulfil their organization's vision.[7]

There are some problems confronting Guangdong executives in the process of implementing strategic management. First, due to the extended period of a centrally planned economy, executives are used to following the quotas and orders issued by the State government. As a result, they are not held accountable for profits and losses, and consequently they are not familiar with utilization of the tools available from strategic management to streamline their operations. Many of them fail to recognize the importance of strategic planning and strategic management.

Second, long-term strategic planning is something very new to them. The formulation of a strategic plan is usually considered as the last priority in the process of strategic management in Guangdong, and very few executives pay attention to implementing strategic plans even if they have one. The deficiency in strategic planning results in a lot of waste of corporate resources.

Last, those executives who recognize the significance of strategic management are unable effectively to implement strategic management due to the lack of business education and training in Guangdong. Not until the early 1990s was the first Western-style MBA education programme introduced to some Guangdong managers. The lack of management talent available with global perspectives is the number-one challenge Guangdong faces if it wants to integrate with the world economy. The short history of market-driven business practices does not provide enough successful experience for Guangdong executives to draw upon. The lack of business and management education and training and limited international exposure will result in poor understanding of strategic management, which will definitely lead to poor performance of Guangdong corporations.

Therefore, it is extremely urgent for Guangdong executives to learn more about strategic management and implement the tools of strategic management better to utilize their corporate resources for long-term benefits. In addition, it is very important for them to stay abreast of the latest technological developments, up-to-date management theories, and constant changes in the competitive landscape. These efforts will enhance Guangdong executives' visionary ability and better shape the future of their corporations.

Dealing with change and uncertainty

The more visionary executives are, the better they handle change and uncertainty. Change and uncertainty now characterize the future. Rapid changes are taking place in many forms, such as governmental deregulation, privatization, technological revolution and financial market fluctuations. All of these generate turbulence in the business environment leading to a future filled with ambiguities, uncertainties and complexities. Most people will agree that the world is now moving faster than ever before and will continue to do so. People also generally admit that the world is now much more complex and confusing and will continually reshape and renew itself. People commonly feel that uncertainties, like the variation in patterns seen in a kaleidoscope, are immeasurable in many respects.

In such a turbulent external environment, it is critical for executives to learn an appropriate method of dealing with the changes and uncertainties they face in the business world so that they may ensure their corporations' survival and continuous success.

There are many methods suggested by experts to deal with uncertainties. Some experts favour rapid response; another group recommends maintaining a high degree of flexibility and adaptability in dealing with both technology and people. Still others advocate staying constantly connected to others in an ever-changing world. Vision, strategies and scenarios can be linked together to decrease the risks from changes and uncertainties, providing a way to observe how interconnected and interdependent sets of trends might lead to a range of conditions in the future.

In Guangdong, one positive aspect is that Guangdong executives do not lack basic experience to recognize the impact of changes and uncertainties, thanks to their own experience in dealing with the very complex transformation in Guangdong's economic restructuring over the last two decades. However, in order to steer their corporations effectively in an ocean full of ambiguities and uncertainties, executives still seriously lack the professional business knowledge and international experience necessary to accomplish their mission. This will become especially clear when China joins the World Trade Organization.

Currently, there are two common types of attitudes towards changes and uncertainties in Guangdong that could be considered inappropriate. The first is that some executives assume that their past experience is a fairly reliable guide to the future. Although they admit that the situation keeps changing and the future is uncertain, they simply think the future will just become an improved version of the world with which they are familiar. The second phenomenon is that some executives lose their confidence in dealing with changes and uncertainties. The pressure created by the changes and uncertainties, and the lack of internal strength to continue the battle overwhelm them. They give up any hope of doing anything to shape and influence the future, negatively assuming the future is totally beyond their control. Undoubtedly, both attitudes prevent executives from truly understanding reality. As a result, these executives will certainly fail to acquire the wisdom, insight and strength to manoeuvre changes and uncertainties into opportunities that can benefit their businesses.

It will be essential for Guangdong's executives realistically to deal with changes, ambiguities and uncertainties which are a crucial part of the future. The unique Chinese business environment, greater foreign competition and the massive transformation of state-owned enterprises will trigger tremendous organizational restructuring, staff layoffs and decentralization. A more turbulent future lies ahead, and Guangdong's executives should psychologically prepare for the changes and learn to deal with these situations from the examples of executives in more developed countries.

Information technology

The proliferation of information technologies (IT) accompanied by the rapid growth of the Internet is transforming the business and competitive landscape in profound ways. The impact of IT on market structure can be classified into three effects. The first is the electronic communication effect in which low communication costs will allow businesses to access abundant information and will enhance market efficiency. The convergence of several traditionally disparate industries such as communications, entertainment and computing through the integration of the telephone, television and computer technologies has enabled the instantaneous transmission of data, voice and video across continents. This availability of information may not only influence information-intensive sectors, such as the financial market, but also reduce end-user prices by eliminating middlemen. For example, through video conferencing, executives on different continents can converse with each other in a relatively comfortable and convenient way and corporate intranets enable employees instantaneously to share information around the world.

The second effect is the electronic brokerage effect in which buyers and sellers are connected. The World Wide Web (WWW) resembles a huge fleamarket where potential buyers and sellers can meet in an environment that is available all the time. These features transcend the time zone and national boundaries in commercial trading.

The third effect is the electronic integration effect, which refers to the tighter buyer – supplier relation. With the help of technology, corporations are able to link with their business partners and suppliers, and this will enhance informational efficiencies and enable better monitoring of exchanges between all business parties. For example, in the automobile industry, car designers from Detroit and Germany are able to work together with customers and partners in real time.

The above-mentioned technological impacts will transform traditional business models completely. Today, IT is one of the major driving forces reshaping the global competitive landscape. For example, in the new economy, the USA leads the world, leaving its competitors, Japan and Europe, far behind thanks to its new technology advantage. In 1998, the USA accounted for 75 per cent of the world's Internet-based commerce.[8]

Because of the power of new technologies, no country wants to miss the opportunity to catch up with the USA. They strive to embrace the new technology. Based on International Data Corp. projections, by 2002 the rest of world will account for 50 per cent of e-commerce, and hence, the US share of the market will shrink.[9] E-commerce technology has at the same time created tremendous threats to traditional business. For instance, Amazon.com, an outstanding representative of the IT industry, has successfully captured 25 million customers all over the world in a very short period. The rapid growth of Amazon posts enormous threats to traditional book distribution leaders such as Barnes and

Noble, founded over 125 years ago. Ironically, the market value of Amazon was several times larger than that of its 125-year-old competitor. Another example is America Online (AOL), the largest ISP in the USA, which also has a short operating history and which announced a US$183 billion deal to purchase Time Warner on 10 January 2000.[10] Even though Time Warner is currently five times the size of AOL in terms of revenues and has a much longer history than AOL, the latter became the acquiring agent.

It is a fact that the stock of many IT companies has tumbled since April 2000, and the recent performance of high-tech stocks has disappointed many of their stakeholders. However, this will not change the trend that high-tech companies continue to create jobs and improve corporate productivity and market efficiency. The new economy, driven by technology, will prevail over the old economy.[11]

Corporate executives, whether they are in the new economy or in the old, need to consider a series of significant issues related to new technology. These issues include (1) how to recognize the fundamental shift in business models caused by technology innovation in their industries; (2) what their companies' strategies in technology investment should be; (3) how to understand the global competitive landscape to build their companies' core competence; and (4) how to recruit, train and retain 'technological' talent. Of course, these questions are not easily answered.

In China, development of IT is still in its infancy, but it is growing extremely rapidly. For example, the number of Internet users increased from 1.4 million in 1997 to over 22.5 million in 2000 and the number of wireless phone users has exceeded 85 million, up from five million in 1995.[12] China is embracing the new technologies and has thrived on it. The Chinese market will become one of the largest markets in the world. All global giants have entered or will enter China to obtain a piece of the market, and learning the new technologies and competing with the world's largest and best corporations will pose one of the toughest challenges for Guangdong executives.

Currently, due to financial limitations and a lack of qualified trainers, most Guangdong executives from traditional industries are not fully aware of the impact of the new technology, let alone have they taken advantage of the new opportunities. The technological revolution will continue to alter and shape the competitive landscape of Guangdong's businesses, both domestically and internationally, and there is an urgent need for executives to understand the trends in technology development and the impact of information technology on their own businesses and industries. They must incorporate new technology into their corporate strategies and use this technology to build their competitive advantages and sustain their market shares.

Globalization

Globalization is changing the world rapidly and radically. Globalization is defined in this case as the international integration of markets in goods, services and capital, and the trend of increasing labour mobility and cross-border information flow and cultural homogenization.

International trade, multinational production and international finance have been the driving forces of globalization. Technological innovations in recent years have expedited the process of globalization through reduction in the cost of transportation of goods and, more importantly, through rapid distribution of information. Internet technology has eliminated the boundaries of time and space, greatly accelerating international capital flows, multinational production and effective communications. The desire of multinational firms to expand their international activities has grown as the costs of moving goods and information have decreased.

As the result of globalization, barriers to trade, such as time zone differences, national boundaries, language and cultural differences, and national protectionism will disappear. Any domestic market will increasingly become an international battlefield. In order to expand market share and acquire resources, multinational companies (MNCs) will continue to exploit any and all new markets.

Meanwhile, the trends of deregulation and trade liberalization in recent years in emerging markets, such as China and countries in Latin America, will further encourage MNCs to invest in these countries. Heavy foreign direct investment (FDI) is a conduit for the transfer of technology and less tangible knowledge assets such as management practices. As a result, FDI will increase international activities and speed up the free flow of goods, services and capital.

Like the two faces of a coin, globalization brings opportunities as well as challenges to corporate executives. Globalization gives rise to challenges and threats that yesterday's business executives did not have to deal with. These challenges include deregulation, privatization, international competition, diversified workforces, currency risks, international market entries, international training, turbulent capital markets, and so on.

For example, Chinese executives in the foreign trade sector now have to create an appropriate strategy that will help them survive the government's decision to distribute export quotas through a bidding system instead of granting them to all trade companies according to a fixed schedule. In addition, they routinely have to deal with the threat posed by international Internet startups and efficient foreign competitors entering China's domestic marketplace.

Guangdong's executives have little international experience, and there are hardly any truly Chinese global corporations. Most Chinese executives face challenges not only in running a company in the new market-oriented environment and competing with MNCs in the domestic market, but also in needing to learn new skills to take their corporations into the international arena.

Whether Guangdong executives like it or not, after China enters the WTO, China's businesses will have to try to survive the battles brought on by internationalization. Those who are unable to adapt to the new environment will be left behind. In order to be better prepared for the challenges ahead, executives need to be fast learners of international business practices, seek more international exposure, think globally and embrace technology. To accomplish all these in such a short period of time is extremely challenging. Guangdong governments at all levels are utilizing a great deal of resources to develop globally-minded business leaders. In recent years, literally every provincial government has sent their best and brightest to developed countries to study and gain international experience.

For Guangdong corporations to survive, some of them may look to the practices of China Unicom. China Unicom, by leveraging the potential of the domestic market, is attracting world-class talent and international capital through public offerings and designing a flexible corporate structure to fit the ever-changing international business environment. These efforts have quickly transformed this Chinese company into a global entity. Through experiences such as this, executives have opportunities to learn from the world market by participating in it. Those possessing the best and most effective ways of learning (companies like China Unicom) will emerge under the management of China's best global managers.

Today, over 350 of the largest 500 global corporations have established their presence in China. It has become critical for Chinese executive to have the vision to recognize and understand the trend of globalization, to anticipate future competition and risk, to learn the necessary international management skills and knowledge, and to spot potential international markets for Chinese products. Only visionary executives have the ability to carry out these challenging tasks.

Culture

Definitions of culture are numerous, and in order to better understand culture, a few cultural attributes need to be addressed:

- First, *culture is learned*. Human beings are not born with the genetic imprint of a particular culture. Instead, people learn about their culture through interactions with parents, other family members, friends, and even strangers who are part of the culture. Culture is learned from the people we interact with.
- Second, *culture involves beliefs, values and norms*. Beliefs refer to the basic understanding of a group of people about what the world is like or what is true or false. Values refer to what a group of people defines as good and bad or what it regards as important. Norms refer to rules for appropriate behaviour, which provide the expectations people have of one another and of themselves.
- Third, *culture affects behaviour*. Within a given geographical area or among a social group, people who interact with one another over time will form some kind of social bond that helps to stabilize their interactions and patterns of behaviour. These stable patterns become the basis for making predictions and forming expectations about others.
- Fourth, *culture involves large groups of people*. The development of culture requires a relatively large of group of people interacting with one another to develop shared perceptions and experiences that form beliefs, values and norms.
- Shared beliefs, values and norms that are stable over time and lead to roughly similar behaviours across similar situations are known as cultural patterns.

Business executives, before entering a particular foreign market, should spend some time to learn the cultural pattern in a particular country and region. This is crucial for business success. There are some theories developed by culture study experts to understand better cultural patterns. These include Edward Hall's High-Context and Low-Context cultural patterns,[13] Geert Hofstede's Five-dimension cultural pattern,[14] and Michael Bond's Confucian cultural pattern.[15] By studying these cultural patterns and theories, business executives can enhance their cultural sensitivity and cross-cultural communication skills.

In the past two decades, the cultural factor has been so closely linked to management success that the study of cultural management has become prevalent. Such issues as the business implications of interacting with various types of culture, effective handling of cultural issues in managerial practice, the compatibility between culture and overall strategy, methods of managing different cultures when mergers or acquisitions occur, and so on, have become key concerns for business executives.

Besides social cultures that need their attention, visionary executives should also understand and help to form another kind of culture – the corporate culture. Every corporation is an independent entity, and, undoubtedly, has its own beliefs, values and norms that form its unique corporate culture. A corporate culture can strongly shape the company's strategic direction and greatly influence the behaviour of all members in the corporation. Corporate culture, though intangible, determines the corporate strategic direction; it is a powerful driving force of a corporation's existence and development. In a business bestseller *Built to Last*, 250 of the most successful corporations with a history of over 50 years were carefully studied to determine the reasons behind their corporate achievements.[16] The authors determined that strong corporate culture within these elite corporations is one of the most important factors attributing to their long-lasting success. Building a solid corporate culture will be one of the most important tasks for today's visionary business executives.

When a corporation is expanding into the international market, the tangible space constraints and physical barriers are easy to bridge. However, the gap of an intangible values system embedded in human minds of different races and ethnic groups has proved tough to overcome. The acquisition of cross-cultural communication skills to build trust among groups from different ethnic backgrounds will be very important for executives to take their companies global.

As China integrates even more with the world community, learning how to interact with global business communities with different cultural backgrounds will be a challenging task for executives. Acquiring cross-cultural communication skills is imperative for Guangdong's executives to play a role in the global market. Meanwhile, due to the influence of a culture that has a history of several thousand years and is slow to change, building a corporate culture that will facilitate transformation and development will prove to be a daunting task for Guangdong executives.

In China, undoubtedly, people are proud of their centuries-old culture and cherish their cultural heritage. However, for the past half-century, China has been operating under a closed and centrally-planned system which has formed a unique business culture. This culture, combined with the 5000-year-old history, tradition and value system, has produced a very different cultural environment and set of business practices. To some extent, it is creating challenges for China to move into a more open, market-oriented era. For example, 'egalitarianism,' perhaps a typical value in a petty-farmer economy, still pervades modern China; both the 'iron-bowl' and the 'equal-pay' systems were cornerstones of the state-planned economy. This kind of cultural perception strongly resists Chinese executives' efforts to establish corporate incentive systems that are more effective.

Another example of a cultural obstacle to changes is *guanxi*, the interpersonal relations and connections that have become a critical part of Chinese life. *Guanxi* is regarded as one of the critical factors to getting things done in China. Usually it is recognized and implemented so abusively that it leads to an observation that the country is ruled by people with connections instead of by laws. For instance, promotion based on *guanxi* instead of merit widely exists in modern Chinese corporations. Obviously, such practices, which violate the principle of scientific management, will create serious competitive disadvantages for Chinese companies.

Leadership

By defining the need for changes, creating new visions and mobilizing commitment to these visions, leaders can ultimately transform organizations. Charismatic or transformational leaders articulate a realistic vision of the future that can be shared, they stimulate subordinates intellectually and pay attention to the differences among subordinates.

Leadership has been a topic in Western management literature for quite some time. Since its introduction over 20 years ago, charismatic leadership has been strongly emphasized in US management literature. The benefits of charismatic/transformational leadership are thought to include broadening and elevation of the interests of followers, generating awareness and acceptance among the followers of the purpose and mission of the group, and motivating followers to go beyond their self-interest for the good of the group or the organization. Transformational/charismatic leadership is usually contrasted with transactional leadership. The transaction leader is defined as one who recognizes what followers want to get from their work and tries to see that they get what they desire if their performance warrants it. He/she exchanges rewards for appropriate levels of effort, and responds to followers' self-interests as long as they are getting the job done.

The evolution of leadership literature indicates that leadership is a multidisciplinary subject, covering the areas of management, sociology, psychology, behavioural science, and so on. In-depth research, observation and study has been conducted on a wide-range of issues, from analysis of leadership styles to leaders' personal traits, from the roles fulfilled by leaders to their responsibilities, from followership to the dimensions of leadership and the complex pattern of interaction among leaders, and from the decipherment of the roots of leadership to fundamental skills of leadership. This rich collection of leadership literatures provides enlightenment to business executives who aspire to be better leaders in their organizations.

In today's fast-changing world, it is necessary for corporate executives to learn the fundamentals of leadership and explore the personal traits of effective leaders. In this way, they will be able to understand the characteristics and actions of leaders and followers in different situations and better understand their own leadership styles resulting in their becoming better and more effective leaders. One of the most recent topics on leadership is the study of how executives can develop their abilities to confront the challenges of the information age. These challenges include handling masses of information and knowledge fuelled by the technology innovation in the new millennium, learning and observing quickly, discerning useful information from explosive data and statistics, and building flexible and adaptable response systems to the changing business environment.

In addition, the process of globalization has raised other concerns. One of them is that the attributes of leadership may not be universally endorsed. In different cultures, leadership attributes are perceived differently; while being ambitious is a good attribute of an outstanding leader in one culture, it may not be perceived the same way in another. Global business executives need to develop cultural sensitivity when they lead operations that span cultural borders.

In order to achieve effective leadership, which is the most important factor to corporate success, business executives need continuously to learn, practise and develop all the key attributes of being an effective leader.

The Chinese have a long history in studying leadership, especially that related to military strategy. The most famous work on leadership is the *Art of War*, written about 2000 years ago by the Chinese military strategist, Sun Tzu. His philosophy has transcended the test of time and today it is still arguably one of the most important works on strategy and leadership in the world. However, studies regarding leadership in modern organizations are still at an early stage in China. In the process of studying Western leadership literature, Chinese executives should avoid two tendencies. The first is to totally give up Chinese cultural merits in leadership such as the principles stated in the *Art of War*, and completely to follow Western philosophy based on environments and situations that are completely different from those in China. This tendency mostly occurs among Chinese executives educated abroad who learn and experience the bright side of Western management, and have somewhat forgotten where they originally come from. The second tendency is to blindly resist studying any Western theories, experiences and practices. Such people dwell on the glory of Chinese traditions, with no thought as to whether the traditional principles are still applicable in today's world or not.

Perhaps a more commonsense approach should combine China's unique cultural heritage and its different social and economic structures with Western theories, practices and experience, always taking into consideration China's unique business environment. To be an effective leader in Chinese culture, it is necessary to value the virtue of Chinese traditions and at the same time acquire skills and leadership attributes to interact with the international community. This is not easy to achieve, and requires extraordinary courage, confidence and stamina. Leadership is an art and a science that requires not only a combination of expertise, knowledge and skills, but also observation and experience accumulated over many years of practice. Learning by doing and improving by practising are the appropriate attitudes that Chinese executives should adopt.

Currently, China is undergoing massive social and economic transformation, and the changes are only going to compound after China joins the WTO. State-owned enterprises are losing their traditional strength and edge, this changing environment calls for transformational leaders in all sectors to lead China through the transition. In short, fully mastering the dimensions discussed above and their interrelations will enable executives to create a clear vision for their corporations' futures.

Basic qualities of a visionary executive

It is not enough to discuss just concepts and theories. It is necessary to explore some basic qualities of a visionary executive to provide some strategic guidance for executives to follow and practise in daily operations.

Broad interests, willingness to learn and openness

This is the first trilogy of basic qualities for visionary executives. These three elements usually interact with one another to integrate into the visionary engine.

Without interests, a person will lack motivation. Extending to corporate executives, it is almost impossible for them to feel comfortable in dealing with numerous and complicated business issues if they are not interested in what they are doing. Today's sophisticated and dynamic business world requires executives to have comprehensive competencies, and broad interests will provide a good foundation to build up such competencies. To a certain extent, broad interests directly determine the potential and future development of an executive.

The willingness to learn should be integrated into the broad interests. Willingness to learn, on the one hand, will be guaranteed by motivation; on the other hand, it enables executive to obtain relevant knowledge to the greatest degree possible. Actually, facing the explosion of information and exponentially multiplying masses of knowledge, executives obviously will not be able to catch up with the changing situation if they stop learning. Moreover, it is also too difficult to fulfil the mission of management if executives are not willing to learn a wide range of topics. Currently, business management has evolved to become knowledge-based; to increase the effectiveness of management it is necessary for executives comprehensively to make use of different aspects of knowledge, including sociology, economics, political science, history, culture, education, sports and natural science.

Openness can be regarded as the extension of broad interests. It is an indication of a person's ability to accept new things, and it will contribute to helping executives to increase their flexibility, adaptability and creativity. It is hard to imagine that a narrow-minded executive is capable of leading a corporation to achieve its vision. If executives always keep their minds open, they will probably learn faster than their competitors. This will help them to create the core competitive capabilities for their corporations, and bring their corporations to an invincible position *vis-à-vis* the competition.

Intuition, intelligence and judgment

Intuition is the ability to analyse data, comprehensively conclude or scientifically reason. It is the power to directly feel and make sense of happenings and changes. It is unlikely that executives can mechanically make decisions if information is not complete and sufficient, and the situation they are facing is not very clear. Executives must use their confidence and perseverance in making decisions, and a certain amount of intuition is embodied in the decision-making process. Intuition is one of the key qualities of executives despite the fact that it is a raw, not learned, ability. Successful executives should possess excellent intuition, and correct intuition will help executives to promptly and clearly identify the direction of corporations.

Compared with intuition, intelligence can be acquired by cultivation. It is not a simple accumulation of knowledge, but involves insight into society and social developments, analytical abilities and competence in solving problems. Intelligence is always necessary for executives when they conduct business and managerial activities. Very often, successful executives are regarded as resourceful, informed and intelligent. However, it should be pointed out that intelligence comes from diligent and deep thinking, constant and serious judging, and studious deliberation. In other words, learning more, seeing more, and pondering more are the sources of intelligence.

Judgment is a sense of identifying certain people, issues and so on to be correct or incorrect, good or bad, acceptable or unacceptable, important or meaningless, and so on. It is an important factor to measure the capabilities of an executive. It is also true that the judgment ability of executives is crucial to the development of corporations. However, it is impossible for executives to achieve excellent judgment through accumulation of knowledge and experience. A good way to improve judgment is by earnestly soliciting suggestions from experts and by learning from others' lessons.

Communication competence

Various studies show that executives spend 50 to 90 per cent of their work time in some sort of communication task. Communication takes place within a corporation almost anywhere and anytime. Technically, corporate communication is a process that collects information from the business environment, develops messages from the information, and transmits them to obtain specific economic results. More and more, experts and executives are convinced of the crucial role of communications in the management process. Without effective communications, the best idea, the most wonderful strategy cannot be articulated and will therefore have no effect. All corporate activities are implemented depending on effective communications.

Studies show that managers and administrators consistently rank communication skills as the most important managerial skill. The changes and uncertainties generated by globalization and technology innovation make communications, in all walks of life, more crucial than ever before. Visionary executives need to take any opportunity to build and sharpen their communication skills and competences. In a broader sense, communication competence includes identification of the communication process, utilization of communication media and tools, perception of the communication climate and choice of communication style. It also includes the ability to write, speak, listen and read effectively. It could be intrapersonal or interpersonal and verbal or non-verbal.

The level of communication competence will greatly affect executives' performance in fulfilling such key functions as planning, organizing, commanding and controlling, or such key roles as a leader, liaison, monitor, disseminator, spokesperson, resource allocator and negotiator. In particular, the ability to articulate a powerful vision for the company's future and to motivate others to put it into action, is vital to the corporations' success

Innovative capability

Innovation is already part of everyday conversation. Different types of innovation, including innovation of products, technologies, management and so on, have gained great popularity. Because of innovation, new products and services are created, new markets and supply sources are developed, new technologies and processes are applied, and new organizational structures and managerial approaches are introduced. Innovation is commonly regarded as an effective tool used by corporations to create competitive advantage. Some people even view innovation as the spirit of the corporation that plays a critical role in bringing the corporation to success.

In the face of a quickly changing environment, increasingly fierce competition and the trends of advocating the 'Rs' (restructuring, reengineering, redesign, reinvention, realignment, rethinking, reform, and so on), innovation is one of some executives' approaches to deal with those challenges. Executives with an innovative spirit and ability can better recognize opportunities and identify the needs and wants of the market. They also have the ability to bring together the expertise, labour, materials and capital required to meet these needs and wants. They are willing and able to grasp venture ideas, develop these ideas and pursue success with unfailing efforts. Contrarily, executives who lack a sense of innovation and competence stick to convention and confine themselves to the old methods. Undoubtedly, this will cause disadvantages for their corporations, and may even result in their failure.

Certainly, innovation should not be simply recognized as risk-taking without adhering to some principles and disciplines. Although spiritual factors such as ideals, beliefs, volition and intuition play an important role in the innovation process, many skills and tactics account for an indispensable portion of innovation capability. Visionary executives should be aware of the integration of both forces to maximize their innovation capability, and lead their corporations to a successful future.

Business ethics

Business ethics seems to be quite an abstract concept. However, the issue of business ethics has emerged as one of the most important managerial challenges in all spheres of the business world.

The question of what is ethical or not ethical needs to be answered by all corporate executives. Today, business success is no longer only measured in terms of making money or seizing market share; businesses have corporate, community and social functions and responsibilities. They need to keep a balance between short-term performance and long-term effects on the environment, and in addition to the physical environment businesses must pay attention to their practices and values as related to the social environment.

Executives need to not only recognize their responsibilities to various stakeholders of their companies, but also be responsible for the impact of their business activities on society as a whole. In order to lead their companies to fulfil their social responsibilities, executives need to have high ethical standards. Corporate executives are business leaders, and their personal ethical standard has great impact on the corporate future. They are the role models for their followers. In all leadership surveys, integrity is considered the most important personal quality for leaders; without it, followers or subordinates will lose trust and respect for those executives. Without the support of their followers, there will be no future for those executives or for their businesses.

Ethics vary in different times and different places and there is no one-size-fits-all model. Many people pursue self-development and self-improvement related to ethical issues, and at the same time strive for establishment of social ethical values. Only in the past few decades has ethics been related to business so closely, and it has become one of the important elements in examining an executive's ability to balance conflicting interests. On one hand, people, to a greater extent, now look at businesses from the perspective of the community and society as a whole; the general welfare and quest of society have taken centre stage in businesses' pursuit of success. On the other hand, market forces often pressure people to act in ways that they would not personally approve.

Ethical dilemmas often appear between what people know is right and what the company expects them to do, and between human compassion and economic benefit. Therefore, it is critical for executives to establish, reinforce and share their own ethical value system with people from their corporations and communities. This will not only help their people and other stakeholders to fulfil the lofty pursuit of their goals, but also provides direction for management improvement and leadership development in daily business operations, and creates competitive advantages for the ultimate success of their corporations.

Action ability

Without action, executives are only 'armchair' strategists, and their vision is just a form of hallucination. In order to turn the vision into reality, a strategy that has ambitious goals and specific objectives must be developed. Executives should also be effective implementers who are able to put strategies and policies into action through developing programmes, plans, budgets and procedures to reach specific goals. What must be done and how it is done are two critical questions in implementation. Executives are required not only to keep their eyes on the big picture, but also to be involved in the daily business decision-making process. The following 10 stumbling blocks, most frequently seen when corporate executives execute their plans, are listed for reference.[17] By learning critical lessons from others, corporate executives may gain wisdom and insight to help turn their visions into reality:

1. Slower implementation than originally planned;
2. Unanticipated problems;
3. Ineffective coordination of activities;
4. Activities and crises that distract attention away from implementation of the main goals;
5. Insufficient capabilities of employees involved;
6. Inadequate training of and instruction for lower level employees;
7. Uncontrollable external environmental factors;
8. Inadequate leadership and direction by departmental mangers;
9. Poor definition of key implementation tasks and activities; and
10. Inadequate monitoring of activities by the information system.

Conclusion

In the visionary process, learning occupies the central part of the process. Self-insight, self-awareness, self-evaluation and self-development, as internal generators, start and speed up the process. Basic qualities such as the ability to observe, think and take action, as necessary ingredients, interact with learning and interconnect with each other. While executives make their choices of 'learning to lead', they always need to remember that to be visionary is not easy. It requires not only good analytical skills and good personal qualities, but also in-depth knowledge of managerial behaviour and systems, intuition and creativity, and much more. It represents a comprehensive ability package of judgment, competence, understanding and insight. To be visionary is a long learning journey that requires painstaking effort.

Notes

1 Peter Burrows and Peter Elstrom (1999) 'The Boss', *Business Week*, p. 76, 2 August.
2 Global 500 List (2000), *Fortune*, December 2000/January 2001, F-13.
3 Performance Rankings of the S&P 500 (2000), *Business Week*, p. 144, Annual Special Issue, 27 March.
4 David J. Collis and Cynthia A. Montgomery (1997) *Corporate Strategy – Resources and the Scope of the Firm*, Irwin.
5 Andy Reinhardt (2000) 'Does Cisco Have a Microsoft Problem', *Business Week*, p. 100, 5 June.
6 *Ibid.*
7 David J. Collis and Cynthia A. Montgomery (1997) *op. cit.*
8 Michael J. Mandal and Irene M. Kunii (1999) 'The World's Next Growth Engine', *Business Week*, p. 77, 4 October.
9 J. Michael and Irene M. Kunii (1999) 'The World's Next Growth Engine', *Business Week*, p. 77, 4 October.
10 Richard Siklos, Catherine Yang, Andy Reinhardt, Peter Burrows and Rob Hof (2000) 'Welcome to the 21st Century', *Business Week*, p. 37, 24 January.
11 Marcia Vickers and Michael Arndt (2000) 'Stock: The Plunge that Refreshes?', *Business Week*, p. 106, 20 March.
12 Ministry of Information Industry of P.R. China (2001) 'The Statistics Report for its Status of the Development of the Internet in China', *The 2000 Statistics Report for Development of China's Information Industry*, CNNIC, January.
13 E.T. Hall (1976) *Beyond Culture*, Garden City, NY: Anchor.
14 G. Hofstede (2001) *Culture's Consequences*, 2nd edn, Thousand Oaks, CA: Sage Publications.
15 G. Hofstede and M.H. Bond (1988) 'The Confucius Connection: From Cultural Roots to Economic Growth', *Organization Dynamics*, 16(4), p. 4–21.
16 James C. Collins and Jerry I. Porras (1994) *Built to Last*, Harper Business.
17 David J. Hunger and Thomas L. Wheelen (1997) *Essentials of Strategic Management*, Addison Wesley Longman, p. 124.

11

Guangdong: China's Economic Powerhouse – The Past, the Present and the Future

Joanna Z. Li and David C. Yang

Guangdong: China's economic powerhouse

Guangdong, south China's coastal province, became the experimental ground of China two decades ago when its central government decided to reform the economic system and open its door to foreign investors. Since then, the province has found itself in the forefront of changes in China. It was among the first to undergo major economic reforms in the drive for modernization initiated by China's late leader Deng Xiaoping, and was one of the first two provinces, including Fujian Province, to establish Special Economic Zones (SEZs). It was also the forerunner of government reform leading to more efficient government administration and increased local autonomy. Indeed, the study of Guangdong will undoubtedly unveil many of the questions and answers relating to China's past, present and future.

China's decision to choose Guangdong to implement special policies that were to allow for greater flexibility was a result of careful deliberation of the Chinese central government. Located in southern China looking to the Hong Kong connection and having a tradition of emigration resulting in a large population of emigrated overseas Chinese, a rich source of investment from abroad, Guangdong was naturally the best choice for the experimentation of opening up to the outside world.

The drive of reform, modernization and opening up to the outside world has resulted in Guangdong's creating something no less than an economic miracle in the past 20 years. Blessed with the special favourable policy from the central government, the province steadfastly restructured its farming community, underwent tremendous infrastructure construction, opened its domestic market, took pains to attract foreign investment, privatized a significant part of its economy and developed export-oriented industries. Taking advantage of its proximity to Hong Kong, Macao and Taiwan and gradually merging its economy with those in the 'Greater China' areas, Guangdong has become China's gateway to the global economic arena. It has created an economic model that is fundamentally changing the economic and even political life in the country.

Guangdong has indeed become the economic powerhouse of China. With a population of about 73 million, or 5.5 per cent of the national total, in 2000, the province accounted for 10.7 per cent of China's GDP, 30 per cent of the country's foreign direct investment, and 40 per cent of its exports. There are at present more than 60,000 foreign-invested businesses in the province, making up one-third of the country's total. Guangdong in 1979 was ranked seventh in GDP. It quickly benefited from the reform efforts and moved up the list to attain top position during the 1980s.

Economic development in the area has attracted not only foreign investors, but also millions of Chinese from all over the country. They flocked to Guangdong, many finding jobs in foreign-invested and private factories, providing inexpensive labour for these two fast-growing economic sectors. Hence the expression 'the peacocks flying to the south-east land' became a popular analogy of the phenomenon of migrant job-seekers from other parts of the country.

As China gradually expands its economic makeover to other areas, from the coast to the river deltas, from the east plain to the west inland areas, and as the country seeks to merge further into the global economic scene through accession into the World Trade Organization (WTO) as a significant step, Guangdong is poised for continuous growth but will face a tough task of repositioning itself in order to maintain the economic excellency and exuberance exhibited in the past 20 years as the pioneer of economic development in China.

This chapter will examine the major factors contributing to Guangdong's economic achievement in the past two decades, discuss the present situation, especially the opportunities and challenges facing the province, and how they might influence future development of the region.

The past: major factors contributing to Guangdong's economic growth in the past 20 years

The economic success of Guangdong is very much the product of China's decision in 1978 to reform the failing economic setup, and to embark on a policy of opening to the outside world in a planned and step-by-step manner. Guangdong Province, thanks to the economic preferential policy and other reform policies granted by the central government, its geographic and cultural proximity to the region's two major international metropolises, Hong Kong and Macao, ready access to ports, its history in international commerce and other factors, has achieved tremendous success in the past 20 years.

The economic modernization and internationalization effort, starting in Guangdong, has created a 'Guangdong model' that has expanded gradually to the rest of the country. The success of Guangdong in the past can be attributed to the following factors:

1. A preferential economic policy and foreign investment;
2. Special economic zones;
3. Natural, historical and cultural factors and overseas Chinese;
4. Hong Kong and Macao;
5. Taiwanese investments;
6. Provincial government restructuring and increased local autonomy;
7. Development of non-state economy;
8. An export-oriented economy;
9. Reform of agriculture; and
10. Migrant workers.

A preferential economic policy and foreign investment

Perhaps the policy move that has influenced Guangdong's economic development the most is China's decision to encourage foreign investment through various incentives in taxation, import duties, foreign invested projects approval and other regulations related to the introduction of foreign investment. As a result, Guangdong has become the biggest destination of foreign direct investment (FDI) in China. In 2000, for instance, more than US$12 billion, or roughly 30 per cent of utilized FDI in China went to Guangdong.

At present, Guangdong has more than 60,000 foreign-invested companies and US$110 billion in investment, both making up one-third of the country's total.

More than half of the Fortune 500 companies now have interests in Guangdong, mainly in the fields of hi-tech, medical equipment, raw materials, power and road building. These investments are steadily shifting from initial exploratory projects to substantive, long-term commitments. Most of these foreign enterprises are small- or medium-sized companies from Hong Kong that have moved their processing and light industrial activities across the border. Over 80 per cent of Guangdong's 'foreign' investment comes from Hong Kong, and Taiwan represents another 10 per cent. The Japanese and Americans are the next largest investors, with Europe increasing its share steadily. The UK is the leading European investor by accumulated stock of investment. Helped by the large influx of foreign investment, Guangdong's economy averaged annual growth rates of 14 per cent during the 1980s and 1990s.[1]

Special Economic Zones

The Special Economic Zones (SEZs) in Guangdong are a significant central government measure to attract foreign investment and to experiment with other economic reform policies. They have become the forerunners and major contributors of Guangdong's economic takeoff. By far the most important is Shenzhen (adjacent to Hong Kong and 327.6 sq. kilometres), the much smaller Zhuhai bordering on to Macao (121 sq. kilometres) and Shantou (52.6 sq. kilometres situated some 300 kilometres east of Hong Kong on the coast of Guangdong Province). Hainan, established as an Administrative Region under Guangdong in 1981, was upgraded in 1988 to a province.

The SEZs were established as doorways through which two-way traffic could pass between China and the outside world. The basic idea was that foreign businesses, joint ventures and the use of foreign capital, technology and techniques could be introduced in the SEZs. This would allow for the benefits to percolate into the rest of the province and the country, without the more disruptive effects that might arise from their wholesale introduction. In this sense the SEZs were experimental workshops in new managerial, and even governmental styles.

SEZs were created in 1980 with all kinds of benefits to prospective investors, from which other areas in China were excluded. These benefits included more relaxed entry and exit regulations, business registration regulations, labour and wage regulations and land regulations, and preferential tax treatment. Significantly, SEZs controlled most, and sometimes all, of their own foreign exchange earnings, a privilege that was curtailed in 1991 to some 50 per cent.

The results of these reforms have led to a startling transformation of the SEZs. Economically, Shenzhen, by far the most significant of the SEZs, has outperformed even the most optimistic expectations of the early 1980s. Its GDP increased by an annual average rate of 50 per cent per year in the 1980s; exports over the same period climbed by an annual average of 75 per cent. Wages for an unskilled worker are some 500–700 renminbi (RMB) per month compared with 150–200 RMB in the Pearl River Delta.

In recent years, the SEZs have led the country in establishing new systems, upgrading industries and opening wider to the outside world, serving as national models. In 1999, Shenzhen's new-and high-tech industry became the one with the best prospects, and the output value of new-and high-tech products reached 81.98 billion RMB, making up 40.5 per cent of the city's total industrial output and coming out in front in the country.

However, as China expands its economic reform and open-door policy to other areas, first other coastal cities then the Yangzhi River delta and recently the vast western part of the country, the 'special' status of SEZs has been undermined with increased competition in attracting foreign investment.

Natural, historical and cultural factors and overseas Chinese

It is no coincidence that the central government chose Guangdong as its pioneer in economic reform and opening up to the outside world. The natural, historical and cultural factors have made Guangdong the perfect candidate for that task and have indeed contributed to the province's economic success.

Guangdong is situated in the southern tip of continental China, neighbouring the international metropolitan regions of Hong Kong and Macao. It faces the sea with a continental coastline of 3,368 kilometers, and has numerous islands as well. In putting three out of four of China's earliest special economic zones in Guangdong, the central government obviously took full consideration of Guangdong's geographical location and economic status. Guangdong was the southernmost province within Chinese territory before Hainan was made a province. It borders the South China Sea, neighbours Vietnam, and faces Malaysia, Indonesia and the Philippines across the sea, thus affording close marine access to Southeast Asia, Oceania, the Middle East, the Near East and Africa.

Guangdong was an open region even in ancient China. Prior to the Tang dynasty (618–907), Xuwen and Hepu (Hepu now belongs to Guangxi Zhuang Autonomous Region) were vital arteries for marine communication. During the Tang dynasty, Guangzhou became a world-renowned oriental seaport, and the Ocean Silk Road starting from Guangzhou was the longest shipping route in the world. In the Song dynasty (960–1279), Guangzhou's merchant ships sailed across the Indian Ocean to Arabia and East Africa, and in the Ming dynasty (1368–1644), two ocean shipping lines from Guangzhou to Latin America and to Lisbon in Portugal were opened. In the early period of the Qing dynasty (1644–1911), shipping lines from Guangzhou to North America and Oceania were also established.[2]

During the course of centuries of contact with foreign countries, many Cantonese emigrated. According to historical records, as far back as the late Tang dynasty and the Song dynasty, Cantonese began to migrate overseas. After the Opium War, colonialists contracted to send large batches of Chinese labourers to America, Australia and Southeast Asia. In 1862, the United States Congress approved the Pacific Ocean Railway Bill, which resulted in more than 10,000 Chinese labourers, mostly from Taishan in Guangdong Province, being sent to the United States.

Although these overseas Chinese labourers were at the bottom of the social ladder, with low incomes and virtually no opportunities for education, some of them managed to save money and on their return home opened factories. These people were the forefathers of modern industry in Guangdong.

In establishing the earliest factories in Guangdong, the overseas Chinese introduced both technologies and the necessary capital, and in the 1980s when the Chinese government decided to put into practice the reform and opening policy, overseas Chinese, once again, made great contributions to the motherland's economic revitalization. At present, overseas Chinese originating from Guangdong live in more than 100 countries, and their number has reached 20 million, representing 70 per cent of the total population of overseas Chinese. Most of them live in Thailand, Malaysia, Vietnam, Indonesia, the United States, Singapore, Canada, Philippines, Australia, Britain and Peru. Additionally, Guangdong has a total population of returned overseas Chinese of about 2 million.

From the history of emigration, it is very apparent that the province has been far more outward looking than other provinces and has had a long association with the outside world. Consequently, Cantonese have been noted for their robust entrepreneurial spirit and a willingness to embrace new opportunities. This spirit was briefly stifled during the Cultural Revolution in the 1960s and 1970s. That economic dynamism was, however, among the first to express itself after China decided to go on the path of economic reform and establishment of a market economy, leading to the thriving trade and commerce in the province since then.

Hong Kong and Macao

Perhaps the geographic feature that has influenced Guangdong's economic growth the most is its proximity to Hong Kong and Macao, two major international metropolitan regions. Even before the British returned Hong Kong to China, Hong Kong and Guangdong had merged together and became inseparable thanks to the geographical proximity, linguistic and cultural links.

Hong Kong and Macao are located at the estuary of the Pearl River, with Shenzhen and Zhuhai, the two earliest SEZs, as their respective neighbours. Residents of Hong Kong and Macao speak the same dialect, Cantonese, as do most people from Guangdong. Many people from these two cities were originally from Guangdong and still have family or relatives in the province. There had been continued communication among these families and relatives before Guangdong opened its door wide to Hong Kong and Macao, typically with the people from Hong Kong and Macao sending monetary or materialistic support to their Guangdong links. These activities were interrupted during the Cultural Revolution when the border was completely closed and any links with Hong Kong, Macao and overseas Chinese were regarded as 'counterrevolutionary'.

Since the implementation of the reform and opening-up policy, however, Guangdong Province has brought the advantage of neighbouring Hong Kong and Macao into full play and has sped up the ladder of economic development of these areas. In the past 20 years, cooperation between Guangdong and these two cities has developed through trade and investment initiatives.

The most significant activity between Hong Kong and Guangdong has been the shifting of Hong Kong's manufacturing to Guangdong. Since the early 1980s, much of Hong Kong's manufacturing has moved to Guangdong's Pearl River delta in search of lower costs in terms of land and labour. As a result, 90 per cent of Hong Kong's manufacturers have facilities in China, mainly located in the Pearl River Delta, and manufacturing's share of Hong Kong's GDP declined from 24.3 per cent in 1984 when the sector was in its peak to 6.2 per cent in 1998.[3] By the end of 1998, Guangdong had signed 189.6 thousand contracts of utilizing investments from Hong Kong and Macao. The amount of investment contracted was US$134.2 billion, of which US$70.3 billion was put to use. Business people from Hong Kong and Macao have set up over 50,000 Chinese – foreign equity joint ventures, Chinese – foreign cooperative joint ventures and wholly-foreign-owned enterprises. Most of these are small to medium-sized companies from Hong Kong that have moved their processing and light industrial activity across the border. Consequently, over 80 per cent of Guangdong's 'foreign' investment comes from Hong Kong.

Besides investing directly in Guangdong, Hong Kong became the middleman and the gateway of Guangdong to the world. A well-established international cosmopolitan area and part of the world's major trading hub, Hong Kong was the obvious place for foreign companies to look for legal advice, accounting practices, tax consultancy and financial advice when venturing into the mainland, and a place for Guangdong's trade companies to seek market information, trade expertise, management skills and financial and transportation services.

Taiwanese investors

Taiwan is the second largest investor in Guangdong, representing 10 per cent of the total FDI in the province in 2000. Investment from Taiwan in the province has been increasing rapidly in the past few years even though total FDI growth has slowed down due to competition from other areas in China, In 2000, for instance, total utilized FDI stayed almost flat (up 0.3 per cent), while investment from Taiwan rose 24 per cent.

This phenomenon is a result of Taiwanese investors shifting their investment from Guangdong's neighbour Fujian Province to other more attractive areas. Taiwan and Fujian share a cultural heritage that has drawn many Taiwan businesses to Fujian to invest. However, as China's economy has progressed and become more open, the lure of business conditions in other places has diminished the relative attractiveness of Fujian as a place for Taiwanese investment. As a result, Fujian's FDI dropped 5.5 per cent in 2000. Guangdong has thus become a major investment destination for Taiwanese. Its Dongguan City, near the Hong Kong border, for example, is a centre for Taiwan businesses because of its accessibility and relatively low costs.

Provincial government restructuring and increased local autonomy

The policy of economic reform led to a major review of the provincial government's administrative structures. The old administrative and political structure was determined to be unfit for effective economic modernization and internationalization. The political reform of the provincial government has greatly influenced the economic life in the area, resulting from a local government with greater autonomy and a more efficient administrative structure that has contributed greatly to the booming of the local economy.

Reforms were introduced to allow for the general policy of devolution of power in economic management from the central government to Guangdong Province. These reforms included liberalization of production planning, technical policy, capital construction, supplies of materials, foreign trade, commodity distribution, wage levels, cultural activities, healthcare and tourism.

Meanwhile, the province was very soon given a significant part of the decision-making power over investment strategies. Financial contracting systems, including those with foreign interests, were reorganized with the province having a major say in these matters. The sharing of foreign exchange revenue was a matter of consultation between Beijing and the province itself, with Guangdong retaining increasingly large balances. General fiscal revenue for the balance of remittance to central government and retention in the province worked most markedly in favour of Guangdong.

After the Tiananmen Square massacre in 1989, conservatives in the central government advocated a slowdown in growth, with Guangdong having to reduce investment and subject itself to greater macroeconomic control from Beijing. However, in 1992 Chinese leader Deng Xiaoping, regarded as the 'designer' of China's economic reform, championing the acceleration of reforms with a growth target of at least 10 per cent. In January 1992 he visited Guangdong with its booming towns and the SEZs, and praised it as a model for the rest of China. In the National People's Congress in the spring of 1992, Deng was triumphant and Guangdong was set for even faster growth based on a high degree of economic autonomy.

Development of the non-state economy

The rise of the private sector is a fundamental indication of economic reforms and crucial factor for Guangdong's success. The private sector in Guangdong has grown from nothing before 1979 to a force representing between 50 to 60 per cent of the province's industrial production.[4] At the same time, the loss-making state-owned sector has been shrinking to a size that is smaller than in most areas in the nation as a result of market competition, and also China's campaign to reform its state-owned enterprises (SOEs) in recent years.

This more modern and market-oriented economic composition will enable the province to fit in better in international competition than many other areas in China, with the sluggish SOEs being a lesser hindering factor and concern.

An export-oriented economy

Another factor for Guandong's phenomenal economic growth has been its resolution to develop an export-oriented economy. After two-decades of effort, the province has achieved this goal and become the most significant place in China in international trade. Guandong's exports account for about 40 per cent of China's total, and continues to accelerate rapidly, growing at a rate of 25 per cent in 2000.

At present, total exports exceed $90 billion annually, making up 80 per cent of the provincial GDP. Additionally, Guangdong's export market has been very diversified. This has enhanced Guangdong's ability to weather domestic or regional economic downturns and laid an excellent foundation for further trade expansion when China joins the WTO. Thanks to the diversity in its trade structure, Guangdong survived the Asian financial crisis without any major problems. Guangdong is believed to be well-positioned to take full advantage of the benefits of China's WTO accession, and its trade is expected to surge.

Consumer and light industrial products such as electronic appliances, clothing, toys, shoes, computer components, furniture, plastics and so on are the major export goods. The province imports raw materials for the production of the export products and also consumer items such as cars, computers, food and cigarettes.

However, in recent years the rising production costs in Guangdong Province have made it increasingly difficult to compete against other areas in the region in the traditional light industries. The province has thus tried to restructure its industries to move to high value-added, high-tech sectors. Consequently, the product structure of its trade has also leaned in the same direction with increased trade in computer hardware, semiconductors, software and telecommunications, while that in the traditional light industries has been shrinking.

Reform of agriculture

Guangdong's success would not exist if it were not for the reform and development of its agricultural sector, which provides a solid economic foundation for the province's industrialization and urbanization. Pioneering this effort was the introduction of the 'household contract system', in which household farming replaced the people's commune. Individual households became the unit to plan and conduct farming activities, and were responsible for the gains or losses of these activities. This is a huge step of rural reform that greatly improved the efficiency and incentive in farming. As a result, tremendous progress was seen in productivity, profitability and diversification in farming as farmers had the decision-making power over their activities.

The increased farming efficiency in farming, leading to an idle workforce in rural areas and the increased freedom of farmers, laid solid ground for the emergence of private and so-called 'township' industries in rural areas and the rapid urbanization and industrialization in Guangdong. It also provided the labour force needed for the fast growth in the cities.

Migrant workers

The economic development in the area has attracted not only foreign investors, but also Chinese from all over the country, who in return have become an undeniable force driving Guangdong's economic development. Millions of people, attracted by the exciting business and work opportunities in Guangdong, have flocked to southern China. During the five years from 1985 to 1990, intra-migration and inter-migration took place first in Guangdong among all the provinces, and that of professionals and workers continues today. The direction of migration was from neighbouring and inland provinces and remote mountainous areas to the Pearl River Delta and from rural areas to urban areas.

Migration of the population from both the surrounding provinces and those in the north has become the contributing for the rapid population growth in Guangdong. For example, net migration increased the population by 2.4 per cent in 1991 alone. It is estimated that more than 11 million migrant workers from poorer inland provinces have flooded into the area.

The migrant professional workers provided the much-needed inexpensive workforce for the developing private or foreign-invested enterprises, and thus were an important contributing factor for Guangdong's development. However, the migration has had major political effects in both the lowland and highland areas. One of these effects has been to exacerbate of the shortage of housing, education and hospital provision and unemployment, contributing to a surge in crime, vagrancy, prostitution and corruption.

The present: advantages and disadvantages, opportunities and challenges

Looking forward, Guangdong is well-positioned for continued strong economic growth. It has a relatively open and developed economy, better infrastructure, well-established markets, well-developed integration with Hong Kong, a skilled workforce, and comparatively good government services. High-technology industries in the Pearl River Delta will play an increasing role in the province's economy.

However, the province also faces strong challenges following the diminishing effects of economic preferential policies, rising labour and land costs and stronger competition from other areas in the country.

The following positive or negative factors are affecting Guandong's continued economic growth:

1. A comparatively educated and skilled workforce;
2. SOE reform less daunting than in other areas in China;
3. Taiwan's increased economic energy affects Guangdong;
4. A relatively developed infrastructure and market mechanism and a well-established network of foreign investors and clients;
5. The possibility of parallel development of high-tech and labour-intensive industries;
6. WTO accession;
7. The decreased effect of preferential policies and increased competition;
8. Competition with Shanghai and the changing role of Hong Kong; and
9. A fragile financial system.

A comparatively educated and skilled workforce

Guangdong has adopted the strategy of 'rejuvenating the province through science and education'. Since the 1990s, the education level of the Guangdong population has improved; illiteracy has decreased from 7.81 per cent of the population in 1995 to 6.86 per cent in 1997.

At present, there are 43 regular higher education institutions and 57 adult higher institutions in Guangdong with a total enrolment of 332,000 undergraduate and 8,043 postgraduate students. As a result, the education level in the province has noticeably improved.

Additionally, the rapid economic development and income growth has attracted thousands of talented and well-educated young people from all over the country, helping to form the most skilled and educated labour force in China. This will provide an advantage for Guangdong to attract foreign investment in high-tech and knowledge-intensive industries, and thus helps the province's drive to upgrade its industry from the traditional labour-intensive sectors to high-tech, high-value-added sectors.

SOE reform less daunting than in other areas in the country

Guangdong has a lighter burden of money-losing SOEs, which can be advantageous over other provinces in furthering economic growth.

Guangdong received less state capital from the central government than most of the other provinces between the 1950s and the 1970s. Most of the SOEs in Guangdong Province were established between the 1980s and 1990s and have more advanced technology, equipment and market-oriented management mechanism. Consequently, SOEs in Guangdong are more efficient than their colleagues in inland provinces, and, though reform of the SOEs has faced the same social and political obstacles as elsewhere in China, the overall challenge is not as daunting.

Most of the province's major loss-making SOEs are in traditional heavy industries such as textiles, sugar and coal industries. The province is trying to solve the problem by restructuring its industries, encouraging the development of high-tech, telecommunications, information, machine and electronic industries and gradually shrinking its traditional labour-intensive industries. As a result, in the first two months of 2001, the export volume of electronic and machinery products was up 13.8 per cent while that of clothes and accessories decreased by 38 per cent.[5]

Taiwan's increased economic energy affects Guangdong

Taiwan's economy, experiencing significant contraction with deteriorating non-performing loan problems, rising unemployment, a weak equity market and dampened local consumer demand, toppled with the adverse impact of September 11, 2001 terrorist attack on export to the United States, has pushed a hollowing-out of funds to mainland China. The government of Taiwan has abolished its 'go slow, be patient' investment policy, and the accession of China into the WTO will further promote that trend. Guangdong will probably become one of the major destinations of new Taiwanese investment.

Right after China was approved for entry into the WTO, Taiwan was formally cleared for admission. These factors will create a dual effect on Taiwan's economy, leading to the further hollowing out of Taiwanese investment capital to mainland China.

China's accession into the WTO in November 2001 offers Taiwan enormous trade opportunities to exploit the mainland's huge market as the island relies on China for both manufacturing and sales. Meanwhile, Taiwan's entry should help improve relations with the mainland as the WTO could serve as a channel for the two sides of the Taiwan Straits to communicate without political wrangle. Taiwan's bans on direct trade, transport and postal links with mainland China would have to ease under WTO rules, and this will result in the further shifting of the manufacturing sectors from Taiwan to China.

In fact, the trend has already been very apparent. In the first six months of 2001, the mainland approved 1957 Taiwanese investment projects, up 40 per cent from the same period of last year. The total value of these contracts was US$3.3 billion, an increase of 66 per cent. In 2000, 60 per cent of Taiwan's overseas investment went to China. There are at present 40,000 Taiwan companies on the mainland that employ as many as 10 million people. [6]

Guangdong, a major production base for manufacturing traditional light industry products, had naturally become the biggest destination for investment from Taiwan as Taiwan gradually shifted its manufacturing industries of footwear, sportswear, garments and some parts of the consumer electronics and computer industries to mainland China. Taiwanese companies play a significant role in China's private manufacturing economy.

However, in recent years the pattern of investment has undergone subtle shifts and Guangdong is facing increase competition from other parts of China for Taiwanese investment. Indeed, competition between local governments in China for overseas investors, including from Taiwan, is intense. Shanghai, already home to 3,000 Taiwanese companies, cannot afford to do without them. The city wants more and vows to cut back on red tape in an effort to woo more of the island's cash.

Taiwanese investment has started to move into the hi-tech sectors. For example, in 2000 for the first time more money went into hi-tech than any other sector and Guangdong was overtaken by Jiangsu province, including the municipality of Shanghai, as the leading destination of Taiwanese investment. It is predicted that the rebound of Taiwan's economy will be led by the semiconductor sector. Guangdong has to restructure its industry accordingly to accommodate these changes and attract Taiwanese investors.

A relatively developed infrastructure and market mechanism and a well-established network of foreign investors and clients

The pioneering economic development in the past two decades has enabled Guangdong to form a relatively advanced market mechanism, a better transportation and telecommunications network and other infrastructure improvements. Guangdong leads the nation in per capita telephone quantity, highway length, port capacity, airline passenger and cargo transportation, and so on. One of China's three Internet outlets is in the province's capital Guangzhou.

As the country's biggest trader and major host of foreign investment for years, Guangdong has set up ties with foreign investors and clients all over the world. It has also obtained more experience and expertise in interacting with foreign investors and trading clients than any other province. These experiences and expertise will undoubtedly provide Guangdong with significant competitive advantages over other areas of the country.

The possibility of parallel development of high-tech and labour-intensive industries

Development in Guangdong has been very uneven, leaving the SEZs and Pearl River Delta highly-developed, and the remote and mountainous areas in the northern part of the province underdeveloped. The gap in disposable income among urban and rural residents has widened. This will allow foreign investors the possibility to bring in advanced technology to the more developed areas and still be able to find sites where labour and land costs are still low enough for traditional labour-intensive manufacturing to be profitable.

WTO accession

As a major exporter Guangdong is expected to receive potential benefits from greater access to new markets for the province's exporters following China's membership in the WTO. It is believed to be well-positioned to take full advantage of the benefits of China's WTO accession, and its trade is expected to surge.

Recognizing the importance of the private sector as a new source of economic growth, the provincial government envisage being able gradually to relax present regulations governing the capital, property rights, land and labour markets over the next five years. It intends to break the state monopoly and develop modern service industries in such areas as information services, finance and insurance, transportation, tourism, telecommunications, public utilities and real estate.

While China's entry into the WTO is generally regarded as the catalyst for such changes, it remains to be seen exactly when and to what extent foreign companies will be given access to these new markets.

The decreased effect of preferential policies and increased competition

In 1984, China opened 14 coastal cities – Dalian, Qinhuangdao, Tianjin, Yantai, Qingdao, Lianyungang, Nantong, Shanghai, Ningbo, Wenzhou, Fuzhou, Guangzhou, Zhanjiang and Beihai – to overseas investment. Then, beginning in 1985, the state decided to expand the open coastal areas, extending the open economic zones of the Yangzhi River Delta,

Pearl River Delta, Xiamen – Zhangzhou – Quanzhou Triangle in south Fujian, Shandong Peninsula, Liaodong Peninsula, Hebei and Guangxi into an open coastal belt. In 1990, the Chinese government decided to open the Pudong New Zone in Shanghai to overseas investment, and opened more cities in the Yangzhi River valley. In this way, a chain of open cities extending up the Yangzhi River valley, with Shanghai's Pudong as the 'dragon head,' has been formed. Since 1992, the State Council has opened a number of border cities, and in addition opened all the capital cities of inland provinces and autonomous regions. In addition, 15 free trade zones, 32 state-level economic and technological development zones, and 53 new- and high-tech industrial development zones have been established in large- and medium-sized cities.

As a result, a multi-level, multi-channel and diversified pattern of opening, integrating coastal areas with river-line, border and inland areas, has been formed in China. As these open areas adopt different preferential policies, Guangdong is facing increased competition for foreign investment and gradually losing its competitive advantage resulted from preferential policies.

Competition with Shanghai and the changing role of Hong Kong

In recent years, the internal and external factors affecting the economic development of Guangdong and Hong Kong have greatly changed. As China enters the WTO, its market will open up to the outside world and the development of a market economy will be hastened in Guangdong and the rest of the country. Development in other areas in China, especially areas in the Yangzhi River Delta centred on Shanghai, is catching up quickly and could become a complementary or competitive force to Guangdong and Hong Kong. Under this circumstance, the economic relation between Guangdong and Hong Kong has raised widespread concern and become a new strategic issue for the both sides.

The rapid growth of Shanghai poses great pressure on Guangdong and Hong Kong. Consequently, many have called for full integration of the two cities to strengthen the regional competitive advantage. Shanghai has evolved into the economic locomotive in the Yangtze River Delta. Hong Kong, while becoming Shanghai's largest foreign investor and aiming to serve the whole of China as an investment and trade bridge, currently serves mainly south China's Pearl River Delta with its financial, legal and other capabilities. The Shanghai region and Guangdong–Hong Kong have become China's two major economic clusters. However, the free flow of resources between Shanghai and the eastern provinces is able to boost the region's competitiveness substantially. This contrasts sharply with the Guangdong–Hong Kong relationship.

There have been concerns on the lack of capability in the existing framework of cooperation of the two territories to take full advantage of each other's competitive edges and grow on combined strengths. The major complaint is that the border has restricted the interflow of production factors between the regions. This will hinder the Pearl River Delta from freely tapping the financial, trade, marketing and management services of Hong Kong and result in duplication and dissipation of resources and lowering in the overall competitiveness of the Guangdong – Hong Kong region. A suggestion is to promote the free two-way flow of people, traffic, cargoes and funds between the two territories.[7]

At present, the flow of people is very unbalanced, with Hong Kong residents travelling to the mainland exceeding the number of people travelling to Hong Kong from the mainland by 12 times. Only a limited number of cars can freely commute between the two regions, falling well short of demand for traffic flow. Cargo flow, though not restricted, is not as efficient as desired due to reasons related to import duties, security and infrastructure facilities, and as trade is expected to grow dramatically after China's accession into the WTO, the problem of insufficient port facilities might further aggravate delays in cargo flow.

The suggested higher degree of integration of the two areas includes solutions to problems. One measure to ease the restriction in people flow is to issue multiple-entry visas of longer duration (up to 10 years) to business people, government officials, academics, experts and high-tech professionals to enable them to come to Hong Kong any time. Private cars should be allowed to commute freely between the two regions to boost traffic flow. To enhance cargo-handling efficiency, Hong Kong is considering establishing several cargo-handling hubs with direct rail links to the container terminals in Hong Kong in the Pearl River Delta.

Perhaps the most complex issue, however, lies in the flow of funds. Exchange control and the inconvertibility of the Chinese currency RMB is an issue at the national level, but perhaps affects the Guangdong – Hong Kong area the most as many corporations have investments in both sides and the need to move funds freely between the regions is inevitable. It is hoped that China's entry into the WTO will ultimately lead to the removal of exchange control and the convertibility of RMB.

The integration of Guangdong and Hong Kong's economies will require the two governments to coordinate closely in the planning and construction of cross-border infrastructure and long-term city planning.

This will enable the two areas to plan with a view to map out and share resources to avoid duplication, internal competition and waste of resources.

Furthermore, Guangdong, as it strives to shift its focus on traditional light-industrial manufacturing to high-tech and other industries, could take advantage of Hong Kong's capability in telecommunication and information services and innovation and hi-tech industry. Through a more thorough integration with Hong Kong, the two areas could jointly develop or complement each other in the above-mentioned sectors, and in tourism, transportation and logistics services.

A fragile financial system

The bankruptcy of the Guangdong International Trust and Investment Corporation (GITIC) in January 1999, the first bankruptcy of a financial institution in China, underscores the fragility of the province's financial system. More importantly, it was a wakeup call for Guangdong to seriously get down to the business of sorting out its troubled financial sector as the central government's decision to overrule the provincial authorities and shut down GITIC has indicated China's resolution to reform its financial system.

The central government, by ordering the ill-managed and debt-ridden company into well-deserved bankruptcy, sent two important signals to two parties involved. For the Guangdong government it sent the message that it was high time to reform the state-owned firms, and the financial sector, with market mechanisms and government backing. For domestic and international bankers, Beijing delivered the signal that lending should be done by commercial criteria and not by personal connection, to bring it into line with international practice.

GITIC was the country's second largest financial-trust company, formed in the 1980s by the Guangdong provincial government as a means of attracting foreign investment to Guangdong Province. The company was shut down by Beijing in October 1998 after a string of ill-considered investments in stocks and real estate left it unable to pay its debts. It was first closed and put into the hands of a liquidation committee in October 1998, but then declared bankrupt at a meeting of investors on 10 January 1999 with debts totalling US$4.5 billion. Almost half of that was owed overseas; it had only US$2.9 billion in assets.

The bankruptcy could mark the beginning of a new era of investing in China. It was reported that the provincial leaders had indicated to foreign lenders that the provincial government would stand behind the loans the bankers made to the trust company. By shutting down GITIC, the central government showed both the province and foreign lenders that government backing does not necessarily bring protection, and that lending decisions should be based on the project, not *guanxi* – the Chinese term for 'connections'.[8]

International banks and financial institutions reacted adversely to the decision by the Chinese government not to intervene to prop up a corporation which many believed had been guaranteed by its immediate owner, the Guangdong provincial government, and therefore by Beijing.

Such institutions often lent to projects connected to high-level government officials, with the deciding factors often being the official's connections into the upper powers of government, not the project itself. This so-called *guanxi* phenomenon was prominent in Chinese investments before the GITIC incident, but *guanxi* has been shown to be a very fragile basis for investment.

China has 240 non-bank investment companies or international trust and investment companies (ITICs), many of which are in financial difficulties. A number of economic commentators have warned that the Chinese government will allow the number of such investment houses to fall to 70 or even less. The exposure of foreign financial institutions to ITICs is estimated to be between US$10 billion and US$15 billion. The financial problems of these non-bank financial corporations points to an even more fundamental underlying crisis of the banking system as a whole. It is estimated that the level of bad loans held by China's State banks amounts to US$212 billion or 25 per cent of all lending.[9]

It is no accident that the debt difficulties have emerged in Guangdong. Over the past two decades the province bordering Hong Kong has been a hothouse of capitalist development. By the end of 1998, overseas companies had signed 200,000 contracts and provided at least US$80 billion in investment, more than one-third of the national total, in order to exploit the opportunities of establishing cheap-labour manufacturing enterprises.

As a result, many nonbank investment companies were established by the local governments at different levels in Guangdong to take part in the investment activities. The economic boom in Guangdong provided tremendous opportunities for these companies to invest or act as middlemen to investment projects. Due to the unfit ownership structure, poor management, lack of experience, the lack of a sound monitoring system of these companies' activities, speculative and imprudent investment decisions were often made. Government involvement in many of these companies' operation, as demonstrated by the GITIC case, worsened the problem.

At the same time, financial instability is part of a broader crisis stemming from the economic recession throughout the rest of Asia, and internationally. China's exports to Asia slumped as a result of the downturn in the region in 1998 and its economic growth rate fell in 1998 to 7.8 per cent. China had to compete with cheaper goods manufactured in countries like Indonesia and Thailand where the value of the currencies had fallen markedly, while China, for long-term considerations and in its effort not to further worsen the regional financial instability, did not devalue its currency to cheapen exports. As a result, China's trade in 1998 fell for the first time in 15 years by 0.4 per cent.

As in the rest of the country, another problem in Guangdong's financial system is more directly a result of its loss-making state-owned companies. China's state-owned banks have long been the major funding source of its SOEs, and loans are made often based on political criteria instead of commercial ones. Consequently, the debt-ridden SOEs have become a heavy burden for many financial institutions.

Since financial institutions cannot simply stop funding SOEs, as SOEs are a major part of the economy and doing so would lead to immediate closure of many of them, with soaring unemployment. Improving their efficiency has become crucial and will probably be the key to solving the problems of Guangdong's financial sector.

The future: economic transformation and a knowledge-based economy

The prospects for Guandong Province in the next few years has been laid out in its 10th Five-Year Plan (2001–05). The targets set are challenging, especially when compressed with the more moderate economic objectives set out in the 10th China National Five-Year Plan. Nevertheless, considering the province's track record of economic development over the past 20 years, the targets are achievable based on three major factors as follows:

High growth and transformation of economy

The Guangdong government expects the regional economy to grow to US$196.4 billion and GDP per capita to rise to US$2,410 by 2005. This will require an average annual GDP increase of 9 per cent, compared to the national target of 7 per cent growth per annum.

The main aim of the 10th Five-Year Plan (2001–05) is to build on the social, economic and commercial progress of the last 20 years, a period of remarkable economic growth and commercial success for the region. The Plan places particular emphasis on measures to maintain Guangdong's status as China's leading exporter, and sets out proposals to upgrade the region's infrastructure with a long-term goal of transforming the local economy from a value added processing centre to a high-tech manufacturing base and knowledge-based economy. The Plan also sets parameters for economic development that reflect a renewed concern for sustainable development and greater protection of the environment.

Much of the planned modernization drive will be centred in and around the Pearl River Delta area, with Guangzhou and the province's three SEZs (Shenzhen, Zhuhai, Shantou) taking the lead. Improvements to the highways connecting these cities to other important economic centres within the province, boosting the province's electricity supply and improving communications by way of installing a wideband telecommunications grid throughout the province, are high on the government's list of priorities. New tax concessions and qualitative measures were introduced in 1999 to attract more foreign investment, especially in the science, technology and environmental fields. Guangdong's Governor, Lu Ruihua, recently established a panel of 20 foreign advisers from Fortune 500 multinational companies to assist in this process.[10]

In particular, the province is to focus on developing three technology-intensive industries: electronic information, electrical machinery and petrochemical industries. The electronic information industry experienced a growth in the 1990s, with its output value making up one-third of the national total. The task ahead is to set up five production bases of telecom, computer hardware and soft ware, audio-visual and electronic component products.

The information industry has played an increasingly significant role in Guangdong Province. In 1998, the output value of the sector was US$19.8 billion, accounting for 16.4 per cent of the province's total industrial output value that year. Computers, switching boards, telephones and other post and telecom products are on the primary list of products.

The electrical machinery industry will focus on developing environmentally friendly, intelligent and energy-saving multifunctional household appliances of high quality to strengthen the province's market penetration all over the world. The petrochemical industry will make full use of petroleum resources and advanced production technology to produce raw material products that are urgently needed to substitute imported material.

By 2010, the output value of the three pillar industries is expected to account for 40 per cent of the provincial industrial total. In addition, efforts will be made to speed up the technological renovation of three traditional industries – textiles and garment making, food and beverages, and building materials – to maintain their comparatively high growth rate with more technological content and competitive force.

Continued utilization of foreign direct investment

Guangdong will try to maintain FDI at its current level of around US$ 12 billion each year. Particular emphasis will be placed on attracting investment from European, American and Japanese multinationals and financial institutions, while at the same time efforts will be made to further cooperation with businesses based in Hong Kong, Macao and Taiwan.

Information and communications technology, agriculture, the export industry, environmental protection projects, service industries and reform of SOEs are the major targets for injections of foreign capital. Tax breaks and other incentives to encourage foreign multinationals to establish R&D centres with local partners are offered in the Plan.[11]

New goals in education and HR training

To achieve its goal to create a knowledge-based economy in the future, however, Guangdong needs to improve further the level of education, especially high education, among the population to provide a foundation for the development of information and hi-tech industries.

The provincial government indicates in the Five-Year Plan its commitment to further education, vocational education, adult education, self-education and distance learning. The Plan foresees a marked increase in tertiary education, with the enrolment rate into universities to rise from the current rate of 11.3 per cent to 16 per cent. To achieve this goal, the provincial government plans to set up 10 new universities by the year 2010.

The Plan also recognizes the need to improve the quality of education by allowing greater access to the education system by private organizations, and the need to attract premier domestic and foreign education institutions to cooperate in managing educational establishments and undertaking more scientific research.

At the same time, Guangdong announced in August 2001 that it was to earmark at least US$36 million annually to help children from poor rural areas with their school education. This move is a measure to shorten the regional gap in education and thus ultimately shorten the gap in economic development between urban and rural areas.

More importantly, Guangdong is making great efforts to improve the human resource (HR) quality of its government by sending civil servants to study abroad to acquaint them with international rules and practices. The province has engaged in an unprecedented HR training programme of its government officials. The programme, started in 1999, will over five years send 300 provincial and municipal officials to the USA and Canada for training in public administration, business management and other subjects.

The programme aims at preparing the province with the needed human resources for entry into the WTO and further integration of Guangdong's economy with the global economy.

With these new developments as background, the acceleration in economic reform will inevitably lead Guangdong to a modern knowledge-based economy. The experience of Guangdong Province contains invaluable lessons for the other regions of China as well as for developing countries in the world.

Notes

1 Guangdong Economic Brief <http://www.britishembassy.org.cn/english/guangzhou/gdeb.shtml>
2 'Long-term Opening up Gives Rise to a Unique Economy and a Distinctive Entity – Overseas Chinese', *China Today*, August 2001.
3 'Hong Kong: Manufacturing in China', Market Information Centre, US Department of Commerce <http://www.infoserv2.ita.doc.gov>
4 *Economic Performance 2000: Guangdong*, Market Information Centre, US Department of Commerce.
5 'SOE Exports in Guangdong Declined', *People's Daily*, 20 March 2001.
6 David Murphy, 'Holding the Purse Strings', *Far Eastern Economic Review*, 5 July 2001.
7 'Strategic Thoughts on Integrating the Economies of Guangdong and Hong Kong', Hong Kong Trade Development Council <http:www.tdatrade.com, February 2001>.
8 Michael Laris (1999) 'Chinese Say Bank Insolvent', *Washington Post Foreign Service*, 12 January, p. A14.
9 Joan Christian and Peter Symonds 'China's First Major Financial Bankruptcy', 30 January <http://www.wsws.org>
10 Guangdong Economic Brief <http://www.britishembassy.org.cn/english/guangzhou/gdeb.shtml>
11 The Tenth Five Year Plan (2001–05), Guangdong Provincial Government.

Index